CLEMENS KUBY
Practised reincarnation

For His Eminence Jamgon Kongtrul Rinpoche

CLEMENS KUBY

Practised reincarnation

*My incredible
experiences*

Practised reincarnation – My incredible experiences

Copyright © 2019 by Clemens Kuby, Blumenthal 1, 86551 Aichach

All rights reserved. No part of this book may be reproduced in any form or by any means, electronic or mechanical, including photocopying, recording, or by any information storage and retrieval system, without permission in writing from the publisher. Should this book contain links on the websites of third persons, we cannot be held responsible for them because we do not make them ours, but we only refer to them at the moment of the first publication of this book.

Translation: Margit Loerzer
Proofreading: Liz Marino
Geographical map: Wolfgang Pfau / www.pfau-design.de
Author Photo: Susanne Krauss / www.susanne-krauss.com
Typesetting: Kai Rübsamen
Printing: Amazon.com, Inc. Kindle direct publishing

P–ISBN: 978-3-932486-30-2
E–ISBN: 978-3-932486-29-6

www.clemenskuby.de

On 25th April 1992 Jamgon, after sleeping at his mother's home, drives to Siliguri with his companions in order to stay at the hotel Sinclairs *near the airport before taking the morning flight. When he and his team get up at five a.m. as usual and have breakfast together, Jamgon says: "Let's go for a ride – we still have time to do a little test ride with the new car." Not far from the hotel there is the National Highway No. 31C that crosses Mohal Jungle for about 7 miles straight north towards the foot of the Himalayans, where you can turn right to Bhutan or go straight ahead climbing up to Sikkim. A broad and tarred road, rather ideal for a test ride.*

The sun is just rising, its golden light shines through the bright green of the jungle on the right and left and a wonderful morning air as soft as silk and pleasantly cool is rising to meet them. They rejoice with the electric windows, unknown in Indian cars so far, they also consider the electric sunroof great fun in this quick ride on this still traffic-free highway. Yet their greatest joy is directed towards the Hi-Fi Stereo system on which Jamgon plays his favourite pop music. He tells his driver: "Don't kill the pigeons!" (that are sitting on the road).

Followed by a screeching noise of the tyres, a terrible bang, dull and shrill ... time shattering into fragments ... silence ...

Contents

Why this book? – Introduction — 13

1 Great excitement — 15
On the road — 16
What has happened? — 16
Feeling guilty — 18
Changes — 19
Topga tortures himself asking why this happened — 20
Jamgon is taken to the temple — 22
Butterflies — 23

2 Surrendering in order to live — 29
We often die before we die — 30
Becoming and passing away — 31

3 Understanding death — 33
Consciousness has many levels — 35
Jamgon makes a decision — 36
I ask Topga — 39
Death is deathly sure – but is it also self-determined? — 41
Reincarnation instead of resurrection? — 44
Explanation models — 46

4 Continuity of life — 49
New experiences — 50
Change of form — 53
The best moment to die — 55

How to reincarnate optimally   59
Thought control   61
Creating a good life-movie   64

5 The cosmos vibrates   67
The truth for the benefit of all   70

6 Karmapa and his seat-holders   73
Death, power claims, waiting for reincarnation   77

7 My search for clues towards reincarnation   83
Flight maneuver, power maneuver   84
Hanging from a silk thread   90
Jamgon's last words in front of the camera   95
A cosmic friendship   96

8 Is it all just coincidence?   101
Soul talk   104

9 "Are you crazy – or do you see more than me?"   113
Those who search will find   114
Karmapa found!   116

10 Good timing, bad timing   121
Time changes   126
Wrangling for recognition   128
The rumination effect – terror without end   130
Transformation by remorse   135
Remembering former lives since the beginning   136

11 Karmapa continues his mission — 141
Triumphal journey to Tsurphu — 143
Where the 17th Karmapa was (re-)born — 145

12 Am I dead? – If yes, what then? — 151
Dying the Tibetan way — 154
Addictions are just a nuisance, even in death — 155
The body as a tool — 158
Jamgon goes, Jamgon comes — 161
The magic find — 163
Intuition has the insight — 166

13 Searching for home — 169
Jamgon visits his former lives — 171
Nepal – encircled by two superpowers — 172
Becoming a better person — 174
True love does not tell lies — 179

14 Reincarnation versus genetics — 181
Is it all a matter of genes only? — 181
No soul without form — 186
With which human image do I look at life and death? — 190
Belief concepts – life's glue — 194

15 Social games – an inventory — 203
Obstinate power systems — 206
Brutalized males — 208
Jealousy — 213
The freedom I mean … — 216

16 The mummy is moved to a new place   223
Waiting for Jamgon in his new form   225

17 Reborn! – Starting the search   231
Tsurphu monastery and its role in my former life 233
Karmapa knows more   237
Tenzin is on his way   245
Is it him or not?   249
Recognition is a feeling   254
At the beginning there is a red plastic bowl   258
Light and shadow of an authority   263
Training intuition   265

18 Life goes on – Karmapa meets Jamgon   271
One child – two mothers   273
For the benefit of the child, for the benefit of all 275
At the right moment   279
The universe is at your service   281
Grandpa says   283
Grandma's wisdom   284

19 Crossing the green border to India   295
Topga waits for a sign   295

20 Jamgon the 4th on his way to Pullahari   303
Among brothers – in the car again   308
Many lives to become a master   309

21 Finishing the circle of life   315
Islands of consciousness   319
The fear may go away   321

Family meeting – Topga's wishes	323
Movie scenes: what happened and being in the middle of it	328

22 Eternal life — 335
Rivals — 335
On the throne, but as a refugee — 337
Surprising changes — 338

23 What a crazy thing! — 341

Epilogue — 345

Annex — 347

Personal masterplan for reincarnation — 349
Who was I in a former life? — 352
How do I recognize who someone else was in a former life? — 354
How do I invite someone to reincarnate with me? — 357
How do I project my next reincarnation? — 363
Practising thought control — 367
Soul writing – in script-style — 372
KUBY – the time after my death — 382
Probing for the next life (Example of a client) — 387

Thanks — 389

Who is who in this book? — 391

Books and works by Clemens Kuby — 395

How to continue — 399

Why this book? – Introduction

This story takes place in Asia, mainly with Tibetans, the majority of whom do not live in Tibet any longer because it has been occupied by a foreign power. The central person of this story is **His Eminence Jamgon Kongtrul Rinpoche** in several lives of his, especially during the transition of his third to his fourth life under the same name Jamgon Kongtrul (Rinpoche being a title meaning as much as "venerable", often used when addressing him). Based on Jamgon's story I try to make the reincarnation concept comprehensible to Westerners, since it is almost unknown in our culture, it is often smiled at for being "esoteric stuff" or it is simply dismissed disparagingly. However Asians have a lot less problems with it. Since we all live on the same planet, it would be enriching if we learnt from one another.

Asia profits a lot from the West in everything regarding technology. It has learnt so much that meanwhile the copied far-Eastern technology comes back to the West in an enhanced manner. This ping-pong effect may also happen with their spiritual knowledge when it reaches the West, as the East loses more and more of its traditional wisdom. If the West learns from this wisdom and enhances it by pragmatic use, it will also impregnate the far-Eastern cultures in turn when being re-imported back there. Partly this is already happening now regarding the general image of women in the Asian countries and Ecumenism (religious unity or cooperation). This is quite a blessing for mankind because our exchange is no longer restricted to commerce and technology, but also concerning spiritual and mind-liberating matters.

Your attitude towards life is distinguished on the lowest level, whether you consider it a singular phenomenon or a continuity without beginning or end. This book deals with just this difference. The challenge consists in openings one's consciousness. I have created the movie, the music, the website, the seminars and this book *Practised Reincarnation*, all of which render a lively concept of reincarnation, for this very purpose.

I am a tool for these five levels and call myself a "channel" or whatever. Anyway I cannot pretend that what I have created has been invented by me. It has rather been like that: while I am writing, I find the words for something that is just in front of me. Thus I am not able to create motion pictures, even if one can transport messages a lot more clearly than with documentaries. The difference between a performance and something happening in reality is decisive especially when it comes to the subject of reincarnation. This is most obvious as far as production time is concerned: for more than 30 years we have followed and shot the present case of reincarnation. As a motion picture we would have finished it in about a year.

This project began with the above-mentioned scene and went back from there to several shootings of Jamgon already existing in his life as an internationally renowned and well-travelled lama. These shootings stem from Valerio Albisetti, a good friend of mine, who has been travelling with the third Jamgon as his cameraman for more than three years (from 1987 till 1990) across four continents. His work had a big impact on my decision to make this movie and later write the book, too. The decision itself was taken at the death of Jamgon Rinpoche on 26.4.1992. Not only because his death was and still is a mystery for many people, but also because in Jamgon's case the hope for finding his reincarnation was very high-flying. However we will see that all this did not take place without great drama and lots of doubts.

1
Great excitement

In Sikkim, on the west side of the large valley below the highest peaks of the Himalaya there lies a monastery called *Rumtek*, just in front of the Sikkim's capital Gangtok. In this very monastery lived the third Jamgon since he was six because it was the main seat of his exiled great master, teacher, friend and leader *His Holiness the 16th Gyalwa Karmapa*. H. H. Karmapa had been absent for almost 11 years (since 1981) because he had died. And all his adepts, in the first place his four so-called "seat holders", with Jamgon being one of them, were waiting longingly for the announcement of their master's reincarnation.

Just now in 1992 thanks to *Situ Rinpoche*, one of the four seat holders, appeared a letter written by H.H. Karmapa in which he gives the address of his next reincarnation, a place in the completely inaccessible Eastern Tibet, an area inhabited by nomads without any civilization. The so-called coincidence made that in this very moment Jamgon was granted a visa by the Chinese government valid for all Tibet which he had applied for six months ago to be able to participate in a social help project. Therefore, the four seat holders *Jamgon, Situ, Gyaltsap* and *Shamar* decided that during this trip Jamgon look out for the reincarnation of their leader in the nomad area of Eastern Tibet. According to the letter they had found, Karmapa had to be 7 years old in the meantime.

I said good-bye to Jamgon in Rumtek on the evening of April 22nd after finishing a last-minute interview about his impending journey. I regretted not being able to join him on this trip since my aim was to continue to document the search for Karmapa's reincarnation for my movie *Living Buddha*, but there was no way for my team and me to get a visa from Peking at such short notice (even less a shooting permit). Instead I arranged to meet with Jamgon once he would be back in three weeks' time as planned, so that he could tell me (through my camera) about the things happening in Tibet.

On the road

On 23.4.1992 Jamgon is riding in his brand new BMW with his three companions: his young assistant Tenzin, his master of ceremony Kunga and his chauffeur Norbu from Sikkim down to Kalimpong in West-Bengal. They started from Rumtek Monastery at five o'clock in the morning since they plan to visit Jamgon's mother *Pema Yudron* in Kalimpong first. Pema will be delighted to see what a generous gift one of her two older sons made to the other one. Kalimpong lies at the Southern foothills of the Himalayans. It is no great detour to pass there from Rumtek in Sikkim before reaching the airport in Bagdogra belonging to the big Northern Indian city of Siliguri.[1]

Jamgon and his team are booked on the flight to Tibet on April 26th at 9 a.m. Even if it is only a stone's throw from Gangtok to Lhasa in Tibet and there is an antique trade route crossing the Himalayans at this point, their journey is supposed to pass Delhi and Kathmandu – because of the restrictive Chinese controls affecting all visitors who want to enter the country of Tibet occupied by them.

All four of them have fastened their seat-belts properly on this ride – and suddenly from one second to the next, three of them are dead.

What has happened?

The phone rings at mother Pema's at 6.15 a..m..

A woman says: *There has been an accident.*

---

[1] See the geographical map of the different sites at the end of the book.

Pema asks: *Has anybody been injured?*
The woman answers: *No.*
But Pema hears that her voice is trembling.
Pema: *Please tell me the truth.*
The woman rings off.

Pema immediately calls her son Topga[2] in Nepal. He instantly feels very guilty.

Topga: *Shortly before the accident he was at my house in Nepal and asked me if I wanted to come along with him to visit our mum. But I was busy and said that I could not come, maybe another time. I thoroughly regret this.*

Topga is tortured by the question: How could this happen? He knew the driver as a very reliable person. The car was brand new, the road completely straight and not at all dangerous.[3] What *had* happened? The wildest rumours got to him. Since there was great tension in Jamgon's monastery as to Karmapa's reincarnation, maybe his death could be related to it. Was it possible that the new car had been manipulated? Had it been murder?

In our last conversation between Jamgon and me in Rumtek in the late evening before his departure, there had indeed been a noticeable tension in the air. In the shooting of our talk this is clearly manifested.[4] However nobody imagined that the 38-year-old healthy Jamgon would be dead in less than 80 hours.

---

2   In Tibetan Topga is pronounced as *Top-gial*.
3   On *Google Earth* you can see this road. See also the geographical map of the sites of drama at the end of the book.
4   See the movie *Reincarnation – Looking for a Sign*/QR-Code in the annex under "How to continue".

Feeling guilty

Rinpoche's sudden death at the age of 38 had an extreme impact on his younger brother Topga aged 32. In Nepal he used to lead a secular life as the owner of a big rug company with many female Tibetan carpet weavers thus giving work to the refugees of his people. The contact to his all spiritually dedicated brother has been very slight since his birth because Jamgon had lived in the monastery ever since and Topga practically grew up at home alone.

Yet they had a very brotherly relationship. For example Topga knew that racing cars was a cool, nerve-wrecking experience for his brother. Jamgon was no racer himself since he never drove cars nor did he have a driving licence. But whenever it was possible and his driver urged the car forward, he felt great pleasure and excitement. It made him jump and his blood-pressure rise. Of course there had never been any accident so far. Yet he was nicknamed the "James Dean of Buddhism", who – as we know – also lost his life driving too fast.

Topga: *Rinpoche loved cars and the BMW was a good one, so I had one sent to him as a gift.*[5]

This was in April 1992. Naturally Jamgon could not afford to buy such a car on his own. Not only because as the lama of the monastery he did not claim any money for himself but also because of his image. What would it look like if Jamgon arrived at his teachings with a Ferrari? It was inconceivable that Jamgon would ever buy a flamboyant car. So Topga was in the position to bestow a special gift on his dear brother.

Topga: *I provided him with a car – a good one.* Mercedes *and* Rolls-Royce *were out of the question since they are well known in India as status symbols. But hardly anybody knows BMW here. So I decided to get a* BMW 525i. *The car was supposed to be a surprise for my brother.*

---

5 See the movie *Reincarnation – Looking for a Sign*/QR-Code in the annex under "How to continue".

So Topga ordered the car at the only available BMW-dealer in New Delhi – the BMW which was handed over to Jamgon by the provider shortly before his death in Sikkim/Northern India.

Changes

The message of his death reached me when I was in Bombay where I had flown from Bagdogra the day before. I thought that since I would be back to Sikkim in three weeks just when Jamgon came back from Tibet, I would use the meantime to continue shooting with my crew on my other movie *At the edge of paradise* with the indigenous tribe of the *Todas*. We had a spare day in Bombay before flying to South India on the 27.4. So I took advantage of being near a well working phone to call my loved ones back in Germany.

My wife says immediately: *Jamgon is dead.*
I: *Impossible, we have just finished shooting with him.*
She: *Yet he is said to have had a car accident.*
To reach Sikkim with these backwater Indian telephone lines in 1992 is hopeless. I change plans immediately and we fly back to Sikkim during four and a half hours. Already at Bagdogra airport I see a newspaper with the news of the car accident on the front page. We drive to the site of the accident immediately. The wreck has already been taken away. I find it in a garage in Siliguri and I am upset by its aspect. The wildest rumours are rife pretending that this accident had been strange indeed.

Topga says: *Some people believe that there has been a conspiracy or a bomb or something.*

I insist on a professional expert examining the car and I phone from Siliguri to the German TÜV (Technical Inspection of Vehicles). I seem to be lucky because a TÜV agent is just dealing with a checking order in Malaysia. By phone and fax I attempt to organize the arrival of this guy here in Eastern India to check the car. Then we drive eight hours up to Rumtek monastery in Sikkim where I meet with Tenzin, Jamgon's assistant, who has survived the accident. Just recovered from the event he recalls how it happened:

> Tenzin: *Suddenly there were some pigeons on the road. Rinpoche told the driver: "Don't kill the pigeons." So the driver tried to avoid them by making a maneuver with the steering wheel. However we drove so fast we went skidding. Then I do not remember anything.*

How has Tenzin survived? After the phone call mother Pema immediately drove two hours from Kalimpong to the site of the accident:

> Pema: *If you saw the car, you would think that nobody had survived such a crash.*

Tenzin only remembers: *When I came to again, I was not in the car any more. I immediately looked for Rinpoche. He had also been ejected from the car. He had a small wound. I took him into my arms and he took his last breath. The driver and Kunga were both dead.*

I get a negative reply from the German TÜV and then try a second possibility through the car supplier, the BMW-dealer in Delhi who sends his son in the end. The latter comes to the conclusion that the car has been completely normal and in order. I remain sceptical because he can also be moved by his own interests to give such a statement.

Topga tortures himself asking why this happened

Without knowing the exact cause of his brother's death Topga feels horrible having fulfilled his brother's dream that directly led him to death. Topga is tortured by the question of why death was brought about by the car he bestowed on his brother. He is afraid that this feeling of guilt will keep him in check for a long time.

> Topga: *If I had come with him to Kalimpong, I would have driven the car and for sure there would never have been any accident.*

To be sure he does not mean to charge Norbu the driver with the responsibility for his brother's death. But in his sleepless nights, a thousand variations of how it could have been race through his head. But no thought brings any solution or even a little relief to his fate.

In his function as a driver Norbu only ever drove Indian cars with a maximum speed of 50 or 60 mph, with these cars starting to shake so much that you would rather avoid going faster. With the BMW 525i they had reached 120 mph at the moment Norbu avoided driving over the pigeons without really noticing the speed.

However the little maneuver to avoid them gets the car unbalanced and skidding. It is a model made for driving on the left so the steering wheel is on the right side and its right-hand door where Norbu sits crashes against a fully-grown tree with a diameter of 20 inches on the left side of the road crumpling the car to the centre console and having an impact on the whole car frame which made the left doors pop open and the rear window pane jump out of its frame completely. Jamgon who sat on the passenger seat on the left is ejected and comes to lie on the grass. Kunga and Norbu remain in the car with their seatbelts fastened and are dead or at least unconscious. (Some time later they are said to have died on the way to the hospital.)

It a great wonder that Tenzin survives this accident: due to the immense impact, his body is ejected backwards out of the seat-belt through the rear window with the pane gone and somersaults through the air, all this causing him to lose conscience throughout. He only comes to when he lands on his feet on the grass behind the car without injuries.

In the next few minutes, passers-by are stopping on the road. Two of them are heading towards the car to help instantly because at this moment mobile phones do not exist yet. Before the police and the ambulance arrive at the site of the accident, Tenzin transports the body of Jamgon with a passing tuk-tuk – a small three-wheel typical Indian motor-rickshaw – to the Buddhist temple of *Salugara* only three miles away.

This is only possible because Tenzin and the passer-by who has rented the tuk-tuk as a taxi place Jamgon's body over their thighs with his legs jutting out on the side. By taking Jamgon's body away from the site of the accident Tenzin saves him from undergoing the standard procedure such as done with the bodies of Kunga and Norbu. Thirty minutes after the accident they are sent to the local hospital of Siliguri.

Jamgon however is laid out in the Salugara temple and six monks are immediately beginning with the death prayers. Tibetan Buddhism, being the highest developed religion with respect to death, offers marvellous prayers for helping the dead. The famous *Tibetan Book of the Dead* was and still is the oldest textbook about what happens to the soul when the body stops living.

Jamgon is taken to the temple

Pema learns at the site of the accident that her son was taken to Salugara temple. "Dead or alive?" Nobody can tell her anything definite. She continues towards the temple and already distinguishes a big crowd outside the temple. "What is all this turmoil?" The police has learnt that Jamgon is inside the temple and requires his body for examination or a post-mortem according to the law. The few present monks succeed in postponing the entrance of the police until the agents threaten to use violence to get access to the temple and already phone for reinforcement. This upsets the Hindu neighbourhood of the Buddhist temple so much that instantly a giant crowd of about 300 people gathers, blocking with success the entrance to the temple for the police.

Mother Pema is let into the temple by the crowd and the monks and finds her son laid out there. Yesterday she had still cooked a meal for him. She can hardly believe that he is dead now … Luckily he has not been injured. Though this is extraordinary if you look at the car. He even looks beautiful and relaxed lying there. Pema gets on her knees and prays with the monks. She knows the room and the bed he lies on. It is the bed of *Kalu Rinpoche,* a fatherly friend to Jamgon who shortly before his death at the age of 90 had this temple built and lived in this room.

The official inauguration of the temple only took place a few weeks ago. Without this refuge at close quarters to his death it might have been unpleasant for Jamgon. In the context of the tragedy everything was as good as it could be.

The city of Siliguri with about one million and all West-Bengal with about 90 million inhabitants is an exclusively Hindu region with Salugara being a tiny Buddhist jewel, but at this moment it is spontaneously protected by hundreds of Hindus. You may take this as a sign of this peace-loving people and Jamgon's liberal-mindedness and cosmopolitan spirit.

If Pema is moved by the death of Jamgon she is also moved by the survival of her other son Tenzin.

In tears she says: *He only has a small scratch at the back of his head and his back is a bit strained but otherwise he is ok. It is incredible that Tenzin has survived if you see the car or what is left of it. It is inconceivable ...*

Butterflies

I have a great idea when I go back to the junkyard in Siliguri to have another look at the car-wreck, about 10 miles from the site of the accident. I go to the military asking for a strong lorry with a crane to transport the wreck back to the place of the accident the next day so that I can shoot what happened to the car. Together with my large Indian film team I stay overnight at the same hotel where Jamgon stayed on the night before his death. We leave at 5 a.m. in order to capture the same magnificent soft morning light which accompanied Rinpoche towards his death.

My chief of production Naveen deals with the transport of the wreck in the morning when I am driving on the highway with the team bus from the hotel to the site. A terrible thing happens: we run over a pigeon! The very thing Jamgon had avoided, meeting death, together with this less than 50-year-old driver Norbu and his 60-year-old master Kunga.

Shortly after we arrive at the tree on the site, the military crane with the wreck is stopping there too. Naveen jumps out of the driver's cabin. Immediately I tell him what has happened and I am shocked when he says: "We too have overrun a pigeon."

"What does this *mean*?" I ask.

Valerio the cameraman is angry about the question: "Why do you ask? Nobody is allowed to stage such a horrible tragedy. Enough people have warned you not to do it, but you cannot be stopped. This is the outcome of you insisting on it."

What a blow for my ego! I consult again with my heart if I am right about doing this. The answer is yes. – I direct the lorry crane towards the tree so that the car wreck can be placed against the tree where it had come to a halt after the accident. When the crane has almost put down the wreck towards the tree with its own weight shifting towards the side, the giant military lorry is tipping over to his right and sliding down the little slope from the road to the tree. And this big vehicle bursting with strength is now completely blocked by the tree between the driver's cabin and the crane making it impossible to move forward or backward. The scene with the car wreck in front of the tree cannot be shot anymore. The lorry crane dominates the picture.

I will never forget Valerio's face. My Indian cameraman is still ready to go on working. Yet suddenly there are unusually dark clouds coming up on this marvellous summer day which has started so beautifully. What can I do? About 30 involved team members stand on the highway which the police has blocked on one lane and is now directing the traffic so it may pass the site slowly. All of them look at me wondering what is up. I say: "In any case, we now need a second crane to tow the first crane back to the road." All people involved make an attempt at putting this into action.

Indeed there is another military monster showing up on the road at about 11 a.m. I am fairly relieved because in the meantime, the Indian police has stopped considering this spectacle great fun and wants to reopen the second lane again. Just then huge, heavy rain drops start falling from the darkened sky. With the immense power of the second crane supported by four outriggers, to maintain it on the road, the first crane is towed up the small slope towards the road until it gets back there again with its thirty feet high wheels.

We can now shoot the scene for which we all have got up at four a.m. Valerio has disappeared into one of our cars with his second camera. I am discussing how to shoot the scene with the Indian cameraman after the two monster lorries have gone from the scene. In reality the car wreck is not properly positioned yet. Should we try to lift it again with the lorry crane and position it correctly …?

While I am still wrestling with myself about what is necessary to do for what I have in mind, there is a bloodcurdling thunderclap followed by a flash and a heavy downpour only the Indian sky can produce which does not consist of buckets of rain but seems like water pouring from a crumbled dam. Everybody takes refuge in the available cars and buses. Then a thunder-storm with heavy hail begins to pour down which makes the car window panes go blind and even makes us fear that they might not resist this inferno. I am also sitting tightly packed among my crew, drenched to the bones. Nobody is speaking and we are all afraid of the next thunderclap. Some are pressing their hands to their ears shutting off the noise and keeping their eyes tightly closed. The turmoil continues for about twelve minutes, then there is silence again. Everybody lifts their head. I also lift my head and say: "I give up."

A wave of relief passes through the crew and for the first time Valerio looks at me nodding his head. The thunder-storm disappears. Soaking wet and sweaty we get out of the cars and buses. Naveen gives instruction to all aides for closing the shooting today. Everyone is busy again but this time there is hardly any noise – we are all in low spirits. I see relieved faces in one half of the team, and the other half shows regret.

Without anything to do I stand in the middle of the steaming road when I notice a thick dark cloud of about one cubic meter in a distance of some 30 to 50 feet in front of me approaching me directly at a height of 10 feet above the road.

"What is this?" I am profoundly surprised and touched while all the crew members, the police and the passers-by on the now completely barred road direct their faces towards me.

They are witnesses of an awesome experience. At least it is for me. It is not a usual cloud but the living shape of a swarm of butterflies. Not normal butterflies however, like the ones known in Europe, but dark shimmering giant butterflies with a wingspan of about four inches and with yellow eyes painted on the wings whose lower sides are coloured with a deep changing purple.

The whole swarm of butterflies is coming to rest on me: not only on my head, my shoulders, my arms, my breast, but also my whole face is covered by this magical animals. The other people are petrified with amazement, like me too, although I feel unspeakable joy at the same time. These butterflies are enchanting my mind and with their tiny feet are tiptoeing all over the pores of the skin in my face and all other places where my skin is showing. All this is happening without any sound except for the cosmic beat of wings. Everybody is so fascinated that nobody remembers to take a picture. To be sure we are not in the era of mobile phones yet.

Before the background of this history I merely dare to use the photos taken of the wrecked BMW for my documentary *Reincarnation – Looking for a Sign* some 20 years later. These are the only pictures taken at the time. This lapse was necessary – together with everything else that has happened in the meantime – in order to be able to inform now about the circumstances. You, dear reader, will certainly understand why at the end of this book. Nowadays even Valerio is at peace with it being published.

2
Surrendering in order to live

If we want to get a deeper understanding of the transience of life in all its facets, it is a good idea to recall the Buddhist ritual of a *sand mandala*. Just to create this mandala five or six monks work between 12 and 18 hours daily for two weeks until they have achieved the symbol of the universe in three dimensions out of the purest and finest coloured sand. The precision of such great skill is breath-taking and beautiful in its magnificent colours and its size of 12 feet by 12 feet on a wooden board.

As soon as the sand mandala is finished it is sacrificed to the masters of wisdom, whose teachings and their spiritual aspects are incorporated in it, by sweeping the sand together on a heap. For most people this very act is an indescribably painful procedure after accomplishing such a perfect masterpiece. At the end there is nothing left but a small heap of many colours that is then filled in an urn and taken to the water. In another ritual for the comprehension of the transience of every living thing the urn is transferred to the water and dissolves there.

This ritual helps us to die. It is of great effect for a life free from fear. Every human being feels the fervour with which they are inclined to preserve the mandala's beauty, such as we want to preserve animals and people. Man himself is such a marvellous mandala to whom we often wish a long life. Sometimes people from outside the monastery wish for the mandala being preserved for a longer time, so the monks decide to let them continue marvelling at its perfection for a couple of days, maximum three. But at the end of this period the mandala's deeper purpose is fulfilled in this special ritual: its destruction. Likewise my form / body and yours and every other form will one day be destructed and swept together in a heap of ash.

May we always be aware of this law of life while we are alive so that we do not cling to transient forms causing us suffering and pain. Due to this pain many people cannot die joyfully. Thanks to the enchanting beauty and profundity of the sand mandala the transience of life is especially felt because one would rather preserve it and cling to it. Nowadays this training of non-attachment can be undermined by the ever-present cameras and mobile phones: one can hardly resist taking a picture of this perfect masterpiece – thus depriving the ritual of its effect. In former times people had to let go of their loved ones completely. Gone really meant gone. An especially insistent exercise in dying.

We often die before we die

We already die when our loved one leaves us; we already die when a fulfilled time is up; we die when we receive a refusal; we die when our expectations are not met. Even our body cells die by millions every day. We can learn how to die during our whole life. Imagine the beautiful and happy things as a wonderful big soap bubble shimmering in all colours as it floats through the air in front of your eyes. You could embrace it, hold it, kiss it, but before you do any of it, it explodes into thin air.

How are you feeling now? "Ohhhhhhhhh", says the feeling of transience, and grief is overshadowing it. – Your soul may know a different reaction towards it: "Ahhhhhhhhh", it says and rejoices seeing the explosion followed by a genuine laugh. Just observe the children, there are always both reactions inside them. You have the choice: to feel joy or grief about transience. The cosmic principle is: all that is created will die. It makes no sense to go against the cosmos. It will only render dying difficult wherever we find it. The great thing with "Ahhhhhhhhh" is that we can repeat it as much as we want in an ever new form: blow a shape into life, give your breath to it, and rejoice at its explosion. In the end the explosion is just as nice as blowing things into shape. My interpretation is made by my feelings.

Becoming and passing away

To spread the awareness of the principle of becoming and passing away, of non-attachment and the transience of life, Jamgon the 3rd travelled with his team from one teaching session to the next, from one continent to the next in innumerable countries during all his life.

He was always accompanied by Tenzin. Tenzin was only four when his mother died. His father had to take care of six children and was relieved when Jamgon took Tenzin to raise him in the monastery like his own son. When he was 16 and had finished his basic formation, Jamgon took him with him on all his journeys around the globe.

Every lecture, every ritual, every visit was a grain to be sown for the awareness of transience. This is what Jamgon did as a mission in life, this is why he incarnated as a human being. His great charisma helped him to be accepted by people of different cultures and beliefs since he embodied the Buddhist image of compassion and wisdom.

In his way of life as a Tibetan monk he maintained age-old rituals of the Tibetan, Indian and Buddhist traditions. The sand mandala has an important role in this tradition as it conveys more about dying than a thousand words.

3
Understanding death

Jamgon's brother Topga as a business man had less opportunity to deal with death in such a way and at an early age. He feels most affected by Jamgon's sudden departure:

Topga: *For me he was a brother, my older brother and a very special one.* He cannot withhold the tears. His mother keeps up a daily Buddhist tradition that helps her in this difficult moment. She does not only think of her own grief, she feels that:

Pema: *It is not only a big loss for me. It is a great loss for everyone.* And there are quite a few of them. The shock about Jamgon's sudden death spreads in no time at all among Buddhists all over the planet. During the 49 days of mourning ceremonies, his adepts come together in thousands from all continents to Rumtek monastery – in the ancient kingdom of Sikkim with difficult access in the North of India.

Naturally Jamgon's whole family takes part in the big death ritual. And of course Topga took time to come with his family from Nepal. He never reckoned that thousands of people would gather there to mourn his brother.

Topga: *I knew that he had adepts and I also knew that he had people to support him* (meaning sponsors), *but I did not know the large amount of his disciples. It is so impressive. I am completely overwhelmed.*

In Jamgon's case the monks decide that his body will not be buried nor cremated but mummified since he is so young and beautiful without any injuries; thus making a relic of this human being which makes it easier for the believers to connect with the spirit of the person symbolizing the relic. In Jamgon's case it is called *Manjushri*, the aspect of wisdom of a realized and purified person.

The mummy will be put in the Vajra position[6] and then put in a box called *Kudung*. To be sure the mummy cannot be seen then but it can be transported. First it is exhibited in the great prayer temple of Rumtek monastery for the 49 day death ritual. A photo of Jamgon and many small and big ritual objects are put all around together with an infinite number of burning candles, in front of which everybody bows or even throws themselves on the floor in Tibetan tradition. This means: one lies down lengthwise, touches the ground with the front and repeats this three times. Every visitor puts a *Katak* on the Kudung, a white silk scarf to greet the deceased and lights an incense stick. Pema and Topga and all their family do so. However Topga – being very sincere – says:

> Topga: *I am a born Buddhist and I believe in this religion, but I could not answer any profound questions about the faith and I am not throwing myself on the ground.*

This means that he ignores why throughout 7 x 7 days and nights this and that mantra, text and prayer is spoken at any given moment and how often it is repeated and he also ignores the effect such a death ritual is meant to have in Tibetan culture which has brought forth the first book of mankind about the phase between death and reincarnation, a thoroughly precise and elaborate manual offering help and orientation to the souls looking for a new form – the *Tibetan Book of the Dead*.

But beware! Already there are various translations in German from Tibetan, none of which is able to convey the contents adequately. This is solely due to the fact that in Tibetan there are 20 different levels of consciousness. What do we have in German or English? There is the colloquial awareness, consciousness, waking consciousness, self-awareness, self-consciousness, the subconscious. Maybe also collective consciousness, but now it starts getting imprecise. Since we do not have an awareness of what the souls go through when changing their form, we do not have any vocabulary for it either. Or is it

---

6   The position of meditation with his legs crossed.

the other way round? Because we do not have a vocabulary, we do not have an awareness for it. This is a matter of mutual pursuit, such as at the computer level where software and hardware mutually support each other.

Consciousness has many levels

In Tibetan the level of consciousness on which one communicates can be expressed by a single letter, such as in our Western languages we can make known to our interlocutor the time in which our statement takes place by merely changing a few letters: future, present or past and various grades are possible (I did, you do, he will do).

More or less we can imagine now how a Tibetan with a high level of education is able to speak about consciousness on 20 different levels, most of which refer to a level without body / form. However I also experienced that my translator told me that he could not convey the words heard from a lama because he lacked the consciousness of this level. He did understand the different words but there was no sense to them because he had not been trained in this field.

This is why the *Tibetan Book of Death* is so difficult to read. One gets the impression that the contents is simply repeated from one chapter to the next. Yet this is only because in the translation we lack the terms from the original to be able to perceive an issue on different levels of consciousness.

In Tibetan the same thing goes for technical matters. I went there six times hiring Tibetan helpers for my team. They took great pleasure in our technical equipment never seen there before. When we showed them our *Nagra* (a professional, big sound-recording device such as those used in the last century) with which they could hear their voices via headset, there was endless joy. They called this device a "moto". When they were allowed to look through the camera, they also rejoiced greatly and the term for camera was also "moto". I wanted them to get a clear picture by trying to explain them the difference between recorder and camera (then still working with celluloid film). But when I heard that our car was also called "moto" in Tibetan, I just gave up.

Yet I can explain now quite well why I have so many problems reading the *Tibetan Book of the Dead* with 20 levels of consciousness being reduced to one term in our language. This can only be boring. The same thing would occur reading a manual for a technical device in Tibetan: "Take moto together with moto and connect it with moto." The same great differences exist in trying to understand dying. Probably they are as big as when it comes to understanding technical devices, if there is no language to communicate the issue or you do not understand this language.

How much Jamgon knew about life and death and the way he applied it for his own death, becomes clear to his mother during the 49 day ritual: "I only notice now how great he was", says Pema.

Jamgon makes a decision

Due to the many adepts from all over the world Rumtek monastery is rife with rumours and stories striving to shed some light on Jamgon's mysterious death. Topga hears a lot of things that make him deduce the following:

Topga: *Jamgon knew very well what would happen and he was prepared for it. For example a few weeks before his death Jamgon gave permission to one of his female adepts to make a statue of him. Such a thing is unheard of in the Tibetan tradition. Nobody makes a statue of a lama who is still alive. It is an absolute no-go. Jamgon's colleagues put a lot of verbal pressure on the artist insisting on her not to make any statue but she always referred to the Rinpoche who gave her carte blanche.*

> *Then there is another thing which also points to his knowing weeks before that he had to die: in the mantra being said after a lama's death he exchanged the name of his former life for the name of his present life.*

Tenzin shows me the text of this death mantra for the 2nd Jamgon Kongtrul – with the correction made by hand of the 3rd Jamgon exchanging his former name for the one in his present life. For Tenzin this is very extraordinary. He only discovered this change after his master's death.

"There are many of such stories which make me believe that he knew that he would leave this life", says Mother Pema too, "It was his decision to leave then. I am convinced of it." – And Jamgon's secretary Michele Martin from the USA, head of his office in Rumtek, states:

Michele: *Before leaving Rumtek monastery on the 23rd of April, Rinpoche was incredibly active. I mean he was always active, but in his last days he only slept a few hours per night and met with even more people than usual. These people told me later that he had given them work – Buddhist practice for three or four years – especially his older disciples. And in the night before leaving for Tibet, I dreamt that he would not come back. I was very surprised by this dream. Other disciples also had similar dreams.*

Mother Pema recalled that Jamgon looked particularly stressed when he came down from Rumtek monastery to her house in Kalimpong on this day of the 23rd of April.

Pema: *I told him that he needed a break. Clemens, you know him quite well, he never had a break. However this time he laid down. This seemed very strange to me. He had never done this before. Normally he only dropped in to eat and left again at once. Very rarely did he sleep in his room here. Yet it was different on the evening of the 23rd. He went to bed early and slept almost all of the 24th of April. This was a very strange thing indeed – extraordinary!*

The next day Jamgon went, like I mentioned before, to *Sinclairs*

Hotel in Silugiri where he used to stay the night before taking a flight. The hotel has quite a good standard for the surrounding circumstances.

>Tenzin: *When Rinpoche woke on his last morning, he called me to come into his room. He called me by my nickname, which he used to do only when he became very confidential. He said: "Do you know that I always pray for you so that you are fine?", and then he blessed me. I did not understand why he did this in early morning, I only thought that he wanted to bless me, nothing else.*

The doorman of the hotel also recalls:

>Doorman: *When Rinpoche left early in the morning and went to his car where his driver and his companions were already waiting, he greeted me cheerfully saying: "We will never meet again in this form."*

This was exactly 20 minutes before his death.

My friend Rosy Findeisen who was cooperating very closely with Jamgon had been in Rumtek/Sikkim for two months before his death. She was an architect from Hamburg/Germany and Jamgon had commissioned her with the structural renovation of the monastery. So she had to assert herself with respect to the Indian construction companies and had to deal with a large contingent of builders. Even in Germany this is quite a challenge in this business, not to speak of a Third World country like India. However with her character and mind trained in Buddhism she managed this task extremely well and put her own money into this project. She and her husband Rüdiger Findeisen, also a capable architect and Buddhist, donated this money to Karmapa's order thus putting Rosy completely at the service of Jamgon Rinpoche's life. She even was president of the *European Buddhist Union* for one term of office.

>Rosy: *The day Jamgon Kongtrul Rinpoche the 3rd died was the saddest one in my life. Although this day had started so warm and beautiful in Sikkim, there were clouds coming at noon setting off a*

thunderstorm with heavy hail.[7] *It was so depressing, so horrible, all the people just ran around in a panic. Only the older lamas went about their business unruffled.*

Meaning that the lamas and Rinpoches started immediately with the 49-days bardo ceremony.

I ask Topga

CK: *How do you feel when you think about Jamgon and the possibility that he might have felt his end being near or even intended to die or planned his death in advance?*

T: *How do you imagine I feel about it? All day long I get told the most varying explanations about it.*

CK: *What type of "explanations" do you get?*

T: *Instructions and advice about how I am supposed to bear my destiny.*

CK: *And how are you supposed to bear it?*

T: *That I should not make any reproaches to myself, and that Jamgon himself had decided to die.*

CK: *Normally one would consider suicide, when someone decides to die, particularly in the case of such a young and healthy man.*

T: *Nonsense. Jamgon was not even driving the car – the idea of Jamgon committing suicide is not working. The two things do not go together.*

CK: *But how do you die when you decide to die – without raising a hand to kill yourself?*

T: *He was in an extremely good mood when he died.*

CK: *Who told you that?*

---

7   This extraordinary thunderstorm – very strange with respect to the season and the region – repeated itself in a similar form some eight days later when I wanted to stage-manage the accident.

T: *Tenzin said it after the accident. Rinpoche was in his best mood. – Nobody reckoned that there would be such a catastrophe. It was simply an accident.*

CK: *Topga, you told me yourself that he knew he would die. Why should he not be in the best mood, if he wanted it himself?*

T: *Because it is gruesome to die at such an early age, when you still have your whole life before you. I don't know …*

CK: *If he wanted it, then we cannot say it was an accident.*

T: *But it could be that he knew that he would die, although he did not want it, could it not?*

CK: *Then he would not have been so happy and he would not have announced his death to the doorman some 20 minutes earlier.*

T: *How could he know that the pigeons would sit on the road and Norbu would lose control of the car? He could not have known that.*

CK: *I believe that if you live, think and act in harmony with the universe which is a universe of love, the universe will do anything for you, all you need is to know what you really want and if it is for the benefit of all. Hesitant decisions cannot receive clear support from the universe.*

T: *Thus his death should be for the benefit of all. Yet I do not see that.*

CK: *But can you imagine that he had taken a 100 % decision for dying?*

T: *Yes, but not for the benefit of all.*

CK: *For whose benefit then?*

T: *I have no idea, in any case not for mine.*

CK: *Maybe for Karmapa's benefit?*

T: *In which way could his death benefit Karmapa?*

CK: *This is what Tenzin asks himself too. Where is the sense of his death?*

T: *If we only knew it …*

Death is deathly sure – but is it also self-determined?

Every human being, even Tenzin, is struggling with the question: what does death mean? Especially Tenzin because for him there is not only the question of what death means for his master, but at the same time what sense there is that he, Tenzin, had survived unharmed?

Tenzin: *I visited many high dignitaries, including those of other Tibetan orders asking them about the significance of Rinpoche's death. Some state that there was a big obstacle for the recognition of our reborn leader Karmapa. Thanks to Rinpoche's death this obstacle has been eliminated now. This was Rinpoche's intention. For everyone else it only was a tragic accident. But all do believe in a higher sense of this death, even if I cannot see it.*

As long as death does not make sense for us, we wish it would not happen. Likewise with meditation: if you do not see any sense in sitting there without moving and not doing anything – then you do not meditate. It just needs to make sense. Or you explain it to yourself just like the Danish pilgrim who assisted at the 49-days bardo ceremony in Rumtek/Sikkim:

Pilgrim: *Jamgon was a lama of the 21st century and he died as such. This is all. Normally when lamas die, they sit down in the Vajra position and just take their last breath. But now we are in the 21st century and he died in a BMW. This is all.*

How else could Jamgon have died? Suicide – we already said – was out of the question, this is why he did not drive the car himself. He must have had a paramount, absolutely conclusive and unequivocal reason for why he died like that and not in a different way.

How is it possible to carry out your own death in this way? Can you learn it like you learn to meditate? It is not possible to learn to meditate theoretically, only by practicing it. Anyhow it seems impossible to practice dying. With meditation I have the choice: either I want to learn it or I do not. With death, choice is limited: everybody must experience it, it is deathly sure. So it is useful to learn to die in good time.

How do you learn to die? Before I start learning something, I reflect on what I know how to do already. If I realize that I do not have any imagination about how to plan my death without committing suicide, I will consider the causes of death which I think possible for me. Most people already find out the first unpleasant belief because they are of the opinion that one has to die from something. If it is not an accident, then it must be a disease. How is it possible to die healthy? Healthy people do not die. Is this a rumour or is it really like that?

To answer these questions we could have a look at the post-mortem documents or at least some death certificates issued by doctors. Nowhere will you find: "Died healthy". In the best case doctors write: "Heart failure". Yet "failure" already suggests disease although that does not necessarily have to be so by any means. "Heart standstill" would describe the same fact but would contradict the belief that humans cannot die by themselves. Doctors are convinced that man has to have some weakness, something that makes them die.

In Jamgon's case such a weakness could be paraphrased by saying: "Bad luck." Or: "Unlucky coincidence" or, as his brother Topga says: "If I had driven the car, he would still be alive." Every single one of these interpretations incapacitates Jamgon. Why should they want to deny his own decision to die at this hour on this particular day? Because they are convinced that nobody could plan or determine that on a deserted, broad, straight tarmac road, at milestone 13, going at 120 mph there would be some pigeons sitting on the street and – in order not to kill them – one would go towards death by himself? On a certain level of consciousness this is just unthinkable. But since there are different levels of consciousness – which in Tibet have also been established in their language -, likewise there are different outlooks on life. Changing levels and outlooks may be learnt and practiced – and not only in death, but even in life.

The change from one level of consciousness to the next consists in interpreting life as a singular and unique phenomenon or as a continuity. If you have been convinced until now that with death life has finished because one has always felt grief – even great or very great grief –, one knows that with this feeling at least you are on a low level of consciousness, the one identifying yourself primarily with the body.

Before you go on reflecting on this outlook and your feelings, it is worth checking: how much of your life energy have you put into your physical existence? There are innumerable things to be listed starting with what you wanted to have, attachment to things and persons, passing by ownership issues and insurances of all kind, and finishing with the wish to live as long as possible. Once your life is ending, it is no wonder that such a mighty conditioning makes you fear the moment you have to let go of everything you have grown fond of and heaped together in the very ramifications of your consciousness. What a gruesome realization for most people since they are unprepared for it.

STOP! Does that mean that I have to stop wishing for a long life? It does not matter if I live a short or a long life. The point is that I have to find out with which attitude I interpret death. If I do not consider life as a singular phenomenon, but as a continuity, I make a conscious shift of outlook from one level to another. A life oriented towards the infinite continuity is a long life anyway, as it is infinitely long, which means eternal. When I change my outlook on life in such a way, I have no need to ask for a long life, because it is given to me in any case.

On this level of consciousness eternity is the principle of life which I can also accept as a materialistic person. I do not have to convert to an esoteric person or spiritually interested being. On the contrary: with the philosophy of an eternal life the materialist takes pleasure in the fact that after death he will not be buzzing around as a spectre somehow, but will become another material being of flesh and bone with his two legs firmly on the ground. *This is the interpretation of life as a continuity– and not as a singular phenomenon.*

Reincarnation instead of resurrection?

Counter-question: *How can materialists be free from their fear of death?* Perhaps you say that this is why the Christian teachings have dropped the concept of reincarnation introducing the concept of resurrection instead. With resurrection Jesus Christ keeps his body with which he had been nailed to the cross. As a proof he still carries the nail wounds on his hands and feet. Therefore he did not have to surrender his body as this is the very thing materialists fear most. With the concept of resurrection this fear to surrender your beloved body can be omitted, even if it is only for a moment or some time. For materialists there is still a certain continuity of the same body despite death.

If you do not relish this belief in resurrection since normal humans obviously do not qualify for it and thus cannot be experienced by them, and secondly because this concept of resurrection appears as extremely improbable, then you have to continue looking in order to learn about death. Because the way most people imagine death to be, is spreading fear and terror.

Let us stay with the concept of continuity then, where death is a deathly sure matter – such as in the level of consciousness in which life is a singular phenomenon. You find the difference between the continuous and the singular outlook on life by asking:

Question: *What dies when you are dying?*
Answer: *The body.*

This answer is valid for every consciousness as long as you do not believe in Christian resurrection in the same body. Yet does the soul also die when you die? Or the spirit? Which consciousness do you need in order to give an unambiguous answer to this question?

It is enough to have a very materialistic consciousness, for example in a physicist or biologist who can establish unequivocally that after death the body disintegrates into its different physical elements. The time of this transformation depends on the type of funeral you choose. If you are cremated, several elements are transformed into the gas phase with a lot of energy (fire). If you are buried, the same thing happens, but it takes much longer. Everything else that once made you a living being stays behind. Nothing is ever wasted or disappears in the universe, merely the physical elements change their aggregate state or dissolve from one molecular composition to another one. Thereby disintegrating the form which we called "human". This is the very act of death.

Can this act also happen to the spirit or what we call "soul"? The physicists and biologists give a definite no. For them it is a certain fact that spirit and soul do not consist of physical elements. As much as you examine your body: you will not find spirit nor soul in it. To be sure you will find a brain consisting of physical elements. You will also find energy establishing the metabolism between these elements and you may even measure how many atoms change their place to do so. In the brain this change of place is called *forming synapses*. However the contents of what these atoms transport cannot be measured (yet), only presumed: they are said to carry information moving from one brain area to another in a living body. Yet we can merely recognize their vibration or frequency but not the contents or sense. This vibration is the physical image of our thoughts which means what our spirit or soul produces.

Exactly there is a difference between matter and what we call spirit. The materialists pretend that spirit needs a physical carrier to exist. In their imagination however God does not need a physical carrier to exist. If there is no such thing as God for the materialists because he does not represent a phenomenon which can be checked materialistically, then spirit cannot exist either for the materialists since it isn't a phenomenon which can be checked materialistically either. Yet every materialist can think and has a spirit. Yet if they affirm that they recognize every spirit that needs a physical carrier, they can also recognize God. Because in this concept the term of "God" – like spirit in general – has a physical carrier, that is the brain.

Logic commands that with the death of the body God loses his existence instantly, meaning that after death there is no God, no spirit, nothing. Matter decomposes and therefore everything spiritual too. Many people call this state the "black hole". Of course this is not a scientific description for the meaning of death, but with death, science and all materialistically thinking human beings have reached the limit of their consciousness. For all that may come after that they do not have an explanation model and thus no language either ...

PAUSE.[8]

Explanation models

How do you die with a model of life that only has a black hole or nothingness at the end? What is such a life about? Is it about the conclusiveness of an explanation model like the atom model or the analogue and digital model or is it about being healthy and happy – until your last breath? No explanation model can explain life. It is always a structure or framework projected on life itself in order to recognize certain connections that may be used for new forms of existence.

An explanation model that is derived from theoretical suppositions is worthless and, if provided with power, only leads to suffering and dogmatism the latter of which is the preliminary stage of fanaticism which in turn leads directly to war.

Let us take for example the following explanation model: *I am the Lord, thy God, thou shalt have no other gods before me*. To establish this explanation model hundreds of thousands human beings were killed under torture because this model is based on the power interest of a

---

[8] The advantage of a printed book or an ebook is that is easier to make pauses than with an audio-book or movie. Such pauses are as important for the digestion of the contents as the pauses between the meals. (The movie is shown in about two hours. This book may take some days or weeks to be read.)

few mighty people and it does not correspond to life in any point. It is a merely theoretical construction, such as the Big Bang or the financial interest model. There are endless life models that having little or nothing to do with life, are diametrically opposed to it and thus cause infinite suffering. An explanation model has to be developed on the basis of observable phenomena of life and be measured by them.

With each of the above mentioned explanation models retracing life there are not only dangers, but marvellous things and ways of life can be created because they were copied from life. However not a single explanation model is capable of representing life as a whole. Therefore it is always only a certain perspective of life seen from a certain angle from which an explanation model is developed.

So it is not solely the question of which explanation model copied from a certain aspect of life is more truthful and genuine than the next. We deal with the question of what serves this or that explanation model.

I suppose this question is answered unequivocally by every human: the explanation model I use for my reality (because I perceive it) is expected to serve me for realizing my plans. If my plans are ethically pure, and I do not exert violence on other persons or nature or animals, I try to use it for my or someone else's benefit. For every human being there is the project of living healthy and happy until the end of their physical existence. If you adopt this project you can decide which explanation model you want to accept as your reality: the one which gives you eternal life or the one which only gives you a single life? Which of them, do I believe, will lead me to a healthy and happy end?

4
Continuity of life

When you look at a new-born baby, you do not get the impression that you deal with a soulless piece of meat. On the contrary: often you discover an old and wise person when you look them into the eyes, not a blank page anyway. If you really take them in, you will find that you deal with a whole personality. This personality has not been formed from zero in nine months. Neither is it the product of the genes of their parents. Genes are biological elements of physical nature but not the person's character. On closer inspection it is a very special and unique character that cannot be compared with anything. More often than not, when you get to know someone closer, people usually say: "Quite the grandma" or "Quite the grandpa, uncle, aunt etc." Such similarity strikes us because the compared person is well-known to us.[9] In comparison with persons in wider surroundings it is more difficult to see these similarities.

According to the explanation model of the continuity of life we judge a parallel to be not "quite" the grandma or grandpa, but as if it *is* the grandma or grandpa. We can even feel this congruence when the person concerned has changed their gender during reincarnation. Thus it always depends on the glasses we are wearing when we observe life – it is as easy as that when it comes to seeing what our explanation models allows us to see. Those who think in an analogue way will never ever understand a smartphone. They will have to put on the digital glasses, only then will they be able to decipher a smartphone.

If I look on the new-born as a blank hard disk in which I have to write an education program I will have problems recognizing the faculties this being has brought here and fail to promote them. So the

---

9   You will find helpful ideas in "Personal Masterplan for reincarnation" (see annex).

little being is stuffed with everything his parents think that it will be good for it and as a consequence create a huge amount of educational difficulties. This means that I have to push the child to do something which does not correspond to the continuity of his evolution from one life to the next. I would rather not push (educate), but only promote and further the things and hobbies the child wants to do. As long as I do not see what the child has brought to this world, I sit and wait, because when I give it the freedom to show me his faculties, it will do so.

New experiences

If we can consider the beginning of life beneath the aspect of reincarnation, it will be easy for us to also see the end of life from this aspect. We were already at the point of becoming aware that in death the body dies and decays, since it consists of physical elements bereft of the energy to maintain their connection. However the soul does not consist of physical elements, so it cannot decompose into these. And at birth we note that the soul is alive when it shows itself again in the new form of a boy or a girl. So it has not been reborn because it would have had to die first. It merely created a new tool for expressing itself and making new experiences. This is exactly what the explanation model of reincarnation is about: to make new experiences so that we can go on evolving. This is the very sense of life.

We would hardly continue to develop if our body was immortal. Since human beings are creatures of habits, it is hard for us to change our own patterns. Especially if we were always in the same body, because the scope of our experiences would be quite limited and therefore the evolution of consciousness we could make in a single body would remain very restricted. This very fact would endanger the existence of humanity even more than the present speed of our evolution of consciousness, as we see that we lack the awareness of maintaining our planet as perfect as it was created.

So we need to expand our consciousness as fast as we can so that mankind on this earth has a chance to experience love on a larger scale: not only love between people, but love towards all creatures and the whole nature – in order to live our life with and not against nature. To do so we urgently require new possibilities of experience going beyond what we can experience in only *one* life with *one* body and *one* identity.

If as an adult I suddenly had to face a completely new situation, maybe even in a different, unknown culture with a new language and a new passport, this would be a great challenge for the evolution of my consciousness. Some people, above all refugees, undertake this experience consciously and often forcibly. Yet this expansion of consciousness is not enough in comparison to what humanity needs.

I can make a bigger leap with a new body and a new identity, even if I have to part from the idea that I will have to continue right at the point where I left my former life as far as the level of my consciousness is concerned. This is quite a challenge, much more than the one I could experience in a physical continuity, i.e. an extremely long life (anyway it is not possible to have an eternal life in one body).

Since this leap is a bit difficult for creatures of habit like us humans, it is absolutely necessary and free from stress if I do not have a new life as an adult like in resurrection, but as a baby. As a new-born I grow softly into new conditions with my new tool, called *body*. Only with a new body and the slow adaption to new circumstances can we accept them, independent of how advantageous they may be or not. As an adult we could never adapt so easily to them as a baby can.

Luckily we develop our (marked) ego merely in adolescence and have already come to terms with the new conditions by then. If we started straight away with our marked ego from the former life into the new one, we could not change around to the new conditions so that we really begin and experience something new. These new experiences are necessary to expand the consciousness of the former life. We first have to be babies who adapt to life and the new situation, so that we learn to endure the new reality that awaits us to be able to make effective use of it.

We live in a time in which the density of events grows with lightning speed (I will come back to it later). Now if technological progress is picking up speed, we can deduce that the evolution of consciousness is also happening faster. It is true that we live longer, almost twice as much as 500 years ago, but we also reincarnate much quicker than 500 years ago. This means that our scope of experiences for the evolution of consciousness is also augmenting because we stay less time in the bardo (the phase without human form).

This is from pure necessity because if now – at the beginning of the 3rd millennium according to the Christian calendar, and in the middle of the 3rd millennium of the Buddhist calendar – the evolution of consciousness is not advancing rapidly, we will definitely destroy our planet. We are daily destroying one species only to expand our lifestyle in the present form on the whole globe. By installing our lifestyle other species have to give way. This attitude is not leading us anywhere good. And it is not only other species that we human beings endanger and destroy, it is nature as a whole. As long as we believe that we only live once, we may behave absolutely irresponsibly in our egoism according to the motto "after me the deluge" (don't worry, there will be future generations who will clean up our mess). If we adopted the awareness of a continuous development, we could learn from our mistakes in the former lives and become aware of the fact that we have to make amends and clean up the mess we have caused in our former lives. Such an awareness would speed up the evolution of consciousness of mankind as a whole enormously and maybe we would still have the chance of becoming better humans in time.

Change of form

For those who practice focusing their consciousness on the continuity of life, death is not the end but a change of forms, not something that could make you feel afraid or even scared. Changes of forms happen quite often in life: you move house, you change clothes, you change your job or your partner. However you do not die in any of these cases, although you may feel like dying. Many people know the pain of separation, especially if a love relationship is concerned. Yet the relationship to your own body is the strongest love relationship for human beings in this materialistic world that focuses on the well-being of the body.

To separate yourself from your body is felt to be a more difficult job for most of us than to say good-bye to a long-term love relationship. This is valid for both persons: the one who is leaving and the one who is being left behind. How often does it happen that you have to admit during a separation or divorce that the relationship had been over for quite a while before it was terminated in the end? Both persons involved would have saved themselves a lot of suffering if they had separated before they started to torture each other.

The same goes for dying. Even there you may spare yourself a lot of suffering when you admit in time that in fact the best time in your life (the joyful relationship with your body) is over and that you could enjoy a pleasant, healthy (or halfway healthy) end. Certainly the explanation model you adhere to is playing an important role for this kind of joy. It depends on whether you relate to a spiritual or materialist concept of belief.

To the term *spirit* you could assign the spiritual aspects of your being like soul, awareness, subconscious, feeling, psyche, thinking, I, identity, reason, sanity etc. The term *matter* could be assigned to the body, the physical movements, the organs, hearing, seeing, touching, tasting, smelling, age, symptoms, sounds, speech and death. If we compare both terms we will notice that during funerals nothing of the spiritual aspect is buried or cremated, only physical matter.

So I may part from the idea that death cannot affect spirit. Everything dealing with physical death has nothing to do with spirit, only exclusively with matter.

If you wish to live a long life, you may desire to keep matter for as long as possible. Yet matter will not persist eternally and we should be thankful for it, because it would be horrible if matter did not decompose. A horrific pile of bodies and vegetation suffocating all life would be the consequence. A ludicrous thought or wish, since the persons we would prefer that they do not die because we love them so much could not even be born. Becoming and passing away are two sides of the same medal. Only becoming without passing away is not possible in universe. So we would rather not wish for an eternal physical life – although the present practice is a different thing.

With the consciousness of a singular life you will surely make an effort to preserve life for as long as possible. Most times this wish leads to a very unpleasant phase of infirmity. You may not be able to imagine another life, then infirmity is still better than the black hole, and people willingly accept a lot of inconveniences and even long-time suffering. How often do we hear or read the news that: "He or she passed away today after a long and serious illness …"? It is gruesome to imagine what happened there.

So what would be a good wish? If life is supposed to consist of joy until the last breath, one would rather adopt the change of forms (in reality death is nothing else) as long as you can still feel joy of life. And when do you feel most joy of life? You feel it when there are still new things to discover daily. Those who are curious to see new things every day will always continue to evolve and will become old in their present body. However not the fact that you get old is the essential thing but the joy of life you daily feel anew.

Therefore some people die very early because they foresee that under the given circumstances life cannot get better. So they look for new conditions and with death they will only find them if they already have trust, vision and hope for a new life under better conditions. Yet if there is no intention in the concept of belief in the person concerned, there will not be any energy going into it. The process of dying may become difficult and more often than not it will take place in depression and a desperate agony.

For the bereaved with a consciousness of a singular life the idea of someone leaving their body joyfully in order to change their conditions of life may seem strange or impossible. I do not speak of suicide as in the case of Jamgon Kongtrul Rinpoche you may think of suicide. I speak of the carefree and conscious process of dying with the soul having a clear idea of the fact that there is no possibility of continuous evolution in the present form any longer.

The best moment to die

Let's draw a profane parallel to the question: What is the best moment for dying? This question is also asked by many car owners. Will they sell or scrap the car as soon as the repairs are getting bigger and more frequent even when it is still working or should they drive it until it breaks down completely? Such a question is answered in different ways. What shall I wish the car owner? The best I can do is not to meddle with his considerations unless he asks me explicitly. Even then I could merely tell him what *I* would do with my own car in that case. This does not mean that he should do with his car (i.e. with his body) what I think is best to do with mine.

In fact it only depends on the sense when changing the body. When does it make sense to leave one's body? Instead of saying: "I wish you a long life" it would make more sense to say: "I wish you a sensible and meaningful death", meaning it to be the only loving wish we can express. We should be able to talk about this sense with our confidants. At least you should agree with yourself when answering the question: *When does my death make sense?* The task is the same as in the case of the car or with all other material goods from which I have to separate some time in the future because nothing lasts forever: if I do not cling to property I will substitute it when it is most sensible. This is what every share trader is doing on a daily basis.

Look at the evolution of your life and ask yourself what made sense and what did not. Every day, month or year when you developed, your consciousness did make sense. This cannot be wrong meaning that as long as the stock index is going up it makes sense to keep the share, the car or the body. In simpler words: it makes sense to learn something that makes you healthy and happy. It surely does not make sense to learn something that makes you ill and unhappy though there is plenty of this feeling in humans.

However when the restrictions of the body increase or the car starts to need excessive repair or the share loses its value many people hope that everything will be fine. Imagine someone saying this when your car has already been driven more than 100.000 miles and gives you serious trouble. Or if the share is going down and someone pretends that it will go up again.

Ask your inner self what prompts you to accept such advice? Which emotion is it? One from the ego or one from the soul? Are you prepared to say: I thank you and let you go? Why should I not die now? Why do I cling to life, to the car, the shares and so on? I have already crossed the zenith and "everything will be fine" has no attraction for me because the only criteria for me is purposeful joy of life. I do not follow the impulse to get more benefit out of this matter/body. My body has served me well for a long time, now I may say thank you and let it go, thus dying with dignity. You may evolve towards this last state of consciousness during your life and you can expand it decisively e.g. by doing *Soul writing*®[10] and communicating

---

[10] In case you want to work with *Soul writing*® practically you can find concrete advice in "Personal Masterplan for Reincarnation" (see annex).

with your soul by listening to your inner self. Do not think your state of consciousness on the subject of "dying" is what you hear from the outside. Normally this is a consciousness which does not promote your evolution. Exceptions are possible though – thank God. Yet most people when they are faced with death will only stammer helplessly, even in official funeral talk. Very rarely reincarnation is mentioned because it has been banned from our Western Christian vision of the world in the Council of Constantinople in 499 a. D. when the Pope removed this subject from the ecclesiastic liturgy on request of the emperor. This only changed 1500 years later!

Is it not arrogant to decide if I want to decide whether to live or to die?

Who else should decide this? God?! – Who is God if not yourself?

I know that this thought is very difficult for most of us. In former times such thoughts have cost the lives of millions of people because the official way of thinking is: "I am the Lord, thy God. Thou shalt have no other gods before me."

I remember distinctly how much the historical aspect was emphasized in my history lessons. The Greeks were the last Europeans to worship several gods whereas the Romans already followed the one Christian God in the end. On the same occasion monogamy was gradually introduced, it being an inseparable part of monotheism.

One common reincarnation question is: "How often do you have to be beheaded before you submit to the monotheist doctrine? – Often!

Even if we are aware of the fact that our evolution of consciousness is continuing from one life to another, there is no reason not to explore the potential of development in every life to the fullest. Certainly there may be conditions being so disadvantageous that you may turn around before even obtaining a form which makes you capable of living your life. Our species usually takes nine months to obtain such a form – a long time in which many things may happen and a lot of knowledge can be gained. This phase can be looked upon as a test: can my mother or the other involved persons like my father, my siblings, grandparents or whoever in my surroundings in which I am supposed to be born into give me the opportunities I wish for? This does not only depend on the mother, but on the whole environment in which you grow up in order to unfold your full form which is reached by man statistically speaking at the age of 22 or 23.

There are also beings for whom the conditions they are born into are not of primary importance. A greater role is played by their own constitution. Only after they start incarnating they notice that their constitution would actually not be capable of developing an intact form. This is why they go back to a non-physical phase. There is nothing reprehensible in it. Some beings acknowledge this fact earlier than others, this is normal – that's life. Even if the bereaved family members feel pain and grief then.

Therefore it may be comforting to look at nature, to which we humans also belong: how many seeds grow to be plants and how many do not even sprout and how many only grow a little? The ratio of the beings who develop to their full form when incarnating and those who stop this development at an early stage is one to one billion, say biologists, if they count every fertilized ovum. How many sperm does the man ejaculate which never even reach an ovum? This ratio is no better than the woman's. Even during menstruation there may be quite a lot of fertilized ova in different stages of fertilization. It will only be noticed by the woman if the foetus is some weeks old.

Even this is completely normal in nature. For all sadness it causes it does not mean you are ill, infertile or a bad character. In the end it only means that the being who made an effort to incarnate did not continue with it.[11]

---

11 Also this subject may be treated with *Soul writing* with concrete advice in "Personal masterplan for reincarnation" (see annex).

How to reincarnate optimally

The density of events is increasing exponentially – like I mentioned before – since entering the industrial age, which is why we incarnate ever more rapidly. Consequently ever more human beings are incarnated on this planet with a physical form. The former ages like the age of the crafts, agriculture, gathering and hunting took always longer than the ensuing age. The industrial age has already been superseded by the communication age around 1982. Since the diffusion of the Internet we can talk of the information age which will soon give way to the consciousness age. One age always conditions the next. No phase can be skipped, but as I said:

The phases are getting shorter, because the evolution of consciousness mankind has gone through in the preceding age and the resulting higher level of consciousness have contributed to an ever quicker process of awareness.

The human consciousness as a whole, however, only evolves significantly if every individual is working on it for themselves. There is a self-fertilizing process as the individual evolution of consciousness is prompted by the general one. Naturally the individual also embraces the new communication possibilities of the new circumstances and conditions in order to speed up their own evolution of consciousness. In a nutshell: the global process of growing awareness is a moving wheel of individual and collective endeavour. The motor for it is the same individual being causing the process and profiting from it at the same time.

The whole sense of incarnating is to make experiences which raise our level of consciousness and thus contribute to the evolution of mankind as a whole. So nobody may complain about the general awareness being so low without including themselves and advancing their own process of becoming aware.

Get this clear: humanity is not incarnating but only individuals. To be sure you may benefit from the rise of general consciousness on a personal level, yet the general consciousness merely evolves as fast as you evolve yourself. In the industrial age this was even more difficult than it is now and therefore development was slower. With the communication age, since the majority of the gross national product has been generated by means of communication (phone, media, computer etc.), for the large majority of mankind it has been possible to access those contents necessary for speeding up any individual process of evolution of consciousness.

In the 1980s there was hardly any so-called esoteric literature available for Westerners. In the meantime we find whole departments of this literature in large bookstores. The online book market is booming right now especially in this kind of books. The term "esoteric" is gradually losing its negative connotation. In many places it is substituted by "living more consciously", "modern life" or "personal growth". Now and then however some esoteric book titles are suspected of being written by sects. But this is decreasingly taken seriously and ever more made fun of.

Yet my daughter aged 17 recently told me that in 2016 the subject of an exam in the public school system was about sects. The then school administration wanted to know how the new generation thought about sects, because they were afraid of sects endangering the established system. My daughter chose the sect "12 Tribes", which had made the headlines several times. Anyway the teacher had allowed explicitly that the choice included the Catholic Church too, as it possesses the very same features of a group of people that may be catalogued as a sect.

Special attention is directed to its sexual behaviour which particularly in the case of the Catholic Church is of unspeakable misery. There are not only "suspicions", but indeed massive crimes. It is a great success of the communication age to have discovered and made public these crimes: sexual abuse has certainly been as wide-spread as nowadays in the Catholic Church but in former times it has been a lot more difficult to make it public.

Thanks to the Internet and mobile phones with photo function the conditions have been met for a speedy evolution of consciousness on this very planet – and it cannot be stopped because it is a cosmic necessity. In the times of the gatherers and hunters there were scarcely any means for developing one's consciousness. And the soul had missed little if it had not been incarnated on earth for quite a while. It did not matter if you were without a body for more than a hundred years. If you stayed away from Earth for some decades or even a whole century nowadays, you would have trouble coping with life. You would be marginalised as old-fashioned and out of sync. If you die now, you had better incarnate again quickly, otherwise you cannot keep up with the speed of events and the potential for evolution.

And the end of the last century we had to wait patiently to get an answer to a letter. Nowadays we get nervous if we do not receive an answer to an email in three hours. The electronical development is so fast that it affects almost every earthly activity. That is why we notice a strong increase in the density of events. Those who remain in bardo (the time between death and conception) for too long have trouble coping with everyday life on earth even after a few years. This means that they have more problems using the tools of their evolution of consciousness. If we want to incarnate quickly we need to learn to control our thoughts, since they are the vehicle of steering us into the next incarnation.

Thought control

How do we learn to incarnate in a way that we get the biggest benefit from it? We may part from the idea that our thoughts do not stop after death. They go on, so it is logical, advisable and reasonable to learn thought control at an early age. What does thought control mean? How can I control what I am thinking? I would have to be able to position myself *in front of* my brain and only let in those thoughts I have controlled and believe to be thinkable and block all the other thoughts. This is not possible because in order to exercise control I have already thought what I may not want to think. From this point of view thought control would be a negative tautology: I think what I do not want to think (e.g. "Do *not* think of a pink elephant …").

So what is thought control supposed to be? It is correct and matches the experience of all people that the train of thought never stops – even if we are asleep. It is true that we are sometimes aware of our thoughts in the form of dreams we partly remember. But nobody can part from the fact that they have stopped thinking only because they do not remember their thoughts. The same goes for the thoughts we have when we are in a coma or as a baby or even before as an embryo. Strictly speaking we also have thoughts during conception and before. The least part of our thoughts is beknown to us. Yet we can revive each thought taking it back into our consciousness actively. But what do we do with the thoughts that arrive by themselves which are bad for us? How do we control them?

The easiest method is to say *Stop!* or *Cut!* energetically at the moment we notice an upcoming thought which is not healthy for us. The energetic *Stop* or *Cut* can consist in repeating this word quickly and often – if possible aloud – until the disturbing thought has been drowned and disappears. In a way we take away the energy / focus from the thought giving it to the sound *Cut* as long as our breath lasts: *cut, cut, cut, cut, cut, cut, cut, cut, cut, cut, cut, cut* … until the last drop of my breath, then there is silence. Almost every thought is dissolved by this method.

Naturally there is another thought appearing just after the *Cut*. Yet we have gone a long way if we manage not to go on thinking this uncomfortable thought thanks to the *Cut* (or *Stop*). Afterwards we can relax for a split second and ask: "What will I think next?" and gain some distance from our thoughts. At least we have reached a point where we have stopped negative thinking which has a toxic effect on us.

There is a detailed manual for thought control in the annex under "Personal Masterplan for reincarnation". You may experiment successfully with this technique. It is worth trying!

Exercising thought control shows you that non-attachment to your thoughts means that you first have to perceive them completely before you can let them go. It surely sounds contradictory: I shall let go of my thoughts, I shall not interpret them so that I will perceive them completely!? It sounds even more incomprehensible when you are aware of the fact that every thought is already an interpretation. Sit down and feel the carousel of thoughts in your brain, then try not to do something that happens anyway: carry out an interpretation. This means that you think of something without interpreting this thought because you would occupy yourself too intensely with this thought so that you cannot even perceive the next thought.

Who tells us that the next thought is not exactly the interpretation of the present thought that we did not want to interpret? Answer: *The freshness of the thought itself shows it.* If the next thought does not feel like a fresh one, it must be an interpretation, or justification, of the last thought (interpretation). This means: we are inside a carousel of thoughts and all the time we think more or less the same thing. A fresh thought is not an evaluative or justifying one, it is better not to waste any thought on the thought itself. It is fresher to look at the next thought and the next and the next and the next ... – from this non-attachment emerges a flow of images which means that we are in the Here and Now.

When we stop seeing the cuts between the different images (thoughts) in our brain, we are in meditation. We do not need a special place for that, no special tuning in. We can also cross the hall of a train station being in meditation.

In reality our thoughts only consist of perceptions we try not to interpret. The film going on in your brain without your intervention is a singular one in the whole universe, it is exclusively *your* film, no other being knows it. It represents your singularity. Only you are responsible for it.

If it comes to relationships and love is in the game, then both partners often intent to imagine a common film. This means both think in parallel ways for a while. Sometimes only for seconds, sometimes it becomes an obsession and mostly it is only illusion. Long-standing couples are used to think only what the partner thinks – at least they think they do. Many people do not want to do this. If there are no more new experiences and stimulating impressions, e.g. after retiring from professional life which has forced them to be active and creative, mental activity gradually stops. Many die very quickly without enjoying their retirement for which they have slaved away during all their life.

The unhappier people are about what they think, the earlier they die. For the Government this can only be a good thing when people do not get old, because it saves them money. Just think of the public outcry concerning the apprehended "demographic age pyramid", which in its generalization means a discrimination and devaluation of the human capacities. Under such sad circumstances it is surely more sensible to die than to stay here. But this is not a good starting position for the next life.

Creating a good life-movie

We should take care to create our ideal film in the Now as well for Tomorrow. This film is created by our own thoughts and best jotted down in detail. (The "Personal Masterplan for Reincarnation" in the annex helps you to get started.) Ask yourself: What would be the best and the greatest thing for me? What will make me really happy and healthy? What will make me remain healthy? What is good for me and increases the well-being of others? You believe this film to be true, you project it with your thoughts and write it down in detail, then it will become your own and very personal, subjective truth: *The observer changes the observed object by observing it.*

As trivial as this sentence may sound, Professor Werner Heisenberg was awarded the Noble Prize for Physics for it when he was 31. From 1942 since 1945 he was the head of the *Kaiser-Wilhelm-Institut für Physik* in Berlin. After the end of the Nazi regime its name was changed to *Max-Planck-Institut* whose director was Heisenberg until 1970 and which later was renamed after him.

Franz Josef Strauß, a powerful German politician and minister of nuclear matters, made Heisenberg the protagonist for nuclear energy. Strauß always wanted the German government to have its own nuclear missiles. Luckily Werner Heisenberg succeeded in talking him out of it. Anyway the then valid NPT (Nuclear Prohibition Treaty) was against the minister's aspirations although he and the former Chancellor Adenauer would gladly have tipped it over. However Strauß held on to nuclear technology and appointed Heisenberg for the *Deutsche Atomkommission (German Nuclear Commission),* where he praised the "Peaceful Use of Nuclear Energy". The company *Siemens* together with its daughter KWU made the biggest profit from it because they built most of the German nuclear power plants.

Also my dad Erich Kuby used to support the peaceful use of nuclear energy with his lectures to a large public, since Werner Heisenberg was his brother-in-law. They considered themselves very progressive, as their mission contained the word "Peace". In spite of the scientific know-how there was a nuclear power station built in Garching near Munich whose waste could be used to make – worse than nuclear weapons – plutonium-weapons, producing waste which will contaminate mankind for millions of years.

Uncle Werner died of tongue cancer, at a later point I interpreted it as the expression of his unsolved conflict to have brought to life something that he would have cared to retract at the end but did not dare to put his reputation at risk. How do you want to interpret such a death? As a form of suicide? My mother, Heisenberg's sister-in-law, the oldest of five children of Hermann Schumacher, rector of the *Friedrich-Wilhelm-University* in Berlin, supported me with the idea of letting Uncle Werner express his last conviction before a camera, even if he was no longer able to speak fluently. Yet Aunt Liesl, his wife, was against it.

My mum would have agreed with it, if he had been her husband. It was not a sudden death – the process took some time. Uncle Werner was disappointed with life; that became clear when he said his last words to my mother with his wife being out of the room:

"In the end everything turned out wrong" – then he took his final breath. He could not announce to the public that he had made a mistake when supporting the nuclear fraction. Very tragic for everybody.

My father had a lot less to lose when he changed his opinion thanks to my mum and questioned the nuclear power plants late but not too late. He was only a reporter, but Heisenberg was a scientist. Both of them worked at a high level but socially, a scientist's job weighs more than a journalist's. So it was more difficult for Heisenberg to change his opinion publicly.

Nevertheless, I am very proud of my Uncle Werner, as one of his theories helps me understand the *KUBY method*® today and why it works so stunningly well as a self-healing method for all the different problems we cannot solve with rational thinking.

His theory states that there cannot be any objectivity in the very sense of the word. This is very soothing because the subjective truth is the overall criteria for our own existence. This means all the possibilities for your life-movie are open to you. You create your own personal truth.

5
The cosmos vibrates

Jamgon also created his own movie naturally. If this film is for the benefit of all, it is in its synchrony with the universe, because there is love and harmony and also death. So how did this work in Jamgon's case? Which thoughts have crossed his mind in order to die, so healthy and young as he was? Jamgon, too, lived his own film created by him such as you and me, such as any one of us. Even Topga says: "Jamgon must have had an important reason to leave." How can we decide to die out of an important reason, but then not commit suicide or be a victim of a potential attack or assassination attempt by others? It rather looks like Jamgon was a victim of the pigeons which he avoided. How is it possible to synchronize such a thing to the second?

At this point you realize that you do not progress with the terms of fate, coincidence, God etc. You urgently need a different level of consciousness. I get the impression that a lot of this esoteric stuff in the book-shelves is only a new form of mysticism stopping people from taking responsibility for their own life. Therefore I prefer physicists like Werner Heisenberg and Hartmut Müller, better known as the inventor of *global scaling*.[12] If you can prove mathematically that time is only a construction, that the past and the future exist at the same moment, your own linear thinking has reached its limits.

There must be change of consciousness, otherwise you can only remain in the mystical and the irrational. If you want to accept that these mystical notions are the elements of the cosmos, it would be an inscrutable chaotic heap. However this does not explain such synchronic events as Jamgon succeeded in creating. Nor can you explain the continuity of soul with these terms.

---

12   My film *Melody of the Universe* (see annex/media shop).

Yet with mathematics or physics there is a crack of insight where we have seen that everything vibrates and that space seems to be 99,99% empty. However space is not empty, it vibrates: not as a reaction to a frequency impact but by itself, like every atom. So space is not empty, dead or might be neglected, but it lives in a non-materialized form. The form is only generated by the communication of the atoms with each other. This is why we cannot imagine anything material with respect to the term atom, though it is (at least) 99,99 percent spirit. What we perceive as matter in this universe, is only a tiny part of 0,01 percent.

Everybody vibrates in this frequency of spirit! In each of us vibrates the entire cosmos. Our breath is cosmos. Every being is part of this cosmic and atom-based vibration. So it is impossible to feel separate and isolated.

Our brain has 1084 synapses. These are more possibilities than the elements of the universe. Although this seems to be a large number, at every moment every synapse can connect with any other one in four steps maximum. *Google* shows us a tiny drop of the blueprint of our brain which is similar to an ocean of drops. We are not able to imagine such a construction neither in a linear way nor as a second, third, fourth or fifth dimension. Only mathematics can help.

Global scaling is based on the mathematics of *Leonard Euler* and many others who have risen to this level in the meantime. However there are still many insights to be obtained which Euler discovered in his Russian period and which are neglected by Applied Mathematics. The letter *e*, the Eulerian nature constant, is well-known. But many of the important insights he had when he was working at the Russian court, are still neglected and not understood in all their scope because, in Germany, people considered the Swiss scientist's thinking as too revolutionary.

Global Scaling does take it into account.

According to *global scaling*, energetically speaking, the universe is a gigantic copying machine every being can use in *real-time* and on its own. What can everyone do for it? Produce a good vibration. How do you produce a good vibration? By thoughts. By what thoughts? Those who serve the well-being of all. The universe itself also does this by serving the benefit of every single being. When I think of war, I get war, when I think of love, I get love and so on. In other words: "The way you shout into a forest is the way the echo sounds." This law of resonance can be expressed mathematically. I am not able to do it, but I know that it is possible. Our thoughts are the strongest force, they are the blueprint for the "copying machine".

Of course the copying machine does not copy every nonsense. Egoism comes to its limits automatically when one starts cutting the tree on which one sits. Our host is nature and it is destroyed by thoughts like envy, greed, possessiveness, jealousy, hatred and ignorance. This is not a mystical thought pattern, it is the course of things. The universe offers abundance and wealth to *every* being. Only the egoists do not believe it. They are permanently afraid of shortage. Mother Earth and Father Sun and everything else in the universe provide for us anytime – nonstop.

Together with the whole universal spirit they fulfil every wish if it means love. Love means harmony – and harmony means: *energetically on the lowest level*. The universe is very economical for the following reasons of logic: acting caringly does not cause friction, everything runs smoothly. However in order to push through egotistic interests much energy is needed in the form of power. But this is *man*-made, it is not what the universe wants.

Yet naturally, the universe respects our free will – even the will of egoists and materialists. If it was not so, it would not be a universe of love and we really would have a gigantic chaos. Those who act ignorantly may do so, there is no such thing as an imposed happiness. Everyone produces their own karma. This will be shown by your way of dying and whether you know why you die. Jamgon obviously knew exactly why he died. Since it was an important and good reason for the benefit of mankind, everything worked out fine, even for the pigeons at milestone 13.

The truth for the benefit of all

"Looked upon from outside", the universe is without sense. In the soul where you create your own universe, the observed changes the observed object. So the universe is created as the result of all projections. An eternally changing, infinite something. The only valid truth, the subjective truth of all beings – this is the universe.

However every subjective truth is a creed and in so far the universe "merely" consists of creed, there is nothing else. Everyone may believe their own creed to be true, that means breathe truth into it and search for proof.

"Looking for a Sign": everybody does this in order to justify their creed. This is ok because it is the principle according to which life works. However it is not really necessary to wage a war in order to impose on other people the creed for which one believes to have found signs of truth – subjective truth.

Each soul is of course a subjective soul. When I am not well, nobody is well. When mum and dad love me, everyone is fine. Whether they do it or not, depends on my interpretation. I feel loved by Mother Earth and Father Sun and boundlessly gifted by them. They love each and every one. This is my reality. It makes me happy and healthy for the benefit of all. Not in the future, not in the past, but NOW.

NOW I experience the world as I imagine it. I only believe what I see with my inner eyes. I look sharp because I want to experience it. I am the actor and at the same time the director of my reality, my scenes. We do not do magic. We create our own reality as credibly as possible. There is a solution for everything for the benefit of all and this is exactly what we create. I wish for complete happiness, not only for half of it.

Every wish is a movie. In script style[13] we write down the scene we want to experience thus creating a blueprint for the universe to copy into reality. The universe registers every syllable, well, rather every *feeling* underlying every syllable. So we get a 1:1 copy and sometimes even better than we can imagine.

If the movie I create is good and is lived by me, this has a positive effect also for dying. This can be seen in the face of a man who has just died. The suddenly unwrinkled and smooth skin of the dead man who formerly looked his age shows in which attitude he has left his body. Most of the old people who die are as beautiful as in their youth. They smile and seem relaxed. They must have experienced death as a positive event, otherwise they would not look so satisfied. You have reached real satisfaction when you die exactly as planned.

What had Jamgon planned? He too had a relaxed, beautiful face after dying in this crash, at 120 mph, in Tenzin's arms and his body was completely unharmed. The thought he had chosen for his death must have been a powerful one with a strong base, otherwise he might have refrained from it in the last second.

Why does a person die so calmly? What makes a person ready for dying? There is only one answer: it must be a matter of relationship. Even if you die of hunger or are a victim of war or perish in a plane crash, for the dying person death always feels like the same experience as love. And love is always a matter of relationship.

Many dying persons do not feel their fear of death in themselves. Mostly they prefer not to die because of somebody else: the partner, the children, the grandchildren, their homeland, or the life span somebody else expects them to have – always someone they think they need them urgently and does not agree if they leave their body

---

13 More about script style in "Personal Masterplan for Reincarnation" (see annex).

now. Which relationship can be so strong that there is a wish to die? The relationship with your homeland? As a martyr for high ethical reasons. For a revolution? For the liberation of others? For love? To protect someone? All these motivations contain a bit of despair. Does any one motivation fit with Jamgon? Was he in despair?

6
Karmapa and his seat-holders

The strongest relationship in Jamgon's life was not with his mother or father (who died when he entered the monastery at the age of six) like other normal people, but with Karmapa. Even before his mother Pema was pregnant for the first time in her life, she had already received a letter from Karmapa telling her that her first child would be Jamgon. He also offered her to care for this child, so that she could entrust Jamgon to him without hesitation. Pema promptly became pregnant and when the child was born, many considered it to be a very special one.

Pema relates: "I was 20 when I gave birth to Jamgon in a Chinese hospital in Lhasa/Tibet in 1954. For a long time I doubted that my son was the famous Jamgon Kongtrul although before my pregnancy we had got a letter from Karmapa's secretary stating that our first-born would be Jamgon. Only when the Dalai Lama confirmed this seven years later, my family took to believing it. This was when I had given birth to my second son Topga.

Other people already recognized Jamgon as an infant. When he was one year and five months old, we went to our temple *Jokang* in Lhasa for morning prayers and when we left, an old man with long hair who looked like a *Sadhu* (a holy man in Hinduism who lives extremely ascetically) gave Jamgon a *katak* with tears in his eyes. After that my child did not want to leave this man again. I thought he had confused him with another person. At the time I was not religious, only a normal Buddhist woman like all of us in Tibet. I only went to morning prayers for traditional reasons.

Later on we knew that this old Sadhu had been a confidant of the 2nd Jamgon Kongtrul who had lived from 1904 until 1952.

I was completely startled that Karmapa knew my name although I had never seen him and that he asked my permission to raise Jamgon. My father-in-law, who was the head of our big family, was strictly against it.

We had no idea why Jamgon often fell ill. He used to have fever a lot. We went from one doctor to the other, from one hospital to the next. They sometimes made him stay in hospital for weeks on end, or they diagnosed TBC and stuffed him with drugs. They even wanted to operate on his lungs. I put a stop to it and went with him to Switzerland to stay in a lung sanatorium.

Karmapa heard of that and wanted to detain me but I would not listen. I felt responsible for my child. Karmapa repeated several times that it was his task to take over responsibility for Jamgon; I did not have to care for him at all, it was not necessary. However it was *my* child. I would not let him out of my hand. When Jamgon did not get better in Switzerland either, my husband went to Malaysia with him, since he had heard that there were especially well-trained doctors. These doctors diagnosed that he did not have TBC at all. We felt completely helpless: some doctors told us that an immediate intervention was necessary, the others said that he was ok.

We then flew to New York with him to get a third opinion. There we were told that Jamgon had to stop all drugs immediately since his liver had already suffered a lot. On this last trip to New York I was already pregnant with Topga. Two months after his birth we received the confirmation of the Dalai Lama that our first-born was Jamgon, so we decided to give him to Karmapa for an initiation ceremony.

In this ceremony my six-year-old febrile little boy drank a big jug of beer in one swallow. I thought he would die. But Karmapa and his monks said that it was a good sign and that the fever would go away. From that moment Jamgon stayed with Karmapa in the monastery with all the other little monks. We only saw him on rare occasions. Kalimpong (India), where we already lived before 1959, is about four hours from Rumtek (Sikkim). When I did take him to our home sometimes, he wanted to go back to the monastery as fast as he could. Jamgon was a healthy child there from the first day. We could not understand anything of it. I have always considered him to be my child. I did not respect him in a special way as others did.

Only now that he has gone I have recognized him. I have never really understood what he has done for mankind. He has achieved more than any other person in his life. During the 49-day-death ceremony with all these many, many people from all over the world who all knew him and told great things about him I became aware of why I had given birth to him."

CK: *You and your family belong to the Gelupa order (the order of the Dalai Lama), how has your spirituality developed in this order?*
Pema: "Yes, both my family and the family of my husband belong to the Gelupa order for several generations. (If you want to compare Buddhism with Christianity, the *Gelupa* order corresponds with the Protestants and the *Kagyü* order of Karmapa corresponds with the Catholics). I first saw Karmapa in Lhasa when I was 21. This was nothing special for me since I was not religious. Only when we lived in exile in India and I went to see Jamgon in Rumtek Monastery up there in Sikkim I saw Karmapa again.

I just cried then without knowing why, without feeling sad or happy. In the end I even rejoiced in the fact that my son had a stronger love for Karmapa than for me. If my son had been raised with me and had gone to college, it would not have been the right thing for him to do.

Destiny, karma or fate provided for the circumstances that in 1957 we had a base for our trading business in Kalimpong (Northern India) and were just staying there when Mao's troops attacked Tibet. As a rich trading family we would have been the first to be executed. We could not go back to Tibet then. My husband, Jamgon's and Topga's father, fell ill when he heard of the attack and his brain became confused. At the same time the Chinese army destroyed Karmapa's monastery *Tsurphu* in Tibet. However Karmapa had fled to Rumtek with

110 of his monks a month earlier. The King of Sikkim had bestowed a gift on him years ago out of gratitude in case that he might need it some time: this monastery near Gangtok capital. Originally Jamgon's initiation should have taken place in Tsurphu in Tibet, yet since we and Karmapa had our exile place in the same region, Jamgon's spiritual life started at the age of six in Sikkim where we settled down.

All his life he came to visit us on rare occasions, only just for a day or for a meal when we was passing through. He never stayed for long, not even if I asked him to. He slept on the second floor where his room was, but only for one night at a time. He was not only our son. He was there for everyone. There in lie his reasons for dying which have a special meaning for everybody, not only for us. These thoughts help me not to despair.

If I consider how he has died, young, healthy, and strong, then I reckon he had to leave in such a way, it was only possible by an accident. Although I do not think it had been an accident. He worked for Dharma (Buddha's teaching) and for the poor. He worked for Karmapa, he was protected. His mission in life was the well-being of others. He never thought of himself, we could always feel that. He bestowed all his time on other people, even as a child. He always wanted to give something to the poor then. At the age of 4 or 5 he used to give away his things to others. Just like that. In the street. He was different from other children. He loved animals. He also let the mosquitos bite him."

I ask Topga: *Do you have sensed Jamgon's connection to Karmapa as strong as your mum did?*

He: *Jamgon's whole life was dedicated to his teacher, everything else was not important. If he had had to choose between his family and his work, it was clear to us that he would always have chosen his teacher.*

Indeed: wherever Karmapa travelled in his 16th incarnation, Jamgon accompanied him. In 1972 Karmapa visited the Occident for the first time in four journeys.

He started in Berlin and ended in Chicago in 1981. Wherever Karmapa showed up, all his existence/being was a mission for the inner and outer peace. Jamgon accompanied and supported him in every ceremony and all rituals.

At the age of 57 when Jamgon was 27, the 16th Karmapa died during a two month trip to the US in Zion, a suburb of Chicago on the 5th of November 1981. His body was brought back to Rumtek Monastery in Sikkim/India where he was cremated according to his wish. This ceremony was led by Jamgon together with his three other representatives or seat-holders. The 16th Karmapa had had four *heart sons*, how he lovingly called the four little monks *Jamgon, Gyaltsap, Situ* and *Shamar* whom he had trained to be his representatives – the same as in several former lives.

When he died in 1981, those young lamas were between 27 and 30 and they had the task to direct Karmapa's order – *Kagyü* – with its large worldwide community according to Karmapa's wishes in an orderly way until he would show up again in his next incarnation as the 17th Karmapa and take up the official business again himself. It was stipulated that the four monks take turns every three years in order to execute this tradition.

However from the moment the 16th Karmapa died, Shamar, who was slightly older than the other three, took over the regency immediately without ever wanting to surrender it again.

Death, power claims, waiting for reincarnation

When Karmapa brought Tibetan Buddhism to the West in 1972 as the first Tibetan – two years before the first trip of the Dalai Lama -, in the following years until today new problems have arisen for spreading Buddha's teaching. As long as Karmapa's activity had stretched to Tibet and its neighbouring countries and even the more distant Asian countries since his first incarnation as Karmapa in 1110, he could still rely on a basic comprehension of Buddhist teachings from which he recruited his followers.

In the West there was no such thing. In 1972 there were hippies and freaks who came to see Karmapa. It is easy to imagine the insecurity of the Governments when creating Buddhist centres in Europe and the USA which then had to be directed according to Tibetan Buddhism. Where would those leaders come from who could be a model for compassion and wisdom for those who wanted to develop their awareness rising above egoism and materialism of the Western consumer society? A very difficult enterprise. Only a few of the lamas trained in Tibet moved westward since 1972. Their status as a refugee hindered many of them to realize their well-meant attempts.

Due to violent crimes against the Dalai Lama in the 17th century Shamar had been excluded from any power position for five incarnations until 1962. Back then he had intended to seize power in Tibet with the help of Nepalese troops. Yet the Mongolian troops came to rescue the Dalai Lama reinstating him as the head of Government in Tibet after 50 days. Only the 16th Karmapa, when he was in exile in Sikkim, enthroned Shamar as one of his representatives and a seat-holder of his order at the age of 12 after being banished for 250 years.

With Karmapa gone, Shamar took over the single rule over the Kagyü order. The other three seat-holders accepted Shamar's power claim and concentrated on their own new clientele outside Tibet. They built their own centres with headquarters in India. Only Jamgon had not founded his new headquarter abroad yet by the time the search for Karmapa's reincarnation started. He lived still at home, at the exile seat of the 16th Karmapa in Rumtek/Sikkim (Northern India) where Shamar ruled in Karmapa's name.

During Karmapa´s former changes of incarnation he had soon been identified in his new form, mostly as a baby, just a few years after his death. And the interim rulers knew immediately to whom they had to surrender their power. Yet after the death of the 16th Karmapa in 1981 there were no clues as to when and where he was expected to reincarnate next. This remained so for 11 years in which Shamar strengthened his power ever more with no regard for the three year turns every ruler was supposed to respect according to the 16th Karmapa's orders. On the contrary, he never ceased to expand his power position causing great tension inside his order. Only the donations which Karmapa had received in Asia was a two-digit million sum. It was not obvious to everybody the immense wealth Shamar had achieved as an interim ruler.

Before his passing away Karmapa, as in many of his former lives, would normally leave a letter stating his address and the day of his next birth. However this time nobody had received such a letter. Neither did Jamgon have any information about where and how the next incarnation would be found.

Ten months before his death in January 1981 Karmapa gave a special present to any one of his heart sons and seat-holders. Jamgon got a golden amulet and Situ a talisman consisting of a small 2 by 2 inches wide pouch of brocade silk with a piece of paper inside, something quite common for a monk: lamas often write a mantra, fold the paper and give it to someone as a secret, effective message which is supposed to stay on the body always. Karmapa gave Situ this talisman saying: *Someday this will help you.*

Situ carried this pouch around his neck for years while he was searching a clue to Karmapa's reincarnation. On his many trips through hot countries the pouch on his breast felt uncomfortable and he put it in his belt where it remained for several years unnoticed.

Only when the search for Karmapa was still fruitless after ten years, he had the idea to take out the paper again to look at it on the 5th of November 1991, Karmapa's death anniversary, even if the saying goes that an opened talisman loses its power: Situ took the scissors and undid the seam of the pouch.

On a neatly folded and sealed envelope with the imprinted coat of arms of His Holiness the 16th Gyalwa Karmapa stood: "To be opened in the year of the Iron Horse" (= 1992). There were scarcely four months left, so Situ could just about wait until then. One might imagine the pressure that would have built up if he had opened the talisman right after the death of the 16th Karmapa. Would the envelope really have remained sealed for ten years? However, on the Tibetan New Year's day at the end of February 1992, Situ opened the envelope and on Karmapa's stationery he found a hand-written poem providing all data of his reincarnation unequivocally: place of birth, date of birth, name of parents and some other features for his identification.

Situ: *On the next occasion I showed this holy letter to the other three seat-holders in Rumtek in March '92. Together we analysed every word in it until the four of us agreed on the fact that Karmapa must be 6 years old in the meantime and the child of a nomad family in Latok valley in Eastern Tibet.*

Who of the four could make the trip to this place immediately in order to establish contact with Karmapa and identify him with the help of the letter? They all thought it to be a lucky coincidence that Jamgon had applied for a visa to China in January for other reasons, which had been granted just now. So there was no other choice than Jamgon to look for the reincarnation of their common master, their guru, ruler, teacher and fatherly friend.

Gyaltsap stressed: *From the first to the 16th, all Karmapas have prophesied their reincarnation. This time the 16th Karmapa had jotted down his prophecy in a hand-written letter on his stationery with his seal and signature. Situ Rinpoche showed us this letter in March 1992, thus fulfilling our wish and we now have our jewel of bliss back. Peace and happiness is with us.*

Shamar, who had analysed the letter together with his colleagues, had agreed upon the further procedure, but only on the condition that the letter and everything they wanted to undertake further was liable to the strictest secrecy. And his colleagues went along with him for various reasons.

Yet when the visa for Jamgon was obtained on the 12th March 1992 and his flight to Tibet was planned for the 26th March, Shamar showed his true interests: suddenly he accused Situ of having faked the letter of prophecy. He said that by no means would he accept as the next Karmapa any boy who was found due to the letter and that he would continue looking for the genuine Karmapa anyway. It became clear to the other three seat-holders that Shamar wanted to install as Karmapa a different person about whose existence he had not announced anything yet.

For the few guests in Rumtek, among whom belonged Rosy Findeisen with her building team and I with my film team, the tension created by this sudden rift overlying the monastery was very strongly felt despite the secrecy.

7
My search for clues towards reincarnation

It was merely by chance that I was present with my team in Rumtek. The story went like this:

In 1987 I was awarded the German Movie Prize for my documentary film *The Old Ladakh*. It was the first documentary film in Germany since 1945 that was successful in cinema – apart from the animal documentaries, especially the one by Professor Bernhard Grzimek *Serengeti must not die*. At the same time, my movie was the first to open the doors to Buddhism in Germany. When I was asked what kind of film I would shoot next with the prize money, I answered: "A film about reincarnation because I want to know if it exists and if so, how it works."

After several efforts to lay hands on such a case where someone dies and where I could get the instructions on how to find him again in his new life, I received the recommendation to document Karmapa's case since there was enough film material about his former life including his passing away. I was told that if I said yes immediately, I might be lucky to shoot the finding of his reincarnation. "Not bad", I thought, "but who will instruct me?"

"Shamar will", it was said in 1987, he is the interim ruler of Karmapa's order *Kagyü*.

As fate would have it, I had an encounter with Shamar in Paris a short time later and after ten minutes of a first contact with him he indeed gave me an incredible carte blanche for shooting with all possible powers, which opened all doors for the successful achievement of my documentary. And so it happened. From all different sides I received a fantastic full funding for this adventurous project with millions of euros. However it stagnated during some years because nobody knew where and when Karmapa had incarnated.

There had been some false starts which made me recognize that reincarnations were also used for tricking people, at least this had been attempted. Of course, there are promises of power and affluence if you have a Karmapa in your own family. This is why I was hanging in the air with this project for several years. However this gave me time to do another film project about the ancient tribe of the *Todas* in Southern India for four years.

When I finished using all kinds of political and diplomatic levers for six months to obtain an official Indian shooting permit for the *Todas*, it was end of March 1992 and my German film team of five and I had planned to fly from Munich via Bombay to Southern India on a Sunday. Everything was packed already when I had an idea on Friday night: why not fly to Delhi first and try to see Shamar in order to ask him face to face if there had been any news in the case of Karmapa's reincarnation? Thought and done.

Flight maneuver, power maneuver

First thing in the morning I call *Lufthansa* airline asking if I can change my flight and first go to Delhi 24 hours earlier and then to Bombay later. I wanted to meet my film crew, who were to fly, as planned, at the gate on Monday morning at 2 a.m. in order to go on to Bangalore and from there to the Todas. "No problem", was the answer. I tell my team that they will have to fly to Bombay without me with all the equipment and then we will continue our trip together from there as planned.

I land in Delhi on Sunday morning at 3 a.m. and have enough time to get to the gate of the Buddhist Centre in the south of the city where I am kindly greeted by the doorman:

Doorman: *Oh, Mr. Kuby, so early?!!*

I: *Good morning. May I ask you, is Shamar Rinpoche in?*

Doorman: *He is just in his morning meditation, but please go up and meet him, he will be very pleased to see you.*

The door to his room is slightly ajar. I knock on the door.
Shamar's voice: *Please come in.*
He sees me: *Oooooh, Kubyyyyyyy – it's you, just in time.*
I say: *Why?* – Good morning, and offer him my outstretched hand in Western fashion. I refrain from throwing myself on the floor full-length as his adepts are expected to do.
S: *Situ Rinpoche has found the prediction letter of His Holiness with the address of his reincarnation.*
I: *Wonderful!*
S: *Hurry up, go to Rumtek. We four Rinpoches will meet you there in the next days and discuss further steps.*

As promised I pick up my crew at the gate in Bombay on Monday morning at 2 a.m. explaining them that we will not shoot the film about the Todas which we have prepared for more than six months and that we will not continue to the South either. I announce to my team that I already have tickets for Northern India at 9 a.m. for all of us in order to go on shooting my other film about Karmapa's reincarnation in Sikkim since it is obviously in the hot phase now. Every respect I usually receive from my crew as the producer and director is completely gone because I tuned them up on the wrong film. It takes them a long time to start showing me respect again. However these so-called coincidences are what you experience when you try to be at the service of expansion of consciousness.

We have just begun shooting in Rumtek when we sense that there is a basic conflict between the seat-holders. Shamar parts from the idea that I am on his side and shoot things correspondingly. Although it was him who gave me the project and authorized this comprehensive and exclusive shooting permit, I feel more committed to Karmapa's reincarnation story than to him. How am I supposed to proceed now? It is not my task to decide which trace to follow towards Karmapa's reincarnation and which one not to. I wonder if Situ Rinpoche will let me shoot him knowing that I work on Shamar's orders.

It is extraordinary. Situ reads Shamar's wording of my shooting permit and says spontaneously: "Perfect! It says here that nobody may prevent you from doing your work, please shoot whatever you want." Some time later, directly after Jamgon's death, Shamar pretends that in the power struggle of who will be the next Karmapa there would be two against two: on one side there would be him and Jamgon, on the other side Situ and Gyaltsap. Yet no-one had noticed that I had shot a long interview with Jamgon in Rumtek only two days before his death where I asked him:

> CK: *What do you think of the prophecy letter presented to you by Situ Rinpoche?*
>
> Jamgon: *It is very precise!*
>
> CK: *Do you reckon to find Karmapa's reincarnation with the information in the letter?*
>
> J: *Yes, I am quite certain. The letter is very clear and accurate. Thus we are sure to find Karmapa.*

Naturally I also ask Shamar what he thinks of the prediction letter presented by Situ Rinpoche.

> Shamar: *I told Situ that I doubt the authenticity of the letter.*

Of course I also interview Situ:

> Situ states: *We have decided commonly that Jamgon Rinpoche takes over the responsibility for the search. The reason for it is that he has already planned a journey to Tibet some time ago.*

Shamar confirms his denial:

> S: *I am in contact with a person who was a very close disciple of the last Karmapa. He has informed me that he possessed important instructions to his next incarnation.*
>
> CK: *Did he mention the exact date? The year in which ...*
>
> S: *Yes.*
>
> CK: *Can you say when?*
>
> S: *Yes.*
>
> CK: *Do we have to wait for long?*
>
> S: *I cannot tell now. No, I cannot say anything right now.*

With this statement Shamar is clearly differing from his other three colleagues, and together with his followers goes his own way about finding the reincarnation of another Karmapa. He seems to be aware that he needs a different person than the reincarnation of the 16th Karmapa, if he wants to maintain his rule over the Kagyü order. There has to be a reason why the 16th Karmapa has not left the address of his reincarnation to him but to Situ. Why does Shamar as the incumbent ruler of the Kagyü order not rely on educating the new Karmapa in a way that his own position will not be queried by the adolescent? Instead of accusing Situ of falsifying the prediction letter, he might have said: "Well, pick up the boy according to the information in this letter and give him to me. As the head of the order I will take care of him."

Shamar has not dared to carry out this maneuver in order to maintain his power because he would then have to admit that he has disregarded Karmapa's instructions to take three-year turns ruling the order together with the other seat-holders. He prefers to look for a different reincarnation serving him as a new Karmapa so that he might stay in power anyway. This means that his power claims divide Karmapa's adepts.

Although all this has not been communicated openly and the prophecy letter has not been announced publicly so far, everybody feels that there is a conflict of historic magnitude. In Rumtek there are about 160 monks for whom the four interim rulers are a united holy leadership. Suddenly this union is threatened. Many are wondering how it is possible that all of a sudden there are two different Karmapas in their 17th incarnation. Does this really lead to a division of the order? Nevertheless Situ and Gyaltsap have got it clear that they will continue to follow the instruction in the letter of the 16th Karmapa.

What will I do? In any case it is not my task to decide which side is right. I try to take up the neutral attitude of a movie-maker who documents both sides. However I note that it is less and less possible to maintain this attitude. Even the little monks of eight or ten years ask me: "For or against Shamar?" As Rumtek monastery is the headquarter of the Karmapa order since the beginning of the exile, it is also the seat of government for Shamar. Therefore all monks who live and study here belong to him. Situ and Gyaltsap – as mentioned before – have their own monasteries in Northern India. Jamgon, to be sure, still belongs to Rumtek, but he travels for most of the year. So a difficult phase has started, even for the monks in Rumtek, because the main protagonists of the rift are acting right in front of them.

Jamgon starts his journey – as planned – to Tibet. With the prophecy letter in his hand he is completely sure to find the address in Eastern Tibet where the new six-year-old Karmapa is supposed to live. I would love to accompany him with my film crew to document this finding of Karmapa's incarnation but it is impossible for me and my team to get a visa on such short notice.

Nostalgically I say good-bye to Jamgon, for whom I feel a great closeness since our first meeting five years ago and further encounters later on. He once helped me a great deal to find the right tone for my film *Tibet – Resistance of the Spirit*. He showed me an inner attitude with which I would not force any aggression against China but could tell the truth about how it treated Tibet anyway. It was extremely instructive. When I saw him off, we had another short conversation. I asked him directly: "Why do you think that Shamar wants to keep a secret of the prophecy letter and in consequence the search?"

Now that we know what happened two days later his answer shows so much more than I first perceived. Let us have a closer look and listen carefully.

Jamgon: *First because it is something very special.*
I understand what he wants to say: the conscious, planned reincarnation of Karmapa discloses the highest consciousness ever known to mankind. Not Dalai Lama, not Jesus, not Mohammed, not Buddha – nobody ever had been capable of predicting clearly the conditions and circumstances of his personal future incarnation. (I will come back to this in more detail later.) Yet Karmapa is a normal person of

our time known by many people. He is someone to be watched on TV, on *YouTube* and even online, someone who will surely meet with countless people in his new life too. This is exactly why there should be a lot more enthusiasm to be displayed now that his prediction letter has finally been found.

Jamgon: *Yes, true, but this is exactly why there could be … – how shall I put it? … there could be many … mmmh? … Let us say … "obstacles" …, and in order to avoid them we keep it secret. And second that …*
Jamgon swallows and struggles for the right words and thinks hard what to say. He is becoming very serious, as if he sees images before his eyes showing the events of the following two days. Right after this conversation he will drive to his mother's house in Kalimpong with the brand new BMW. He will stay there overnight and remain in bed almost all day long, drive to the hotel in Siliguri and die in the car-crash on the way to the airport. Is it that what he is seeing or feeling just now?

Jamgon continues to speak hesitantly (my film shows much more than what I can transmit in writing), struggles for words: *… only to … the whole process of it is like … the way, it is really … everything is ready … in reality …*

He is stammering, from his face it is evident that there is a lot happening inside him. Obviously everything indicates that he himself has decided to die and has committed himself to act accordingly – including the change of his name in the death mantra.

It is only now that I understand why he – shortly before that happens what he thinks to be necessary – wanted to choose his words so carefully. It is the last time in his present life that he is standing in front of a camera. These words will survive him. It is an enormous act he must go through and in which he will take with him two of his very close colleagues: his master of ceremony Kunga and his driver Norbu. What justifies this act? Jamgon has a highly developed sense of responsibility for all he does. Why do these two have to go to death with him?

Hanging from a silk thread

Seen from a very high viewpoint, from a meta-level, this can only mean that he was perfectly aware of what was at stake at that moment. If the six-year-old Karmapa cannot appear, the hope for liberating all humans on Earth is gone. Jamgon is very aware of the magnitude of this hope, otherwise he would not have the power to carry out such an intervention in the global political process with the help of the universe. The consciousness of mankind is hanging from a silk thread in these hours. Something similar to an event some years ago when the Berlin Wall was opened due to an apparent communicative misunderstanding. In most cases, mankind does not realize where the changes of their evolution lie and how to set the course of evolution.

For "normally" thinking human beings these considerations may sound completely exaggerated because they part from the idea that you cannot plan your death just as you cannot plan your fate – not to speak of knowing when and where you will be born again. Yet Karmapa has done just this 16 times before and is about to do it a 17th time. Apart from that he has not only been able to predict his next reincarnation exactly and in writing, but he has also done the same thing with other people. It is all about being conscious that life is a continuity. This consciousness has so far merely been practiced and diffused in Tibet, far off the beaten tracks, for 900 years. Now, in 1992, the time has come when this consciousness can be obvious to the whole world. However this quantum leap in consciousness is now extremely threatened by the internal power struggle.

Often in our evolution it is like this: the next leap in consciousness arises from a single person who has a great effect on mankind: i.e. Thomas Edison from Ohio who turned on the electric light for every one of us, or Carl Benz from Karlsruhe who moved mankind from horse-back into cars or Steve Jobs who lifted humanity to a new communication level and so on.

Yet with this reincarnation something much more significant is at stake: it is about a man showing that death does not exist. Just for that, for this evolutionary leap of consciousness Jamgon uses his death. Karmapa will not manage to do this step without help. Who could help him better than the person who was closest to him in the past? If Karmapa is not recognized and honoured as Karmapa, the consciousness of the continuity of spirit will not be spread on a large scale.

There are many cases of highly developed persons who have died early when they had not been acknowledged, mostly they pass away as a child and quickly. These are failed incarnation efforts. This is no wonder if you consider the general situation of human consciousness. Even in Tibet where reincarnation is part of people's consciousness it happened now and again that people did not recognize who was born into their family and thus did not grant the child all the possibilities to express the capacities achieved in all of its former lives. Such children often die in order to incarnate in different circumstances hoping to be reared in a family who gives them a chance to come to their true greatness or at least provides conditions which allow them to continue their own evolution. Not to be acknowledged is an energy-consuming detour for the being who wants to serve mankind.

When Jamgon dies two days later, it should be clear that his own reincarnation must work accordingly. He certainly takes this confidence from his lives at Karmapa's side – especially his present life as the 3rd Jamgon with the 16th Karmapa until the latter's death in 1981. Therefore we will trust that by his planned death he may be able to help Karmapa to incarnate as the 17th Karmapa with certainty and despite all challenges, and that in turn Karmapa will hopefully help him to reincarnate and be recognized as the next Jamgon. However he cannot be sure of that.

Each death is a new challenge. For everyone, even for Karmapa. In fact everyone can do what Karmapa does. We simply do not do it, but he dares to do it. He is going full risk. The difference in general is that some say: "I *am* God", and others say: "I *believe* in God". While

God cannot be anything else than what you are thinking about Him. Yet who is aware of this? How do I recognize the film in which I am? Is it *my* film what is happening? Am I the director and actor at the same time? Or am I in a film in which someone else is the director?

In a whodunit it is always someone else who wants to kill you or you want to kill to avenge evil. How does a story change in which people live according to the motto "for the benefit of all"? When we do not make this dimension of "for the benefit of all" the measure of our thoughts and actions, we separate from the cosmos, because the universe only functions exclusively "for the benefit of all" (see also my interview "I ask Topga" in chapter 3). The Universe is a harmonic fractal as modern physics state. We are all cosmic beings, whether we are mindful of it or not. We are part of this universe, nothing else. So we must get it clear: which hope do we carry in our hearts? What shall liberation consist of?

This question is answered easily: to be really liberated means to be free from death. Nothing less than that. In order to show us disbelievers that this is possible Karmapa has reappeared after his consciously performed deaths under the same name: from Karmapa 1 to Karmapa 16 so far (but he has planned to continue till Karmapa 21), so that we are driven to understand what it is all about in this case. So that we get it clear that this is not a simple transmigration of his soul. Very concretely he states the day, the place and the name of his parents and also the name by which he is called, when he shows up again in a physical form. These are not only vague promises, but clearly planned and comprehensible announcements coming true exactly at the given times.

Naturally there is also a Before and After for the 21 Karmapas since our souls are without beginning or end. Yet we materialists are conditioned by the expectation of a beginning and an end. Therefore it is a lot more convincing for us to recognize the continuity of 21 lives under the same name. This rather suits our way of thinking.

The Before and After are in dimensions beyond that. Only step by step can we lift our own consciousness while we subjectively experience every step as a leap, sometimes even as a gigantic leap. However no step can be skipped. Sometimes a thought or a word or a picture is enough to make a considerable leap in consciousness. For example understanding life as single or as a continuity, these are two different dimensions but we may change from one to the next in a leap.

As I said before: analogue and digital are also two different dimensions and many people took a great leap from one to the next by replacing their analogue phone with a smartphone. The change of consciousness from the analogue to the digital dimension was and is an experience of a leap which has not been easy for everybody. Once an expert told me that if the digital era had 100 steps of evolution, we are at step 7 in 2017.

Also the expansion of the Internet does not only happen in a linear way but suddenly, exponentially, in a leap, when e.g. the State or *Facebook* or *Google* decide all of a sudden to invest billions of dollars in the diffusion of the Internet. Moreover the research for *G5* (generation 5) project is in full swing, preparing a global all-round network linking the ever growing demands of digital use, thus permitting even more evolutionary leaps for mankind stemming however from single individuals.

It is possible to switch from the materialist to the spiritual-emotional perspective by just one word, to remain in the spiritual-emotional perspective then and only look back now and again on the materialist attitude to understand this very perspective. How surely and normally such a new consciousness gets established, is shown in daily life by those who have completed the leap towards the digital era with their smartphone, since they look upon the analogue model in a half-smiling way.

Two days before his death Jamgon is aware of the fact that his plan may fail, it is visible on his face in this interview. Yet only seconds later confidence comes back. The chances to get it right or wrong affect the whole world politics, since it is about whether the international state community should go on allowing China to kill the reincarnation of highly acknowledged Tibetans as babies, like China has done so far in many cases. Although the Chinese do not believe in reincarnation officially, they do have children killed of whom it was said that they are especially honoured personalities who have a great impact on the population.

During its occupation China has learnt so far that Tibetans offer their trust immediately to such a reincarnation. As a consequence the Buddhist belief may gain strength again in Tibet, the very thing China is trying hard to avoid by turning it into a purely egoistic and materialistic concept. This is why China has prohibited Tibetans to speak their language and why the Chinese idiom with its ideological doctrine has been compulsory to learn for every Tibetan child at school for more than 50 years.

Instead of eliminating these highly appreciated personalities, in some special cases where the killing would give a bad impression internationally China has started to identify these reincarnations itself – although it despises the belief in reincarnation and considers it nonsense. However Tibetans do not get unsettled by this. They do not accept these persons the Chinese government wants to establish as highly acknowledged Rinpoches. Peking has just announced that it will find the next Dalai Lama on its own.

Such a thing could also happen to Karmapa at the moment. According to his own prediction letter he must be six by now, so he is not as small as Panchen Lama, the second-in-command in Old Tibet after the Dalai Lama, whom the Chinese had changed overnight at the age of two. The whereabouts of the person reincarnated as Panchen Lama who in 2017 must be about 40 is unknown, while nobody who is cooperating with the Chinese wants to know – and all others are not told.

Jamgon's last words in front of the camera

Before this background Jamgon says the following words in his last interview about the secrecy of Karmapa's reincarnation: *Well, as you know, since we have the letter of his Holiness Karmapa, it is no big deal really. But we want to make sure that we do not commit any mistakes and really find the genuine Karmapa. This is why we keep it secret.*

However: it is no longer possible to maintain the secrecy about the address where to find Karmapa since the prophecy letter has been found. The leaks keep growing by the hour. Indeed it is only a matter of time, a few hours in which China may still make Karmapa disappear. How could Jamgon have an impact on the politics of the superpower China to this effect and in real-time? Jamgon knows how. He is extraordinarily clear-headed and oversees world politics as clearly as the continuity of his own life. Extreme concentration is imperative. I can see it in his face. Besides the Chinese politics there is a second, not less explosive problem to be solved when Karmapas 17th conscious reincarnation is to be established: Shamar – as we have seen – has decided to sacrifice Karmapa for staying in power himself by introducing his own Karmapa loyal to him only. Therefore it is necessary to stop him as well as the Chinese from eliminating Karmapa. If both of them cooperate, then it would be extremely difficult, Jamgon realizes. What must be done?

Jamgon continues: *Besides you know the character of human beings. They have very strange ways of conduct, warped ideas and peculiar expectations etc.*

Jamgon knows what he is talking about, he even smiles at his own words. He still shows his compassion for human weaknesses which create such enormous problems. He knows of the vanities, the power hunger, the diseases and the greed of egoistic characters, the envy and the jealousy which drive people to follow their ego and not their soul. He knows exactly the expectations of his adepts concerning Buddhism. In this mixture of emotions, speculation and deformities of character a solution is needed which is superior to all these disruptive forces. There is Jamgon's confidence coming to fruition in a self-explaining way and without any doubt. His confidence to plan his own death in order to solve the problem is a special spiritual challenge.

In this sense Jamgon ends the conversation with the sentence: *It is all about stopping these unnecessary things from happening.*
Afterwards he goes to bed and has an early start the next morning on the 23th April 1992 setting out for his last trip in this body.

A cosmic friendship

Jamgon's motivation to solve these problems at both a national and international level stems from his love for mankind and his deep friendship with Karmapa. He knows that Karmapa needs help now, no matter how high his consciousness may be. As Jamgon is Karmapa's closest friend – because nobody else but him has been so deeply linked to Karmapa all his life –, he wants to grant him this help from the bottom of his heart now that he requires it and grant it as best as he can. After all he owes his present life to the 16th Karmapa, who had brought him to the monastery at six, where he was instantly freed from his several life-threatening diseases.

The relationship between Karmapa and Jamgon cannot be envisaged as a marriage – even less as a homophilic marriage. Both are united in a friendship of cosmic nature because it is not limited to time nor space. Death is no obstacle or restriction for this relationship. Death is rather a kind of test, some call it *initiation*. It may be imagined as the spark of a spark plug which ignites the concentrated energy of the air-gasoline mixture with an explosion. And this explosion must make sense. A senseless death is a terrible death. Of course many people consider that dying in a car-crash does not make any sense, above all when you are completely healthy and in the midst of a very successful life.

The question which death would make sense should not only be dealt with when your body is declining (see chapter 4), because then it may be too late for the preparing steps initiating a purposeful perspective with which you reflect on your next life. This perspective may – should – bring you joy. This is really the one ingenious thing with dying: you will receive a reset, and will start over. However this reset must be shaped into a form and for this we need firm intentions, then the universe will deliver things accordingly. Those who enter a new life with vague convictions, will receive vague conditions. How do you say in English? "Make up your mind." In my own language – in German – we would put it like that: *Decide where the next phase of your infinite journey through existence is supposed to be.* Probably you have already realized how short one life is. Much too short to make your dreams come true.

In 1110 Karmapa had calculated that the realization of his dream would take 21 lives. One of the conditions for achieving his aim was that the *"Iron Bird"* would fly. This is what he wrote about 800 years before the invention of airplanes! It gives me goosebumps just to imagine a word which neatly describes a technical invention only made about 800 years later. Which capacity must you have now to give a name to something which will only be a reality in the 21th century? Something you can assign a term to, such as the "Iron Bird", e.g. a *747 Boeing* with which Karmapa flew to Germany for the first time in 1972.

This alone was not enough for Karmapa to project the mission of his life. Then in the 12th century he further restricted the point of time with a second image by writing: *At the same time the Tibetans are on the run like ants whose hill is upturned.* He was also inspired by this image 800 years before it happened by the invasion of Mao's army in Tibet and one million refugees, he himself forming part of them in 1959 during his 16th incarnation. With these events he described the moment for the fulfilment of his dream about a peace mission which would reach the "West".

Of course it may be difficult for us Westerners to really project 21 lives. However we could make an effort to have at least an idea for our next life even if we do not believe in reincarnation (yet). Life is too short to master just one discipline. Maybe you have a passion you are already pursuing a second or third time but you are still not satisfied with your performance. Then this is probably something you may want to go on developing. However you do not need to wait until your next life, but you could already pursue this hobby now and give a noticeable contribution to humans, animals or plants – something that corresponds with your dream.

When you have figured out such a vision, the next step would be to think about the best conditions for your next life so that you could really make this dream come true optimally. Which culture, which parents and which surroundings would you need? Which circumstances would be favourable? You cannot master all these projections on your deathbed. Such an intention receives much more energy when you start planning it ahead of time, why not now? It is paramount to do it in writing, because it has a greater effect. Get inspired by my movie and my music. You may also find support under "Personal Masterplan for reincarnation" and also in my seminars (see annex).

Jamgon's decision to die rather than live in the present situation must have had something to do with Karmapa then. Yet why exactly, when he had already reserved a flight for the next day bringing him directly to Karmapa's new incarnation and when he could have entered China with a valid visa easily? This is a question also Topga is asking in vain.

Topga: *I cannot see how my brother's death could help Karmapa more than his being alive?* – And he takes his incomprehension wholly on himself by saying: *This is merely my limited thinking.*

In the meantime we know: as soon as Karmapa's existence is known, there is a high risk of him being eliminated in one way or the other, because at the present moment even the contents of the prediction letter with his address cannot be held under lock and key any longer. It is also possible that the child who fits the description may be substituted for a different one. Such a thing would not happen for the first time. Just imagine that out of the 14 Dalai Lamas – who have ruled in Tibet until now and who in the 15th century have been preordained by the Mongolian Khan to do so from one incarnation to the next – six have been murdered at infant or adolescent age, because the incumbent interim rulers did not surrender their power at the end of their interim phase.

Gyaltsap is very aware of it all and says: *It may be really dangerous if we do not act immediately after Jamgon's death. Therefore we have assigned the task of looking for Karmapa based on the instructions of the letter to a trustworthy person in Tibet – Sherab Terching. Since Jamgon Rinpoche's death every day, every hour and every minute counts.*

Parallel to this search, Shamar sets out for a worldwide journey directly after Jamgon's passing away in order to present himself as his successor in all the places where Jamgon disposed of a large amount of followers. However Shamar still does not know about Jamgon's statement in front of my camera about the authenticity of the prediction letter of the 16th Karmapa. So he goes on spreading the tale that Jamgon as well as himself had doubts about the authenticity of the letter and supported Shamar's efforts to find another Karmapa. First Jamgon's adepts believe him – but not all of them.

In a Buddhist centre in France Shamar – under the enthusiastic cheering of Jamgon's followers – has balloons rising up into air with the inscription *Karmapa Chenno*. This is the traditional call for Karmapa. Yet it is not for the Karmapa whose address is already known to Shamar, but for "his" other Karmapa, of whom nobody knows anything yet. So the chain of reincarnation threatens to come to a halt after about 900 years and a division of adepts is imminent. All this drives the conflict to the extreme.

Only in view of this drama can the car-crash be considered and understood. In this tension-laden situation the universe however has a whole lot of aces to play: why are the pigeons Jamgon asks his driver Norbu not to kill sitting just on this long, straight, empty tarmac road – right on the place where the BMW is skidding and crashing right into the tree on milestone 13?

Is this a strange kind of black humour or a tribute to our superstition? How should we evaluate that if we do not believe in coincidences? And even if we want to believe in coincidences: how often is such a thing happening on a 10 mile-long road which is lined by milestones and trees on either side? These are real mysteries to which we me may have an access with *Global Scaling*[14] (see chapter 5).

In the meantime Sherab Terching in Tibet has received the petition by Gyaltsap and Situ Rinpoche via Fax to look for Karmapa and he is overwhelmed by this petition.

> Sherab: *It is a great honour for me to have been named the representative of Situ and Gyaltsap Rinpoche in Tibet. With the help of the prediction letter I got from them by fax it is a very responsible task to look for Karmapa where the letter indicates. This was really supposed to be Jamgon Rinpoche's task. His death is a great loss and I am very sad. I try to give my very best.*

So now it is not Jamgon who will salvage Karmapa from his incognito but Sherab with his team. What is better now? Does Jamgon communicate with Karmapa from soul to soul and does this help Karmapa more than Jamgon's physical support and possibilities to act?

---

14 My film *Melody of the Universe* (see annex/Media shop).

8
Is it all just coincidence?

How can we as living beings imagine how the communication between two souls works? Normally we deny it because we are inside a body and thus we believe that we need the body for communicating with other beings. Is this true? Are we not able to communicate with someone, above all with humans who are close to us without any words? How often does it happen that we think of a person and then this person appears physically or calls us?

Just yesterday while I was dancing tango with a random partner this person told me that two days ago she went to Berlin to visit a friend after many years. She had figured out whom else she knew in Berlin. She came up with the name of her nephew with whom however she did not have any contact anymore and whose address is unknown to her. She regretted this but did not try seriously to find out where he could live and if it was possible to meet with him. She just dropped the whole thing but she felt an affection towards him that could not be expressed personally. Maybe you can guess what happened next: she gets off the metro at the main station and who does she run into? Her nephew ... and Berlin is not a small town.

Every human being makes experiences at the soul level more or less frequently, depending on whether they are open to them or not. Indeed it is like that: those who are not open to them do not experience this soul level at all or only in such moments when these experiences are appearing massively. And even then many people of our era denigrate them by declaring them coincidences.

What exactly is this phenomenon *coincidence*? Does it really exist? If yes, with whom? Only with you or is there a universal principle, such as logic or the law of cause and effect? For reason-oriented people the law of cause and effect works on the whole planet and beyond.

Also the astronomers know it and recognize it in our planetary system. Certainly this law does not stop suddenly at the edge of our solar system. We may rightfully say that the law of cause and effect is a universal law. How are things with coincidence? Does coincidence contradict the law of cause and effect? In reality it does. Coincidence would be at least an exception to the law of cause and effect. How many exceptions are there? And when do they appear?

Albert Einstein once said: "God does not play dice with the universe." Exactly because coincidence cannot exist. *Coincidence* is merely a word for not knowing. There are more commonplaces to express this ignorance such as "fate" or "God's ways are inscrutable". Just imagine that coincidence would be a cosmic law like the law of cause and effect. Then it could be possible that due to a coincidence the moon would stray off its orbit and crashes with Earth or that Mercury also moves away from its orbit and attacks Venus. If coincidence existed, it could be recognized in the universe. Yet what you do see is the exact opposite: all processes run smoothly in an absolutely perfect order and, as I mentioned before, at the lowest level of energy. This means that every function and every modification in the cosmos works in such a way that no energy is wasted. The cosmos is the most intelligent being, superior to any human imagination by an infinite margin.

Therefore soul contacts cannot be coincidence. Neither could be my accident. To be sure, materialistically speaking the tiles on the roof were somehow slippery and I simply slipped on them. Those who believe in coincidence will just say: *Bad luck*. Yet the truth is that I have steered towards this so-called accident for the last seven years and on the 27th May 1981 the barrel was full to the brim and spilled over. Exactly this experience – lying in hospital for a whole year and thus having all the time in the world to thoroughly rethink my life was what I needed for my further evolution of consciousness, including the recognition that I can transform my body in a spiritual way. This recognition is what I can and may transmit today. So all this was no coincidence but an evolution elaborately planned by my soul.

I admit instantly that I did not understand this "elaborately planned evolution" right away, but I knew immediately that change was imperative. Of course change would also have come about by sitting in a wheel-chair from the moment of the accident for the rest of my life. Yet I would not have fulfilled my task, i.e. being a teacher for the expansion of consciousness. And I had carried out this mission even before falling from the roof but two months earlier I had to acknowledge that this had been done by means that were unsuitable for me. I had thought until then that I could fulfil my vocation to work in this life for the general expansion of consciousness by going into politics. This is why I founded the Green party and wanted to carry out this vocation by being a member of the German Parliament.

However it did not work. The envy, the jealousy, the competition and rivalry – all these negative human features became so rife in this party as soon as it soared in the elections that I would have felt shame and disgust to continue attending the meetings. As a politician I would have to be able to behave diplomatically in every moment and only announce my opinion once I was sure I would not be marginalised. The thing to do for a politician to be successful is not to have any opinion of his own, at least not a firm one, and to prefer to be pushed towards a decision without losing his dynamic appearance.

I have to admit that I was not apt to be a politician although I had worked to found this party since 1973. So the Green Party was first elected in Baden-Württemberg (in South-West Germany) and six months later in all of Germany (by then West-Germany) and served as a model as the first so-called ecological party on a national and international basis. However I quit in February 1981.

Without wanting to admit it to myself I had lost my perspective and mission in life. A German popular saying goes: those who are not fit for doing anything else, become a publican. So when I left the Green party, I opened a pub in my own house and henceforth I draughted around 200 beers per night and smoked about 2 packs of cigarettes passively. The pub was a complete success. My wife and I were booked solid. But my soul said: "You are crazy!" Those who will not listen, have to feel – this is another of those sayings. I still heard my soul but I did not do anything to change this situation. I even mentioned this feeling of frustration to a good friend of mine merely 11 hours before the accident, but his only comment was: "Pack your things and go on a trip for a while." This was no option for me. I figured that my responsibility would not allow it. And then it happened …

When you enter into something happening, then you understand that there is no such thing as coincidence, that it is solely a synonym for not knowing. I can accept that for 100% because: how often do you not (instantly) recognize the cause of the phenomena you cannot change in your life and to which you have to surrender. This only means that this cause is not (yet) known to me but it has to exist.

Soul talk

Let us go back to us humans as soul people. It is much easier to communicate at the soul level than you may imagine. It does not make any difference to communicate with a soul who is sitting before us in flesh and bone or with one who is without form at the moment. A soul is a soul. You only have to address it as light-heartedly as if this person stood right before you. The first person with whom I had such a soul contact was my two-and-half-years younger sister Bettina. At 33 she liberated herself from her body which had become a great nuisance to her. At that moment she had been restricted to a wheel-chair for eleven years. I only came to think of it much later that my being able to walk again for a year then had contributed to her passing away. I felt then and I still feel that this is extremely tragic.

Clemens: *Tina, do you want to talk to me?*
Bettina: *It is years that you have not communicated with me.*
C. … *But I have thought of you a lot. You often accompany me in my thoughts.*

B: *Yes I know, but we have not talked for quite a while.*
C: This is correct. I would like to talk to you because there is still something untalked-about in the air.
B: *What?*
C: Something very delicate. I fear that I am partly responsible for your passing away.
B: *Why?*
C: On the 1st of April 1982 I was released from the same clinic in which you had been to also.
B: *I know.*
C: But I left it walking on two legs and you left it in a wheel-chair eleven years before.
B: *So what?*
C: Has this not affected you deeply, the fact that I could heal myself and you could not?
B: *Anyway I had been completely cross about the stupid paralysis I had inflicted on myself.*
C: Me too.
B: *But you were able to undo it. I would have loved to do the same thing but it was unthinkable.*

C: Why? Because the doctors said so?
B: *They said so anyway, but even I had no perspective for myself, I was struggling with depression and resignation.*
C: Since when?
B: *From the very day after I first wanted to end my life because it was not what I had expected it to be.*
C: You had passed the graduation exams superbly, you could dance incredibly and had a fantastic charisma.
B: *I could not do anything with it. I was always torn between wanting to be a star and wanting to be dead.*
C: I know, the conflict of our parents weighed on you and you did not receive any support to develop your great capacities.

B: *I was too weak to bring myself to the top by myself.*

C: *It is true that the conflict of our parents weighed less on me because I could leave home at 13.*

B: *Yes, this is why I felt jealous and wanted to go to the same boarding school called* **Odenwaldschule**, *but it did not work.*

C: *Because you must have felt responsible for mum, that she was ok?*

B: *Yes, she needed me. She once said that she would have committed suicide if I had not been there.*

C: *This is quite a burden.*

B: *I could never stand on my own feet.*

C: *Yes, therefore you needed the wheel-chair.*

B: *This was no solution either. I would have loved to become a real good dancer and actress.*

C: *Then our parents would have had to finance your training. They did not do this.*

B: *They were only busy with themselves and dad was busy with his girl-friends.*

C: *Was it not very depressing for you to see that I could walk again? Were you not even angrier about your fate than before?*

B: *Yes, I think so. Before I saw you walking out of hospital I had already tried twice to leave the wheel-chair by dying.*

C: *I know. Once on the city highway and once by throwing yourself out of the sixth floor.*

B: *Yes, do you still remember?*

C: *Sure I do. Both times you were not even injured. It was incredible. When you rolled your wheel-chair into the four-lane highway traffic going at 65 mph, it only caused some slight disturbance and when you jumped out of the sixth story you merely broke two ribs.*

B: *I was not supposed to leave my body yet. I had not put my things in order yet.*

C: *Yes, when you finally succeeded in leaving your body, you had*

restored order all around. You had even paid your debts and written a letter to the Pension Fund that you would not need any retirement pension. You had cancelled your accounts and stopped your tenancy. You had only forgotten Facebook.
B: *Facebook was not even existing then.*
C: *Ah well, it was only a joke.*
B: *In my present life I am on Facebook.*
C: *You may stay on Facebook from one life to the next.*
B: *You only have to remember your Password.*
C: *This is why you should bequeath all your passwords to the correct person before changing your body.*
B: *Whom to?*
C: *To those who have to identify you in your new form.*
B: *How did you succeed in doing that with me?*
C: *It was a gift. It means that it was a strong feeling.*
B: *But is it not possible to fool yourself? If the wish is too overwhelming.*
C: *It is your eyes, your character and there are also special signs.*
B: *Which signs?*
C: *You left your body with a handicap and came back with one.*
B: *I thought if I took my life I would get rid of the handicap.*
C: *The handicap simply is an expression of the condition of the soul which can be enhanced by the evolution of consciousness. Obviously you were not completely aware what your handicap stood for at the time of your death.*
B: *What did or does it stand for?*
C: *For what it shows, for a handicap. Who or what was a handicap for you then and now?*

B: *My parents ....* (Bettina starts crying)
C: *Why are you crying?*
B: *Because in my present life it is the same.*

C: *Why?*

B: *You know that my father B. had been our brother and my twin brother.*

C: *Yes. Unfortunately I do not have any contact with him.*

B: *This does not surprise me. You live in two completely different levels of consciousness. You are what is called an esoteric person dealing with spirit and he is a craftsman working with matter primarily.*

C: *Yes, I have the same view on this. So why did you reincarnate with him then?*

B: *Because I love him. I have always loved my twin brother even if we have lived on two completely different levels of consciousness.*

C: *Do you wish to achieve that both of you get synchronized?*

B: *Yes, but it means a heavy struggle. It is even more difficult now than it was in my former life. He was my brother then, now he is my legal guardian and I still love him as much as I did before.*

C: *In both lives you wanted to get more affection and care from your parents thanks to a disability?*

B: (cries and gets angry) *I only want them to understand me.*

C: *Don't they understand you in this life?*

B: *They believe it is complete rubbish what we are talking about.*

C: *This was quite the same in our last life, we could not share our conversations with anyone.*

B: *That's true.*

C: *You want to force him to expand his consciousness with the help of your incurable disability. However he thinks your handicap is fate. So you do not achieve your aim in this way.*

B: *What I am supposed to do?*

C: *To give care and affection to yourself.*

B: *How do I get there?*

C: *Considering yourself as a continuity and pursuing your dream you already had in your last life, but could not realize then. Take your destiny into your own hands.*

B: *I am already doing this.*
C: *But you still want the recognition of your parents.*
B: *Why the bleep not?*
C: *You can even give this recognition to yourself as a virtual being.*
B: *How does this work?*
C: *By soul writing.*
B: *What is "soul writing"?*
C: *The very thing we are doing right now. We are talking to each other on a soul level and I am writing it down. You can also do this. You talk to your soul and write down what it says to you. You could ask e.g.: Why could I not fulfil my dreams after finishing my graduation exams?*
B: *I know why.*
C: *I do not believe that because the answer must never be: I will end my life if I cannot make my dreams come true.*
B: *Why not?*
C: *Because you had enough possibilities to realize your dreams after passing the graduation exams in your last life.*
B: *This is not true!*
C: *Do you have more opportunities now?*
B: *Yes, my present parents at least pay my training as an actor in a drama school.*
C: *This is great. It is true, your parents in your former life did not do that.*
B: *But now I am not in the best conditions.*
C: *Why?*
B: *I squint, I cannot move my left hand properly and I am an epileptic.*
C: *All this has to do with your former life.*
B: *Do you think so?*

C: *I ask you with what consciousness did you leave your last life? Is it enough to fulfil your dreams in this life?*

B: *In fact I only ended my life because I was fed up with sitting in a wheel-chair.*
C: *I see. However this is not enough to make your dreams come true. There is still the problem that your parents are responsible for your happiness.*
B: *This is what they are!*
C: *They are not. This would be horrible indeed, we could never be free then.*
B: *That is it.*
C: *Of course you can free yourself. You can create your own reality which makes you healthy and happy.*
B: *And if my parents do not participate?*
C: *In your own reality they do exactly that. You see to it. You are the creator, you write down what you need and how you need it in a way that is credible to you.*
B: *Then I am manipulating others by it.*
C: *For the benefit of all.*
B: *Is this possible?*
C: *It is. This is how the universe works. The best solution for each individual is the best solution for all.*
B: *Only if all participate in it.*
C: *This is exactly what they do in your imagination.*
B: *And all behave accordingly?*
C: *Yes, because it is also the best solution for them. Every being in this universe wants to be happy and healthy and this is what each individual creates in their virtual reality.*

B: *Just like this conversation.*
C: *Exactly.*
B: *Sounds really fantastic.*
C: *I think so too. Let me hug you. I can feel it.*
B: *I can feel it too!*
C: *This is just what we are talking about. With this emotion we*

created on our own we are continuing our real life.
B: *The physical one.*
C: *Yes. All the best for you.*
B: *Let's continue talking tomorrow.*
C: *Yes, with pleasure.*
B: *See you then.*
C: *Good-bye.*
B: *Bye.*

9
"Are you crazy – or do you see more than me?"

Karmapa and Jamgon do not have to fix a date to meet in the next life, it goes without saying that the love between them will attract them to each other. I remember that in 1992 when Jamgon has been dead for five or six months and Karmapa, 7 years old, is sitting on the high Tsurphu throne in his temple with crowds of people watching his enthronization, he says to Titi, his servant:

Karmapa: *Please give Jamgon a cup of tea!*
Titi: *His Holiness, Jamgon is dead.*
Karmapa: *But there, just look. (Karmapa indicates some point between the pillars of the temple as if his was following Jamgon's steps with his finger.) He is thirsty. Bring him some tea.*

Titi looks in the direction again where Karmapa points to straining his eyes even if he knows that Jamgon is dead; perhaps he is seeing the same as Karmapa.

How would you look at such a situation as a materialistic? Who would say that he can really see Jamgon when Karmapa says: "There he goes", with the full knowledge that he has been mummified five months ago? – Or do you think that Karmapa is crazy anyway, that he sees things that are invisible? Which group do you want to belong to? Maybe you answer diplomatically: "To neither of them." Which means more or less: you connect with Jamgon imagining him. This would not be any problem for Karmapa since he has already heard so many stories about Jamgon, especially about the closeness of the connection between him and Jamgon the 3rd.

This is what he confirmed me when he came to Berlin in 2014 and

> said: *…I have such a strong feeling for Jamgon because I have heard so many stories about our close relationship in our former lives.*

When the 7-year-old Karmapa asks his servant Titi to bring Jamgon a cup of tea as an expression of his friendship with him, how is Titi supposed to behave then? Should he say: "OK, boss, I go and bring him some tea."? Or should he say: "Right! But I do not bring him any tea. " Then Karmapa would smile a bit and that is it. But Titi does not say this.

What would you do, dear reader? Would you try to see Jamgon? Unlike Karmapa Titi knows Jamgon in the physical reality. Can you imagine, can you make an inner picture of something that your intellect cannot hold? Would you allow yourself to accept such a picture as the truth? I always say: "Reality does not need to be true – reality is what produces an effect." Therefore our capacity for imagination is as important as the real experience, perhaps even more important, because it makes you clairvoyant.

Yet this does not explain why the dead Jamgon should be better than the living one. At the moment it only means that Jamgon is not able to go looking for Karmapa and has to leave this task to Sherab. What sense does this make?

Those who search will find

Instantly Sherab and his confidants set out riding towards the place of Karmapa's address in East-Tibet, in the completely inaccessible nomad land. Here in the Latok valley Sherab Terching together with his escort find the tent of a nomad family in which Karmapa is expected to be living since the beginning of his 17th incarnation according to the prediction letter he left in his last life. Indeed: there he is. A six-year-old nomad boy with his father to whom he said a couple of days ago: "I will go to Lhasa." The father was surprised as Lhasa is about 900 miles from here.

Just during these days while Karmapa is secretly found and identified, on the other side of the Himalayans (at an air distance of about 150 miles) thousands of his adepts meet at the funeral of his friend Jamgon Kongtrul Rinpoche. What perfect synchronicity! Such masses of people would never have come together if they had been sent a newsletter saying: "We have found the prediction letter of the 16th Karmapa. We will now search for him according to its contents." Similar news were spread in the past years when nobody had a reliable clue yet about where and when Karmapa would reincarnate – all this had been done solely to placate Karmapa's community.

His interim rulers, the so-called seat-holders – Shamar, Situ, Gyaltsap and Jamgon – had become nervous already four years after Karmapa's death because they did not have any clue about when, where and how their great master would be born again. They and the Kagyü adepts feared that the reincarnation chain of the Karmapas might have ended although the founder of Tibetan Buddhism *Patmasambava* had predicted 300 years before the first Karmapa that there would be a Karmapa who – in 21 lives as Karmapa – would serve mankind as a teacher of wisdom.

Owing to this concern the four seat-holders deliberately produced a fake. They put some hand-written document of the 16th Karmapa in a holy place and announced to the Kagyü-Buddhists something like: "We have found a prophecy letter written by him, yeah – but we do not tell you yet what is says!" They did that supposing it could not take long until Karmapa showed up and then they could say that this event was written in the alleged document. Everything was staged because they wanted to keep their followers confiding in Karmapa's reincarnation. However: it is an incredible story which seemed to be suspicious to many Buddhists. Years later the 17th Karmapa was still missing.

There was also a high-nobility family pretending that one of their babies born in 1990 was Karmapa. The family in which Karmapa was born would be automatically regarded very highly. So a second family was also tempted to make manipulations so they could pretend that their baby was Karmapa. I even had to visit this family with my film crew to document the case because Shamar had asked me to. But the behaviour of the infant and the alleged documents warranting his authenticity turned out to be embarrassingly false and totally unworthy of a Karmapa.

Karmapa found!

What happens now in June 1992? Sherab and his confidants ride back until they find a Chinese post office to fax the marvellous news to Situ and Gyaltsap that they had identified a six-year-old nomad boy as the new Karmapa owing to the prediction letter.

At the same moment Shamar is on a world-wide journey to tell the Kagyü disciples that he is about to find the genuine Karmapa and to ask the support of everyone now, especially of those who had known Jamgon and had declared to be on his side. However it is no plea. In true Tibetan guru-tradition he is converting it into an obligation. His adepts have to testify their compliance by throwing themselves on the floor in front of Shamar and touching the floor with breast and fore-head.

Situ and Gyaltsap immediately contact the Dalai Lama announcing him the finding of Karmapa. Thanks to all the documents being submitted to him the Dalai Lama is convinced that the nomad by really is the true incarnation of Karmapa and gives his official blessing. – Shamar declares that the Dalai Lama has been deceived and that Situ's Karmapa is not genuine. He continues to say that he, Shamar, who by virtue of an interim ruler is competent of finding Karmapa, would soon present the authentic one. Wherever Shamar is passing through on his trip cannot be retraced from Sikkim.

Nevertheless Situ and Gyaltsap in Rumtek – where right now hundreds of Jamgon's and Karmapa's followers from all over the world have gathered to attend the 49-day-death ritual and funeral festivities – move to action and convoke a press-conference to announce to the world that Karmapa has been found. They do not consider themselves bound by Shamar's wish of secrecy any longer since he himself has spoken of the prediction letter distancing himself from it.

As eleven years have already passed since the death of the 16th Karmapa and now and again there have been rumours about if Karmapa's reincarnation chain would or not go on, a wide-spread insecurity and confusion has reigned among Karmapa's adepts. Hardly anybody knows of the big conflict going on behind the scenes owing to Shamar's rejection of the announced Karmapa.

In the press conference on the 12th June 1992 everything is laid on the table. To be sure the guests have come from far away for the funeral festivities and hardly anyone suspects that all is about Karmapa. Yet the tension is noted by all. At 10 a.m. Situ and Gyaltsap appear with their colleagues in front of the gathering crowd among which a lot of local and national journalists are present. They start by disclosing the whole reincarnation story since the death of the 16th Karmapa until today. It is mainly Situ talking who speaks English. Gyaltsap adds some pieces in Tibetan which are translated to English too. Questions are made which are answered in detail.

As Shamar's shooting permit and exclusive rights for me have been welcomed by Situ too, I can continue to shoot now at the outbreak of the quarrel in the Kagyü order. With my Indian cameraman and his assistant I am in the midst of the crowd to hear what Situ and Gyaltsap have to tell the public about Karmapa's reincarnation. My German cameraman together with his assistant has found a good position for shooting outside of the crowd on the roof over the yard.

Situ speaks frankly and sincerely about everything including the fake actions, especially the ones they have been part of themselves. This self-critique is taken positively in contrast to the fact that during this event – which might be the most important for the continuity of the Kagyü order in the 21st century – the incumbent ruler Shamar is missing without any explanation. He has been missing since the outset of Jamgon's bardo-funeral-ritual, and in Sikkim there are only rumours of his whereabouts.

The prime message on this press-conference is the official recognition of Karmapa as the authentic reincarnation of the 16th Karmapa by the Tibetan head of Government – the 14th Dalai Lama. Although his Holiness Gyalwa Karmapa spiritually represents the older line of Tibetan Buddhism, the power is still with the Dalai Lama as he has a double function: he is not only the head of the Gelupa order, which has more members world-wide than the Kagyü order, but he is also the head of Tibetan government. As a consequence Karmapa would not be able to exert his office without having received the official letter of testimony by his Holiness, the Dalai Lama, which Situ has presented in this press-conference. This news is taken up immediately by the present reporters from many countries and prepared to be spread around the world.

Despite the great news that the 17th Karmapa has been found in East-Tibet now, there is no real atmosphere of joy building up during the whole meeting. An eerie threat lies over the entire event. Many attribute this atmosphere to the tragic death of the young and healthy Jamgon Kongtrul Rinpoche. Others note a division of the Kagyü order because Shamar is not present, which makes them feel unsettled. Nobody really knew what kind of power struggle was taking place behind the scenes since the death of the 16th Karmapa. Now Situ reports about several strange occurrences and even about a massive quarrel in the Kagyü order, this is also causing more tension. Moreover no-one knows what Shamar is prepared to do if he wants to implement install his own Karmapa.

When the press-conference is coming to an end at about 12.30 a.m. after two and a half hours of explaining and answering several questions, suddenly three military trucks with about 100 armed soldiers appear in the yard of the monastery. They jump down with their machine guns at the ready encircling the crowd on three sides.

At the same moment, a white jeep dashes into the crowd whose members leap apart to make way shouting wildly. At the steering-wheel there is a highly decorated official with white gloves, a peaked cap and several medals on his breast. At his side there is Shamar sitting like a commander – incredibly – with a dark red robe. He gets off and protected by the army makes his way through the crowd towards the table under the arcades where Situ and Gyaltsap have held their speech and who now stand up to see what unheard-of thing is happening in the yard of the monastery.

Shamar reaches the table gesticulating wildly and snaps at Situ who just turns his back to him and together with Gyaltsap goes to a large door at the back which leads to the interior of the monastery. Shamar shouts orders to some soldiers and follows them. The 100 soldiers are nonplussed and do not know what to do. Evidently their mission was to disperse the gathering which has taken place already anyway.

I cannot shoot because the soldiers drive away my Indian cameraman when he sees them coming. However my German cameraman shoots in the direction of Situ when the soldiers arrive. And when he notices what is happening, he turns the camera in the direction of the soldiers but instantly gets a strict warning not to shoot and obeys right away. I try to get my Indian cameraman back to work but he resists by saying: "I know them, they will shoot" – and disappears into the crowd. I take down the camera from the tripod and take refuge among the crowd too. So both cameras have been saved. Yet we do not have any shootings of this event.

After about ten minutes Shamar, still accompanied by several soldiers, comes out of the monastery, climbs in his jeep and drives away. His action came too late. The information that Karmapa has been found and recognized by the Dalai Lama has spread.

The next day at 6 a.m. some police agents stand at my bedside. "Come with us!"

It is about an hour's drive to Gangtok, the capital of Sikkim. We drive down into the valley and up again to the city. During the whole ride we do not say anything. I simply remain quiet. Of course all agents including the ones who are in my favour try to make me talk. I keep silent until all questions cease. It is the same in India as in China. I have already been arrested several times. At the end they want me to write a humility statement but I tell them that I cannot write in English. Finally they write what they want and I sign the document.

10
Good timing, bad timing

Shamar was a bit too late when he arrived with his soldiers. They were elite soldiers who monitor the delicate frontier from China to Sikkim, in that part of Sikkim which the Chinese government has claimed as their territory until today. The commander-in-charge justified his action telling me that he had not known he was to assault a monastery, otherwise he would not have carried out the order – yet it is always easy to say so afterwards. I believed him since it was the first time it happened to him as a Hindu. He had come too late anyway, so there was nothing to fight for. How do you want to take away something that hundreds of spectators have heard already? The day after, the Sikkimese civil servants went on strike because even the Sikkimese prime minister had not been informed of Shamar's action. It is clear that Shamar's contacts reached even higher – straight to the Indian government in Delhi and to the military.

I was released after having been interrogated for hours in Gangtok and forced to sign a humility statement stating that I would never say or write anything against the Indian government and that I had not seen any soldiers assaulting a monastery. Three days later all our confiscated stuff was returned to us. As nothing really serious had happened and they believed me when I said that I had not shot the attack in Rumtek, I was free to continue working with my crew. The frontier to India was opened again.

Sikkim is in the focus of world politics. If China, as it has often threatened to do, took military action to snatch Sikkim from the Indian government, this would lead to an enormous shift in the delicate Asian balance between the super-powers China and India since China would have crossed the Himalayans. For India and all the neighbouring countries this would be an intolerable constant threat.

The barrage of foreigners who had come to Sikkim because of Jamgon's death crossed all plans by which Karmapa's opponents wanted to keep control. These people from all over the world with their own contacts to the world press made it hard for the Chinese and Indian politics as well as for Shamar to set off on their own course. Around a total of 5.000 foreigners had been present daily during the 49-day-death-ritual. At that moment a special visa was still necessary for entering Sikkim and passing the checkpoints where all cars were scrupulously checked. So our cameras raised quite some stir, yet this international event needed to be shot. With all the hobby photographers who had taken pictures of it, it would have been ridiculous to stop me from shooting just because I had a better camera.

Without Rinpoche's death these masses of people would not have been present in Sikkim physically when the press conference took place to inform of the discovery of Karmapa's reincarnation. This was exactly the protection that Jamgon had seen when I had interviewed him, and he had figured that Karmapa would need him right in this very minute.

Situ said once: *Just after Rinpoche's death we received very good news of Karmapa's reincarnation.*
So the timing between Karmapa and Jamgon worked to the minute with highest synchronicity. Only two souls who are linked by selfless love are capable of doing this.

Most lovers do not trust in such a timing. They fear that they might not see each other again in the next life and so they play it safe by incarnating in the same family. However they forget that they are subject to the incest prohibition prevailing within the family and moreover they have to accept a generation leap. These are bad conditions for lovers. As a consequence sexual abuse often takes place because they do not know about the continuity of the soul and only follow their instincts blindly. In most cases the stronger one abuses the weak one by using brutal force.

Nevertheless this force is united with some kind of unconscious love, therefore this violence is not denounced as such and exposed as a failed incarnation effort. Yet this would be a prerequisite for respecting and honouring the chosen family order. With it the driving force for sexual abuse would be neutralized thanks to the expansion of consciousness and the world would be fixed again.

With Karmapa and Jamgon the confidence in their intuition is so great that they do not worry about timing. However in order to use the time-slots for the coherent deployment of one's fate, you must not be bound to the interests of your personal ego to which everything belongs forming your present physical identity. Jamgon was free from it and therefore he could feel intuitively what was necessary to happen right in this minute to help lift his beloved friend and master Karmapa from the adversities of his spiritual mission into a materialistic world. In this egoless freedom even death may be an option. In this case, however, it was not an option because there was no alternative to solve this problem. Even Situ Rinpoche understood this once the accident had happened and he stated:

Situ: *Whenever Jamgon dies, there will be a ceremony with many of his adepts attending it. And this is exactly what will happen, no matter when and where.*

And this is exactly what happened then. Jamgon was sure of it. He could estimate his popularity pretty well. Most people who want to be popular are not able to do this. Jamgon never wanted to be popular. He wanted to spread dharma but not as a dogmatic religion, but as a life-style. This life-style is what he perfected by his well-timed death. I am convinced that he knew fairly well what would happen when the news about his death travelled around the world.

No other news would have caused thousands of people worldwide to decide instantly to spend so much money to visit a monastery in Sikkim just now. If Jamgon had wanted these honours for himself, for his ego, as an expression of mourning, this would have meant that he himself would have been sad about his early death. Yet this was unthinkable because then there would be another grave problem (as long as you do not believe in coincidence). But at the moment there was no other big problem in Jamgon's life which only could have been solved by his death.

So this death was not an event which sprang from a trouble in his life, but one that stemmed from his love for Karmapa. Therefore it was the best (and the only) thing that would really help Karmapa to come safely into his new life despite the counterforces raised by China and Shamar.

Jamgon knew that most people equate death with mourning, even Buddhists. He knew that people refer to his physical presence and thus want to mourn him. This consciousness is oriented towards the finiteness of human existence. Yet spiritual persons are oriented towards the infinity of life. Therefore it is decisive with what you identify yourself: with the transient body or with the immortal soul? Those who believe in the soul only perceive death as a change of form. Such a change of form may even be considered as gratifying because a new and thrilling potential of evolution is released. With such a perspective of death mourning eventually is converted into feelings of happiness.

As heroically as you may interpret Jamgon's behaviour there is still the tragic fact of the death of Kunga, the master of ceremony, and Norbu, the driver. Nevertheless this term does not do justice to the end of these two lives in any way whatsoever. Yet perhaps their death was not even tragic. You may question yourself if the two have taken part in the drama knowingly or unknowingly.

Since Jamgon's death should not be interpreted as a suicide by any means, he must not have driven the car himself nor must he have told Kunga beforehand: "Stay in the hotel with Tenzin, I will just undergo transformation quickly with the help of our driver." – No, nothing should have looked as if it had been planned, absolutely nothing. The best thrillers are the ones where everything runs normally, but at the same time you recognize the driving force which is at work. Jamgon could not have said either: "Stay at the hotel both of you, Tenzin and Kunga, I will just take me and my driver out of life. But I do not want the two of you to die. Do not worry, I will come back soon to live a new life together with you."

Jamgon's attitude towards death was no secret nor a sudden impulse, but a philosophy which he could transmit to other people, not only during his teachings but also continually by his carefree and completely fearless charisma. This attitude was felt by everybody whom Jamgon dealt with. I can confirm this from my own experience. Therefore I am sure that with his sudden death Norbu will continue his evolution towards mastery. With this death he will by no means be reborn in a worse incarnation than before. Presumably his next life will be a better one than his former life. Jamgon will see to that.

However a Rinpoche does not speak about this, even if he defines himself as a spiritual being. The physical death is still what counts as an end for most people on Earth although they believe in reincarnation thanks to their religion. For normal people spiritual continuity hardly has a psychologically liberating significance – in the Occident even less than in Asia. The norm is: with death life has ended.

Even Jamgon could count on that among his adepts. For most of them his physical death caused such a shock that they immediately took a flight to Sikkim undertaking a very arduous and expensive journey with countless bureaucratic hurdles in order to pay their respects to their idol. This is important even if as Buddhists they had already been taught in the philosophy of continuity of spirit. Thousands of disciples came in the end, yet they could not be aware of the effect this had. With regard to Jamgon's mission and his helping action for Karmapa this was not essential. The main thing was that the friends came in large numbers.

The tradition of the reincarnation culture is decreasing among Tibetans, whereas it is spreading in the West, although in absolute numbers a lot more Tibetans know persons with two lives than we do here.

When things get started here on a large scale and not only lovers recognize each other (again) at first sight, but also babies are acknowledged as old friends, reincarnation will be taken for granted. Often it is not the face which triggers recognition, but a dream that mum or dad or some other family member has about the new being. Or when the baby – as soon as it starts to speak – tells the family who it has been in its old life. There are so many traits of recognition as there are human beings. The most convincing is a strong feeling which gives you the certainty that you know this new person.

In order to perceive this feeling and to trust in it, we require a change in the hierarchy of being we believe in. In the West reason is still at the top and the feeling which stems from intuition is subordinate to it. This is exactly what has to be changed. However this shift is blocked by all the objections which destroy trust.

Time changes

Those who live now in the third millennium may trust in things being altered by cosmos right at the outset of this millennium. To be sure this cosmic influence can already be noted now – otherwise this book would not exist – but human consciousness will only shift massively after 2047. Why?

Then our solar system will enter in the new cosmic influence of the *Sattva era*. Sattva era (empathic, uniting, solidary, caring) will replace Kali era according to the Vedic teachings. I can write this because Sattva era is already approaching even if it looks as if Kali energy (ego-centred, separate, and violent) is just beginning to rule the world. Yet this is merely the usual lashing about of the dying dragon.

It is mostly like that when one era replaces the former one. It does not happen rapidly. There is a process of dissolution with great drama whereby the date 2047 is only giving the apex. This means that from then on, Sattva energy is getting stronger than Kali energy, just like Kali era started to shape us some 5.500 years ago. However there have always been persons less Kali-oriented than the masses meaning that everybody who is already orienting his character towards Sattva qualities, is part of the solution. Nobody can resist such a gigantic shift in which all the solar system is reaching a more Eastern position in our galaxy. To be sure it is possible to cling to old values of mainly rationally and egomaniacally oriented energy but by doing so you will become a problem for evolution – and this may invariably cause casualties.

If we imagine that we are only a very tiny solar system with nine planets in our galaxy called Milky Way and that this system in turn is part of a much larger solar system revolving around a sun which is immeasurably bigger than our sun, then we may figure out that nothing will stay what it was. Especially when our solar system is advancing at a speed of two mach.

If you watch the sky on a cloudless night and figure out that every clear spot represents a solar system that is a lot bigger than the Earth because you can still see its shining light, then you know that you should feel humility and devotion as not to make your mind blow. In this universe you may feel completely embedded in your whole infinity if you do not cling to your body. Because this is what would make your mind blow. Being attached to something causes you pain.

Since these changes will happen exponentially, i.e. that they will not occur continually increasing or decreasing in a straight line but dramatically, meaning very suddenly or violently, you may ask instantly: how much do I trust in a cosmos which teaches me and mankind many things we would never comprehend on our own? Where do I get the confidence that this happens to my benefit?

The answer is very simple for me: without this confidence nothing happens for my benefit. This is a decision I make, this is not a matter of knowledge. The decision is based on a feeling of satisfaction. Jamgon must have felt satisfied during his death. In any case Tenzin reports that he had felt fairly at ease in this new, fast car. With a dramatic act at 120 mph Jamgon blows up all rigid concepts thus unblocking the way for Karmapa. This is only possible if you feel completely embedded in the cosmos – dead or alive, with or without form and spiritually present at every moment.

Karmapa's opponents who have acted out of egoist power motives cannot count on things getting fixed in the same way as the pigeons come to Jamgon's help at the right moment in order to fulfil what has been going over in his mind weeks before as the best solution and after clearing everything for the fulfilment of this vision.

Wrangling for recognition

When Sherab Terching faxed Situ that he had found Karmapa, Situ and Gyaltsap Rinpoche asked the Sikkimese government for permission to bring Karmapa to Rumtek as quickly as possible. Before the Sikkimese government gave any statement, they first wanted to make sure that it was the real Karmapa to whom they had conceded exile in his last life. Therefore two high official of the Sikkimese government were to interrogate the Dalai Lama personally. This in turn alarmed Situ and Gyaltsap and made them travel to the Dalai Lama immediately in order to receive his recognition of Karmapa first-hand.

When they reached Dharamsala together with the representatives of the Sikkimese government, the Dalai Lama had just left for Brasil. So the whole recognition procedure went by fax and phone. Yet the Dalai Lama had already been convinced by Karmapa's authenticity when he saw the photos of the valley where Karmapa was found. This valley corresponded exactly with the dream or vision he himself had had from the place where Karmapa was discovered. The Dalai Lama had already explained me his vision when I asked him a long time before Jamgon's death if he approved of my documenting Karmapa's reincarnation process (this was to be my film *Living Buddha*).

When he eventually saw through several documents stating that the facts were congruent with the prediction letter, he agreed to it. I am sure that his intuition was playing a decisive role in his agreeing or denying it.

I ignore in which former incarnation of the Dalai Lama, of Karmapa and Situ the following story happened but it was about Situ asking the then Dalai Lama to recognize the new incarnation of Karmapa. They collected all the facts and submitted them to the Dalai Lama, but he would not sign the paper. This did not only cause surprise in Situ who was absolutely sure that he had discovered the authentic reincarnation of Karmapa. Everybody who had to do with it was taken aback. This denial went on for several years until the biological mother of the new Karmapa admitted that she had committed adultery and that not her husband was the father, but a Chinese general who had visited Tibet. So Situ crossed out the name of Karmapa's supposed father substituting the name of the Chinese general for it. The Dalai Lama instantly gave his signature to the paper. So intuition also plays an important role in bureaucratic matters among Tibetans.

Now in 1992, with the case of the 17th Karmapa there was not a shadow of a doubt for the Dalai Lama and he sent his written acknowledgment from Brazil. So the way was free to inform the whole world about the successful reincarnation of Karmapa in the press conference in Rumtek.

As the Dalai Lama is the head of all Tibetans, his recognition of the 17th Karmapa is the decisive move in the struggle for leadership of the Kagyü order which Shamar would not surrender to anymore. Therefore Shamar needs his own Karmapa who lets him rule. Without the recognition of the Dalai Lama however it is not possible to succeed in establishing a reincarnation succession politically and legally. Only the one who can say: "In my former life I was this or that person ...", receives the official document confirming his statement with the signature of the Dalai Lama (the Tibetan administration in exile) and inherits everything he possessed in his former life. In Karmapa's case this is quite a lot. The worldwide real estate possessions alone rise to a billion euros and the donations also reach millions.

It is no wonder that even in spiritual traditions the ego might prevail and wage war for his advantages with all possible arms. Still you should think that somebody would not struggle so much for power and wealth when they are convinced of the continuity of their own personality owing to their belief in reincarnation. Do they lack confidence in eternal life? It has to be a deep fear that arouses their ego. All the fears that seize and motivate you to fight may be ascribed to an original fear: the fear of existence. Although the Tibetan belief in reincarnation dates back to the 7th century and is virtually part of the popular consciousness, there are some people who are driven by this fear of existence. So much more are in our culture without the belief in reincarnation.

So let us look at the origins of this deep-rooted fear. We have already recognized that it is closely linked to the imagination of what is death. Even if you are completely safeguarded materially and know that you will not die of hunger, the fear of existence is still there. It is responsible for our obeying to superiors and for not protesting against injustice. Only recently I came across a blatant example of the fear of existence and how it is perpetuated when I was on my trip to Krakow in Poland.

The rumination effect – terror without end

Cracow, the venerable old capital of Poland, lives of holocaust tourism. The whole stream of visitors for the concentration camp of Auschwitz passes through this city. First you drive through the magnificent old town in small electric vehicles for eight or ten persons. While viewing the ancient, dignified buildings in the slowly passing cars and sitting comfortably under a canopy you listen to a voice coming from a cassette in the desired language who informs you about the atrocities committed by the Nazis during their relatively short rule there.

It all starts with the invasion of the German army in Poland in September/October 1939. In merely 48 hours, the invading Nazis dragged about 7000 Jews from their houses deporting them to the newly erected camp in the neighbouring town of Auschwitz in order to kill them systema- tically. After the sightseeing tour a bus takes you to the camp while the voice keeps informing you about many outrageous things that happened in this city. The most perverse of all in my opinion is the fact that in this town, where since time immemorial Jews and Christians have lived peacefully together, no neighbours had protested when the Nazi mob kicked their friends, colleagues and acquaintances out of their flats to gas them.

What does this say about the character of man? This is not an individual case. It repeats over and over at small and large scale on the whole planet. I reckon that it is due to the fear of existence. And this fear is maintained exactly with such sightseeing tours and Nazi atrocities memorial days and places. In school we have been told of these scandalous deeds at the age of ten. When we finished grammar school every one of us knew that a small minority of powerful persons can keep a large majority in fear and terror. This is not only possible in Germany but in all cultures and among all nations. No matter where you go, these gruesome stories about all that happened there are immediately told even if you merely show a slight interest in the place. Sometimes there are even monuments commemorating the massacres, above all of the World War I and II. In every child remains the feeling that terror and fear are ever present and can irrupt at any moment.

This sightseeing tour in the beautiful city of Cracow was also destined to arouse this feeling. I did not want to believe what the voice from the loud-speaker in the nice little electric car told me: "The memory of the inhuman actions committed here is kept alive since it may happen again at any moment." Indeed this is so: ruminating the inhumanity produces more inhumanity. Man cannot escape from this psychological mechanism. We wonder why the upsetting acts do not come to an end although we stir up memories of it in all places investing huge amounts of money in it. The holocaust is ruminated with a gigantic effort wherever it is possible. Officially it is said: " … so that it will not happen again."

In reality it leads to a deep fear of existence in my opinion. Those who visit such memorial sites of terror or study the corresponding literature or films often react with a feeling of dismay and physical nausea and are pursued by these impressions for a long while. Only a few people can shield themselves in such a way that they are not affected by these incredible crimes they are supposed to commemorate. Yet normally this horror leaves behind a feeling of depression, impotence, menace and fear in the visitors.

These emotions are not solely produced by memorial sites, but they are transmitted on a daily basis by horror messages and pictures in the news reports. We are bound to become insensible to these news, in consequence the terror has to be evermore intensified in order to keep us in fear because only then man can be ruled and oppressed.

I protect myself against this. I do not possess a TV. I got rid of it when my children were still small and I became aware of the rumination effect. Even such unsuspicious series as *Tom & Jerry* spread fear and terror in little children's souls, though covered by malicious joy. I do not read any newspaper either, even if people stick my nose into it unwanted. In the car I often have to react lightning-fast in order to switch off the radio before I am told what horrible news have just happened somewhere in the world. You may call me a hopeless ignorant person who opts out of the rumination of horror. I am in favour of razing to the ground all memorial sites for horrendous acts. I am in favour of people caring for real transformation. I will explain in the following paragraphs why I am of this opinion.

From my professional healing work I know that the peaceful,

courageous, loving character of man only shows when he has overcome his fear of death. I am totally aware of why it is so hard to restrain the monuments and horror memorial programs of all kinds: because the people in power have a mighty interest in maintaining the ruminating effect. This is why it is firmly anchored in our education system and in public with these media-effective memorial days, although it is widely known due to many studies that deterrence does not work, not even with death indications: e.g. the consumption of tobacco is only declining thanks to prohibitions.

The delusion that the gigantic effort to commemorate horror, death and destruction serves to impede its repetition, is systemic. The psychological mechanism already works without repeating horror in real all over the planet in order to rule people, to exploit them and to impoverish them. The rumination effect alone causes such a great fear of existence that many people do not protest but let the high and mighty oppress them and shut them up solely because of the omnipresent fear of existence. This mechanism is at work with man and animal equally.

I have protected myself from this rumination effect in the paraplegic clinic by asking the staff not to let anybody visit me by any means: not my wife nor my friends or relatives. They were all convinced that they would help me by ruminating the doctors' diagnose and demanding me to accept it. I remained consequent and when visiting time came, there were often terrible scenes going on behind the door of our six-bed-room with all visitors of the other patients being let in, but my visitors being kept out. Yet later I was the only one to leave the room on his own legs.

No matter how miserable I felt, I fought back from the beginning: "Stop telling me that I have to accept my fate and be strong. I do not want to hear this horrible thing otherwise I will end by accepting it and then my fate is sealed indeed." They sent me the hospital psychologist. He should work on me so that I would rejoice to be able to manage to squeeze myself in the wheel-chair on my own one day.

"Bullshit", I say. "Stop it!"

"But Clemens, be sensible. Take a look at your X-ray, the second lumbar vertebra is shattered and will remain shattered. So be brave and attend the training for the wheel-chair …"

"No. Get out! Go away!"

"Clemens, if you do not participate, the insurance will stop paying for your stay – do you understand?"

"It is all the same to me."

"Clemens, now come on. Please let me put this strap around you so that you can start with the training ….."

I stopped listening and shut up until everybody stopped convincing me of my paralysis. I did not know yet that this was part of my healing method. I did it by instinct.

The reader will hardly understand why I believe that all these horror memorial sites should be razed to the ground because of their rumination effect. However it is a fact that while we think of horror and put our focus on it, horror persists. The memorial sites have exactly this function. When I have to think of terror since they remind me of it, even if I have not experienced it in person, or – as in my case – I am supposed to experience it as a life-long paralysis, then I am obsessed by fear. And those who feel fear may be abused, exploited, ruled, dominated, intimidated, weakened. They will then feel worthless, have a low self-esteem and become cowards etc.

Such masses of fearful people are ideal for the very small ruling minority. It is not necessary to put these people into chains, they are obedient anyway. They do not protest when their befriended neighbours are led away to concentration camps. This is perfect for the rulers because they do not have anything to fear. Almost every ruling system of then and today has operated with this fear of existence.

The crux with the fear of existence is the fear of death in every person. This is why I write this book (today being Good Friday while I am jotting down this passage, the day when horror has been ruminated for 2000 years). This is why I made the film and why I give seminars: to become free. The fear of death has to be overcome. As long as man is a prisoner of his materialistic thinking, he believes death to be his end. Exactly this causes his fear of existence, the original fear per se. Those who experience this fear, may be blackmailed and are obedient. Liberation means reincarnation – no ruling system can impede it.

Transformation by remorse

How can we keep the young generation from experiencing horror and fear? By introducing the subject "reincarnation" or – less provocatively titled – "intuition training" at school from the 3rd to the last grade. I have already carried out my first experiment in teaching this subject (I will come back to it in the next paragraph). How can the reincarnation concept work? The horror, e.g. the holocaust committed against the Jews, has not happened by itself. It has been committed by people. These people reincarnate as well as their victims. Therefore they are amongst us by millions.

As I have experienced in my daily practice for years, remembering your former life only takes 5 to 15 minutes when I apply my questioning technique. If the continuity of spirit was a philosophical part of our society, then every human being would be capable of remembering his former life/lives. *Remembering the horror suffered or carried out personally is something completely different than commemorating horror in memorial sites where the offenders remain anonymous.* Those who become aware of their personal crimes in one of their former lives, because they now – thanks to a new life – have the necessary distance, may decide to become a better person. If they had to regret their crimes in the same life, such as the Nuremberg trials after World War II or the Eichmann trial in Jerusalem, this would not work.

However with the perspective of your new life, it is possible and it is so effective that a relapse is excluded, as my practice shows since

2005. This new understanding, this remorse and deep, serious plea for forgiveness indeed purifies people. And in consequence they change their character by establishing new traits with which they cannot commit such atrocities anymore. In my other works I show how such a process of transformation works in practice, no matter what the subject is.

I want to make it very clear that I am not a person who denies these crimes, by no means. I do not want to repress them either. I want them to be transformed effectively, i.e. at their very source: the offenders whose traits of character have not died when they left their bodies. I want to give them a chance to evolve into authentic, good-hearted beings. By doing so they would manage to put a stop to committing crimes in this life or in their next lives, so history would not repeat itself and mankind would stop continuing their self-destructive program perpetually. By reliving the horror time and again with memorial days, we feed the old trauma and make people feel fear and horror. This should be outlawed.

Sometime in the future we will learn that living in harmony and love is a lot more fun than living in fear of existence and oppression. It is our own free will that decides how long we want to wait for it to happen. However with the ruminating effect we will postpone this moment. Instead we could already support our children by training their intuition.

Remembering former lives since the beginning

I had the chance to teach remembering former lives seven times for four hours at a German school for twenty 9 to 12-year-olds and for five 17 to 18-year-old students. To reach a sustainable effect, though, it would be necessary to teach this subject as often as English or Maths: from the first to the last grade without interruption in order to establish a consciousness of what has to be transformed and what you were already capable of doing in a former life. For your own development it is good and important to know both sides of your past. It would be counterproductive if you only wanted to know your advantages, since the inconveniences also work from the subconscious.

When you become aware of them, you may transform them and get rid of them. If you do not dissolve the negative conditionings in your subconscious, they repeat themselves from one life to the next – until you harmonize them, even if it takes you ages (several hundred lives). Harmony is the law of the universe to which everything has to assimilate. The quicker we learn to live according to the cosmic laws, the more suffering we spare ourselves. It is a waste of energy and the denial of evolving your consciousness if you do not use the knowledge of your former life.

I prefer employing a person who has already worked for my company in a former life if this company had existed then. The disbelief in the face of the people who consider such staff politics impossible to realize reveals how far they are from such levels of consciousness. If they had been trained in the evolution of their consciousness from their first day of school, they would just nod instead of denigrating the whole thing. Every year there would be more cases in which continuity would have been become a reality.

The Tibetans who have possessed the consciousness of reincarnation for 1300 years plan this continuity at least for the upper class and thus reach a high stability in their traditional Buddhist behaviour. Only now that the monasterial societies frozen in tradition do not manage to remain in isolation anymore thanks to the Internet, their behaviour is transformed in just one generation, and in such a dramatic way that the expected connection to the behaviour in the former life does not work any longer. Certainly this is regretted by many. But for the general evolution of consciousness it is a blessing because spiritually highly developed persons are increasingly facing the challenges of normal life.

So when remembering the standard behaviour in our last life there is no need to be afraid that it could make us too conservative. We merely have to deal with the velocity of change increasing exponentially and with traditions that have a much quicker expiration date.

If school senators and big industry recognized the enormous potential for education which lies in remembering your former lives, they would strongly encourage teaching this subject instead of having every generation learn things again from scratch. Once you have obtained the consciousness that life is a continuity, you do not understand any longer how anybody can tolerate such a waste of resources. It seems idiotic that we have not taken for granted the continuity of the development of consciousness.

We most suffer from this lack of consciousness in our incapacity to deal with nature correctly. We do not seem able to learn anything from the destruction of our environment which is growing from one generation to the next, although in the course of our life we note the increasing price we have to pay for this incapacity with regard to life quality. If we remembered the level of consciousness we had towards nature in a former life, we could not treat nature so disrespectfully, because we would be ashamed to repeat the same mistakes over again. We would be aware of sawing the branch off the tree we sit on, when we keep living according to the old biblical belief pattern: "Thou shalt subjugate nature".

The ego spends a lot of energy to put this pattern into practice and to create the man-made human being (see genetic modification). However this effort is bound to fail, exactly as the ape-made ape. Time and again agricultural seed giants are making the headlines owing to the commercial seed production because they often use inferior, infertile and also genetically modified seeds to expand their monopoly. Healthy plants reproduce themselves on their own. Yet when man interferes with the breeding to exert control on nature, there will eventually be men designed by men if we tolerate these developments.

The madness of this scheme is ubiquitous. Even our youngest ones in kindergarten notice this, because they are on the receiving end of it. And some say outspokenly that "adults are crazy". We live against nature and do not realize that we are nature ourselves. Strange indeed!

So every one of us starts afresh with learning in every new life. This is as detrimental as inbreeding and cultivated infertility in plants. "Cultivated infertility" … Dear reader, do you also feel the paradox in these words? The Earth is flooded with such attitudes. So a counterforce is imperative.

11
Karmapa continues his mission

About the same time the press conference was held announcing Karmapa's discovery on the Southern side of the Himalayans, Karmapa travels in a triumphal march the 900 miles from Latok, his birth place, to his main monastery Tsurphu near Lhasa. This is where he had lived since 1110 during his last 16 incarnations before fleeing to Tibet in 1959. In its 900 years of history Tsurphu monastery (the letter "h" is not pronounced) has been destroyed three times by war and earthquakes. During the Chinese occupation of Tibet, the heaviest destruction took place in 1960 since the monastery was one of the largest teaching facilities in Tibet with hundreds of pupils then. In 2020 it will again be as big as it was then. However all the monks to be trained will be under Chinese supervision. Since 2000 the Tibetan language has at least become a minor subject. Despite all this repression the reincarnation philosophy has remained intact, even though it is declining.

Karmapa's homecoming in 1992 as a seven-year-old is happening at the same time as the resurrection of the reincarnation concept. In continuing his mission even under the Chinese rule Karmapa feels a life-fulfilling joy. All those who know Karmapa – I reckon there are about 12 million in the inner circle and other 4 million who have heard his name and about 100 million Buddhists who already know something about the Tibetan faith in reincarnation. For the Tibetans Karmapa is one of them. This is why he did not reincarnate abroad, and even less as a non-Tibetan. Socially speaking he has reincarnated as one of the poorest people existing who, however, are still the freest of the non-free people in Tibet.

In Tibet the colonialists domesticated the nomads by force but in Latok, Karmapa's place of birth, being a nomad is a completely accepted and practiced way of life. Naturally the Chinese are also present as supervisors and controllers but at the time of Karmapa's birth they still lack the power and the means to transform the nomad tribes to their own way of life.

From his older brother Karmapa learns to jump on galloping horses and to drive, protect and care for a herd of sheep and goats. This life ended abruptly for the still six-year-old nomad boy when the search group with Sherab entered his tent.

Escorted by a large group of riders Karmapa first travels several days to reach the road starting from *Kalek* monastery. From there he goes in a convoy of more than 20 jeeps, trucks and even horse-driven carriages all the way to *Tsurphu* (900 miles). He stops at all the important places of the Buddhist-Tibetan tradition for a ritual with all the people gathering from the surrounding areas. All vehicles are decorated with good luck ribbons. On his way, wherever large groups have come together on the edge of the road Karmapa stops and blesses the people who are crying of bliss and are wishing him well with great humility. Every Tibetan man and woman, including the children, know what a great act of victory it is that Karmapa has incarnated again and is continuing his mission at such early age in the nose of the Chinese.

Though there have not been any mobile phones or Internet in 1992 yet, the news of Karmapa's reincarnation is travelling fast all over the world. From the *New York Times* to Germany´s *Stern*-magazine the papers publish that this seven-year-old boy is the new 17th incarnation of Karmapa, the *Living Buddha*. In no time at all the little nomad boy has become famous in the whole world. With this background, Jamgon's intervention regarding his death cannot be evaluated deeply enough.

The face of the seven-year-old who enters Tsurphu monastery on the back of a small, white, magnificently decorated Himalayan horse is full of emotions. Words cannot describe it. The film shows everything:

Karmapa is completely composed as if he was an old man, but also as amazed as a small child. He is the boss from the first moment and he is aware of his power: all his orders are carried out exactly as bidden. To be sure he is being led by the guides and very tolerant with people but only as long as his feeling is consistent with it. The look on his face when entering his main monastery says: *I remember all this.*

Triumphal journey to Tsurphu

When Situ and Gyaltsap leave for Tsurphu right after the press conference, they get a visa immediately. I will accompany them. Situ is no timid person, he leaves me on my own when we reach Lhasa. He is travelling with more than 60 monks, Gyaltsap with 20 monks, I with six-member team. We all have tourist visas only. Unfortunately our filming gear is so bulky that my luggage consists of three aluminium boxes of 40 x 16 x 16 inches which are of greatest interest to the customs officer and later to the PBS-police (Chinese police with military powers).

"Where is your shooting permission?", asks the customs officer.
"I do not have any", I answer.
"Then go and apply for one".
"With you?"
"At the ministry of information and culture in Peking."
"I have come to document Karmapa's enthronement."
"You need a permission for that."
"Very well. From whom?"
"Peking."
"But this is a Tibetan matter, is it not?"
"Peking."
"Peking is very far. I want to speak to the responsible person."
"Wait here."
I wait for 35 minutes.

The customs officer comes back with a man in plain clothes who speaks a better English.

He asks me: "Are these your boxes?"

"Yes."

"You have to go to the ministry to Lhasa."

"OK."

The officers take our luggage and put it in a small extra bus together with my crew and me and drive us to the ministry. – All on my own I have to deal with the subject if my plans to shoot the event are to come true.

I am sure that the PBS police remembers how I tricked them last time and how I could promote the solidarity with Tibet thanks to the published film documents. I can just tell Situ that we will try a special way, that I will go to Tsurphu on my own and that he please wait for me to arrive in order to document everything.

In the end I obtain all I need within 24 hours. China has a vehement interest that I document Karmapa's enthronement and that his recognition be shown in the West in order to demonstrate how liberal they are. To have everything documented by one of their opponents is supposed to emphasize their liberalism even more.

China speculates that they may replace Tibetan's adoration of the Dalai Lama by Karmapa. This includes the fact that Chinese police agents, laden with boxes of photos of Karmapa, go to the tourist markets where Dalai Lama-photos are offered (illegally) and replace them with Karmapa's photos without punishing the merchants. China also hopes to educate small Karmapa in such a way that he can make Chinese rule acceptable to his adepts. (This is where the rulers were totally wrong because when Karmapa was 15 he went fleeing to the Dalai Lama in India by crossing the Himalayans on foot in the deepest winter of 1999/2000.) The cameramen with whom I shoot in Tibet consist of one German, one Indian and one Chinese employed in Lhasa. Every night the Chinese takes the exposed Beta cassettes to his bedroom equipped with a Beta-copying machine by *Sony* and transmits my entire material to Peking. He is certainly making good money from it because he seems to be prosperous. I am ok with it.

There is a Chinese officer at my side who watches me around the clock, until the last day. This means that all I shoot is legal. (Only once did we have a big problem with him, when we shot the birth place of Karmapa in Eastern Tibet).

Right now we drive up to Tsurphu with our official shooting permission where Situ and Gyaltsap are waiting for me to shoot their first meeting with seven-year-old Karmapa personally and within the rigid tradition of throwing themselves to the ground in body-length.

The great event of Karmapa's enthronement is fixed at a date seven weeks from then. We use the waiting time to go to Karmapa's birth place by car and on horseback: Bator in the region of Latok, some 900 miles east.

Where the 17th Karmapa was (re-)born

Even before Situ discovered the letter of the 16th Karmapa and anyone saw Karmapa as "the Karmapa" face to face, the Dalai Lama had the before-mentioned dream of a valley where he lived. When I follow the tracks of Sherab Terching and his search group some six weeks later together with two of his confidants in order to fully document Karmapa's reincarnation, my group and I are crossing a pass at an altitude of almost 15.000 feet in order to reach Latok valley. When we ride into the valley I instantly recognize the picture that the Dalai Lama gave me of Karmapa's birth place. In the valley below I can distinguish several black dots – that must be the yak-tents of the nomads. In one of those tents Karmapa grew up.

I make my group halt. This view must be shot. It takes a while until all the horses have got together and we can unload the tripod, the film camera, the box with the material etc. in order to get a good position for this picture. Eventually the picture is taken without any of us or of our horses to be seen in the picture. All are quiet, the sound is on and I give my cameraman Klaus Moderegger the thumps-up for shooting.

At this very moment there are two gigantic eagles with a wingspan of almost seven feet flying towards us from behind with lightning speed and past the camera at a very low altitude, then they rise a bit and like stunt pilots they veer to the right and left of the valley. I do not dare to breathe. I stand near the camera and do not understand what is happening right in front of my own eyes. I must not say anything either as to not ruin the recording. I only hope that everything has been shot. When Klaus stops shooting (using Super-16mm filming material) and switches the camera off, I only ask him: "Have you taken everything?" Klaus nods and says:

"Yes, but I have put on the 2.5 wide-angle lens, so they appear unproportionally small."

I regret this but then it was done by my own instruction to get the whole valley where two rivers join from both sides into one single picture. It is just how the Dalai Lama described it to me. The eagles have swept away any remnants of doubt I may still have had. Their appearance is the most majestic reward I have received for the immense trouble I have taken to get here, a reward that I could never have imagined. It is a divine experience and very special to me since I am so obsessed with eagles and never have seen any except in the zoo – and now I have just seen two majestic, beautiful specimens! This is an experience at Dalai Lama-level. At this moment I take the birds as a confirmation that we are in the right place.

Then we start our way down to the nomad tents, which we reach two hours later. However it is not difficult to find the right tent, just as the search group of Sherab Terching did six weeks ago. When Sherab arrived with his people, there was a six-year-old nomad boy sitting in the tent of his father saying: "Daddy, I will go to Lhasa." His father was very surprised because Lhasa is about 900 miles away. From then on everything went really fast, every detail of the prediction letter was confirmed and it became clear: *This boy is Karmapa*. Instantly they prepared to obtain a permission for his journey to his main monastery Tsurphu near Lhasa.[15]

Right now when I get to Latok with my crew, Karmapa is already in Tsurphu. It is my duty to capture his origins in picture and sound. Apart from me no other film crew has ever managed to reach this far-off place. Moreover this region is and was barred to all non-locals. For quite a good reason, as the following story shows:

I ask for the camera to be positioned about 300 feet from Karmapa's birth tent for a total which allows the countryside and the surrounding mountains to be included in the picture.

The Chinese officer says: *No!*

I: *Why?*

He: *No shooting!*

I: *My permission says that I may shoot everything connected with Karmapa's reincarnation. It is obvious that the birth tent has something to do with Karmapa.*

He: *Yes and no.*

I: *Why?*

In general it is not advisable to ask the Chinese police "why", it may have devastating consequences. They just do not like why-questions. What they say is the law – and that's it. The answer is very simple though and I can give it myself: next to the Amazon, Latok and all East Tibet have been a coherent forest area of about the size of West Germany. It was considered to be the second lung of mother Earth almost the size of the Amazon region. When we reached this area in 1992, the profiteers had already eaten away almost all of the second lung of mother Earth. For this reason alone mankind should abolish the ruling profit system. – This is yet another helpless thought I

---

15 You may find all the details of this history in my films *Living Buddha*, *The making-of Living Buddha* and the book *Living Buddha*.

have. – Wood was the first thing China could plunder in Tibet apart from the riches in the monastery since they have occupied the country. The trunks of the East Tibetan trees – an uncle of Karmapa told me – often had a circumference for which ten adults had to stretch their arms in order to embrace the trunk. They were gigantic trees at 13,000 feet above sea level. In Europe the treeline is at about 7,000 feet. What a gigantic profit for China. In the meantime, China has already cut down around 90 % of the second lung of the world.

Due to the lack of roads the Chinese lumberjacks threw the tree trunks into the rivers which spring from there and run to China. Merely 20 % of the trunks are really getting there whereas the rest is rotting away in the unregulated rivers which are as majestic as the Danube in Passau even in their headwaters. It is incredible how many of these washed-up tree trunks we see in the river bends and we cannot film this because it is not about Karmapa! When I want to shoot the birth tent of Karmapa the problem is that the mountain with the tree stumps will be in the picture.

With *Photoshop* or *After Effects* we could fix this easily for the Chinese government, but this is not my job.

I: *Dear Mr. Chinese Officer, I am not able to avoid shooting the lumbered mountains when I take a picture of the birth tent.*
He: *You will see what you will get for this. When we are back in Lhasa, all the exposed material is shipped to Peking for control.*
I: *This will be exciting.*
He: *I will guarantee it to you.*
I: *I believe you will.*

Yet he cannot scare me. I will play a trick on him. We are shooting in negative and when he opens the film-boxes everything will be exposed and in consequence deleted. If after our return the officers really want to confiscate my filming material, I will just give them the boxes with unexposed material. When the officials in Peking understand what has happened, I will be at home again with my crew.

Postscript: It did not get to this extreme. As usual I had to sign a paper that I would not publish anything negative against sacrosanct China when I left Tibet. Paper is patient, but anyway I have no intention of visiting China again. This was my sixth and last trip to Tibet, I stayed for ten weeks. – At our return from East-Tibet the enthronement was to take place. As soon as this event had happened, we could say: *Karmapa had managed to become Karmapa again.*

So far Jamgon's plan has worked: Karmapa is discovered and the now seven-year-old boy will be enthroned as the new Karmapa at his mean seat – with the honours of the Chinese minister for religious affairs from Peking and his entourage. However Karmapa must not sit on his throne because he is not supposed to sit higher than the minister. Chinese protocol is very strict about that. Karmapa takes it serenely.[16]

---

16 DVD: The making-of Living Buddha (see annex/Mediashop)

12
Am I dead? – If yes, what then?

This ten-week shooting trip in Tibet about the "roof of the world" was what most challenged me in my life. In the *making-of*-film[17] you can see that I have black hair when I leave and after ten weeks, upon returning to Germany you see that my hair is grey. Throughout the whole trip I got out of my clothes maybe five times to get a full-night's sleep. There were often between minus 30 to minus 38 degrees Celsius. During the day temperatures rose to plus 30 degrees Celsius and you got burnt or a sunstroke if you did not have any protection. I loved these extremes. I loved every day and every night.

Energy was not a problem. It seemed always available. Even for overcoming once some 2,500 feet height difference in a run because Rinpoche, the boss of the monastery, where we only arrived after sundown would have been gone the next day. So we had to hurry up. However the camera alone weighs 7, 5 kg (about 15 pounds) and at this height it seems to weigh double. We arrived completely drained at a height of 15,000 feet when we reached his small retreat hut in a moonless night with all our filming gear – those who have already been at such a height know what I am talking about, because there is always this feeling that a weight of 4 pounds of lead is hanging from your feet.

"He is up there sitting in this retreat", we were told. Cameras, recording devices and everything that had to do with foreigners – especially with interviews, no matter which topic – is strictly forbidden to the Rinpoche from the moment he was dismissed from prison where he had been tortured for 25 years, so that he could die. He is one of the few persons in Tibet who still do the *Pohwa-dying-ritual*.

---

17   DVD: The making-of Living Buddha (see annex/Mediashop)

After celebrating this ritual you know what dying means, because it is earth-trembling. Nomads and other Tibetans who have not yet been "civilized" by the Chinese bring their dead loved ones on the back of a yak, even though the distance is very long and death has come weeks ago. The body is wrapped into a thick yak-wool blanket and tied up with a thick rope. Two relatives take the package off the yak and lay it on a white line on the ground leading directly to the Rinpoche who is sitting in the Vajra-position at a distance of 13 feet celebrating the ritual. Since he has to leave on horse-back instantly after finishing the ritual, I only have time to interview him now, tonight, even though it is forbidden.

The *Pohwa*-ritual is also prohibited but it is not possible to scare someone who has been tortured for decades. However I was bidden not to mention any names in the interview although in Tibet everybody has almost the same names anyway. The Rinpoche does not say much. He does not want to stir bad blood against the Chinese. They have asked him every year whether he still believed in reincarnation. He answered his torturers: "As surely as you believe in the sun rising every day." As a consequence they chopped off half an inch of his right arm every year. 25 chops in 25 years. Now he is celebrating the dying ritual illegally.

One might ask why dying is illegal. Everybody dies, so how can you prohibit it? It all depends on HOW you do it. This HOW is being controlled in the strictest possible way. This is so in almost the entire world. As long as they want the man-made man to remain stupid, the HOW in the dying ritual is decisive. Since dying like self-healing cannot be prohibited, we have a chance of freeing ourselves. To be sure the HOW is decisive for the intelligence of mankind.

The Rinpoche is talking to the body, indeed he is talking to the soul and not to the body. He even shouts at it saying that the soul has to understand once and for all that its body is going to be cut into small pieces for the vultures in the next minutes. This is about the same feeling as if you will be eaten by worms, only a lot faster. When you are being cremated, things happen quickly too. These are purely physical processes, but if you have been more in love with your body than with your soul, you might not be willing to let your body go, although it does not work anymore. Then you have a problem. This problem, the lamas say, many people have.

So it only depends on how easily we can let go. According to spiritual experiences most people need many weeks until they accept that they have died. Many still cling to their body for several weeks and have not understood that it is dead. There is a great confusion in their mind.

Most people know what disputes, violence, fear and pressure are. These things take place above all on the spiritual psychological level. For those who cannot let go of their life harmoniously, things continue in the same fashion right after death. The grumbling and scolding is just going on and on. The deceit and all the other negative experiences we had in life remain present.

Our strongest emotions are the addictions, because they make you cling to your body firmly. You may even feel insulted when your relatives do not lay the table for you any longer. In some houses people instantly cover or take down the mirrors when someone dies since the soul may get a shock as it passes in front of a mirror without seeing its own reflection. More or less like the phantom pain in an amputated leg.

I have experienced this the other way around: when I was paralyzed from the waist down, someone could have put down a hot sauce pan on my thighs without making me wince. Although only half of my body was dead, I could easily imagine that this would affect my whole body – so that I am merely the acting spirit. Normally the physical life is primarily controlled by the vegetative brain in an automatic way but in death this is no longer so. Nobody wants to admit it and would like to fancy that there is still something physical going on there – however it is only the spirit. I ignore what is giving more emotional pain: the loss of the body or clinging to it?

Dying the Tibetan way

This is what the Rinpoche is explaining to the dead person now, he is talking to his soul. And when time has come (even with a soul you cannot continue discussing endlessly as when the body was alive), the Rinpoche is putting his concentrated severity into his voice which makes me shudder. He is exhorting the soul for the last time to separate from its body. If you happen to see the stump of his right arm peeping out of his robe you know where this strength comes from with which he now says: "Jump!"

However we are not on a 30-feet-tower in the swimming-pool from where we may climb down again if the fear of jumping down is too great. Everybody has to die, therefore the Rinpoche is so severe. Naturally he is not angry. It is the loud voice: "Pah – Pah – Pah" (you can hear it in the movie[18]). Later on the undertaker takes over the body and transports it to a place outside the monastery in order to be fed to a large flock of big vultures.

I am absolutely amazed when I follow the undertaker and the body with my camera and there is not a single vulture to be seen in the sky. And in this crystal-clear air I can see into a far-off distance. Even when the body is unpacked and placed on a stone, no bird is appearing yet. But as soon as the undertaker starts cutting large pieces off the body with his big, sharp knife (I am not allowed to film this, the Chinese forbade it), there are gigantic vultures arriving out of the blue. I gather that there are more than fifty of them. They come sailing out of the great heights. After landing I can assess them better: their wingspan is between 5 and 6 feet and they reach to my waist. I am feeling a bit queasy when I stand among them watching how eager they are to eat the human meat – of which I am made of myself.

Their disgusting cries to snatch the best titbits is not only deafening but also scares the hell out of me. They are eating out of the

---

18 DVD: Tibet – Survival of the spirit (see annex/Mediashop)

hand of the undertaker. He is making space on his big stone block on which he is smashing the bones with his giant stone hammer so that no part is bigger than 1.5 inches. This is the size the vultures can just choke down their throat inside their long, red, naked and warts-covered neck. There is no term to express the ugliness of these fanatic and helpful animals.

Eventually the place of the funeral is completely clean, there is nothing left of the body, I cannot even see any blood. The undertaker knows what his work was worth when the flock has taken off with full stomachs. They fly high and far away until they disappear in the sky as small dots. To be sure the Chinese shoot their guns on everything moving, but it seems to me that these vultures cannot be shot. It is not possible to bury the dead in Tibet since the ground stays frozen even in summer from 6 inches down. There is no wood for cremation either, so there only remains air funeral. The element water is not apt for mass funerals, only for dumping the ashes.

As we do not have any air funeral with vultures in our latitudes – how do you want to have things done when your body dies? Do you want it to be eaten by worms present in your body inside a coffin? Or do you want to be consumed by flames so there will be nothing left of you but a small heap of ash? Would you like then that the urn with the ash receives a place for the relatives to remember you and maybe pray or that your ash is scattered over the sea or in a certain place? Is it important for you to know that it is exactly the ash of your body or would you agree to a mass cremation and receive only a part of the ash? It is best to set something in writing at a notary.

Addictions are just a nuisance, even in death

No matter with what ritual your body is treated after death: you should have left it before it is sent to funeral. Normally the lapse of time given for it is three days minimum. This is only just fair. Everything shorter than that is unkind for the dying person because most of them have not been enlightened before dying about what happens during and after death. The dead are completely overwhelmed by the situation. Who has been taught how to leave their body after death? The phase until the heart stops is only the small part of the process. The big part begins when there is no going back. Some people already have doubts and think: I had rather not died at all! Yet dying can be real fun.

Again it is important to know how to do it spiritually. It all depends on how free and grateful you feel when leaving your body. And how your body and mind have been imprisoned in all kinds of attachments with an addictive trait. Which addiction drives me? Yearning? Jealousy? Sex obsessions? Addiction to harmony, discussion or depression? All these are different desires.

The greatest desire is love, but often it has not been experienced truthfully before death, nor has it been practised or taught. In most cases it has worn out for a long time. The end of a relationship often has little to do with love, but a lot with addiction. True love is primarily self-love and the constant new discovering of the other. Only then may partners succeed in living together in an authentic and lively way. But this is what lovers do not care to hear. As lovers they rather live through the other partner – and without the other's love they do not feel love. A couple thinks: ... *I think that you think what I think – and you think that I think what you think ...*, however everyone has to die on their own. There is no-one else who you may make responsible for your being or dying. Only self-responsible love is what counts.

How do I reach this? On your own! It is more difficult to reach it as a couple, though it is still feasible when the two lovers are treating the other consciously and give inner and outer space to the partner. Ask yourself if you have a space of your own within your house or flat? Even if it is only five feet by five feet. It is important to be able to meditate or relax on your own. Not everybody can go out into nature for that. It should be possible to do this inside your house too. When you are alone, you can practise dying. You can observe your spirit, what it thinks about it and which emotions it presents you. In the first place it is not about changing these emotions but getting some distance from them. In death this is very useful, when you are in *bardo*.

When an addiction is getting to me and I can perceive it with some distance without clinging to it, I have come a long way. I observe my feelings and remain curious, i.e. I am amazed by what it discloses me. Thanks to the distance the thought is neither threatening nor does it wake any yearning desire. To maintain a distance, to look at the thoughts and temptations without being seduced, allows me to make a choice. The easiness to be seduced leads to great irritation. It is a good thing to master it when you are still alive, then it cannot trigger you anymore in bardo. With temptation everything comes to life: addictions, co-dependence, expectations, illusions, my ego, the whole selfish program.

It is liberating to die without any obsessions of a psychological nature. All of a sudden everything is possible provided that it was so before dying. Without the body it is even more so.

Everybody has fun with different things. It is only essential where I am going to. Which parents do I choose? How important is this or that to me? With what sovereignty do I notice where I am attracted to? Thanks to the distance I can distinguish between being seduced and electing myself: I may become aware of the fact that I am just being seduced by my projections. When I choose myself, I can recognize consciously why I am attracted to one person and may then make a clear decision.

I may also stop and even change direction. Many only do so when they have already bitten, i.e. they have nested in an ovule and suddenly they note that it was not the right place nor the right time. And then the future mother loses the ovule again – with her menstruation or later as a miscarriage.

This is the game many also play in life: bite or nibble here and there and then let go again. Short incarnations. Does this not look familiar to you, especially in love affairs? She is in love, he only wanted to seduce and run, although she was happy to think that maybe there would be a genuine relation starting. Of course it is possible for it to happen the other way around, since many women do not want to bind themselves either. Men and women are both searching and often find their definite partner late in life.

Why should it be different with incarnation? When you nest in an ovule you do it with the same consciousness with which you have lived until death. This is why it is paramount to prepare dying properly by transforming your detrimental habits and addictions. This is most easily done with e.g. *soul writing*®.

The body as a tool

During our whole life we use our body to make experiences by which we develop our character in the relative speed of a male or female life. Our different bodies are two basic tools in order to make experiences: vagina, conceiving and giving birth on the one hand and penis, begetting and providing on the other hand. These are the two poles from which we expand our consciousness. These are two completely opposed experiences which vary so much that two totally different persons are necessary to make them. For that alone the principle of reincarnation is essentially significant for evolution. The development of human consciousness could not come into harmony if every human being did not experience and develop the male and the female principle in several lives.

Mankind is merely as wise as every single human being who is achieving wisdom. To change your gender is in harmony with the cosmic principle of yin and yang. At some moment everyone changes their gender. It is true that sometimes you get the impression that some persons have not changed theirs for a long while. But everybody can imagine how fantastic it is to be a man and how fantastic it is to be a woman. How fantastic is it when both are mating? How fantastic are other constellations like man with man, woman with woman, man with woman and man, woman with man and woman, well anything? Any imaginable constellation is possible in nature.

According to our Occidental understanding the ideal of a couple relationship is monogamy. The commandment for monogamy is laid down by men who officially live in celibacy and have no experience with monogamy at all. Yet they do not want to live according to their own laws nor are they allowed to do so. They derive the commandment of monogamy from the above-mentioned monotheistic commandment: "I am the Lord thy God and thou shalt have no other Gods before me." However this law does not say: "Thou shalt have no other Goddesses before me." This means that men may have several goddesses, whereas women may not have several Gods by any means, otherwise they will be killed. Since the beginning this moral law has created great problems for mankind.

This law is continuously disregarded as it does not correspond to nature and cosmos. More than half of the marriages have ended in divorce and not everybody is happy in the remaining ones. How often do children wish for their parents to divorce rather than having to experience constant quarrels? So we may estimate that monogamy does not work for most people and is laden with jealousy, secret adultery, power struggle and rigid habits. Adultery with prostitutes is a socially accepted exception for men.

To be sure women also commit adultery massively but men are more unscrupulous in doing so. After all religion does not say anything about how many goddesses a man may have. Biologically speaking women are under more pressure when cheating on men. So men are less inclined to forgive their wife an affair for fear of raising a child who is not their own. (Every fifth child is an outcome of adultery.) The monogamy law has been made for women to obey in the first place. – If both want to live happily, they cannot cope without a sincere, commonly agreed-upon form of life, in writing. This concerns everybody, you too. Once you are a couple, be clear about your positions and put them down in writing.

As I have experienced Buddhism in Ladakh it permits free love. The Buddhist faith the *Gesche* (the priest) represented in his community, the valley of Temisgam, did not interfere in the way men and women lived together. All forms which were possible to imagine and to live by were tolerated by him. He merely established the law that every combination of relationship has to serve peace and that nobody must be in social need. This tradition of different constellations of people living together has often sprung from economic reasons, however it is mostly lived in rural areas. For someone like Jamgon, who has decided to live a life of celibacy since his third incarnation, the question of how to live together as a couple does not arise in the first place, the same as for every monk. They all dodge this difficult question too. Therefore it is essential that they principally eliminate contact with the other sex even before entering adolescence and that life in the monastery is oriented purely in a male fashion. But how is this going to work nowadays when every monk has access to the Internet and learns everything he wants about sexuality?

This is creating the same problems as when the monks enter monastery during or after adolescence and have already had feelings for the female sex. Then it is much more difficult for them to repress these feelings.

In any case those who live in celibacy solely have limited competence to give advice on sexual matters, apart from saying that everything should work out in peace and harmony.

When you live your sexuality, this has a significant influence on the reincarnation wish. It is advisable to have lived in a carnal relationship with the other sex before changing your sex from one life to the next. In most cases it appears to be a prerequisite for it because I need to have a certain knowledge of what I want to be in order to give the incarnation process the desired orientation. The changes of reincarnation are strongly dependent on the sexual emotions experienced between two persons.

Someone like Jamgon, who already dies with the wish to be in a team with Karmapa again, does not question celibacy (yet). In so far sexually fulfilled or unfulfilled yearnings do not play any role in his reincarnation wish. He concentrates on re-establishing his spiritual friendship which is more than a normal one. In principle they are not different from lovers who wish to have and do receive another life together because the wish for love is the strongest one in universe.

When this wish did not first come true in his last incarnation, although Jamgon already knew before his own conception that he wanted to be with Karmapa again thanks to this family, he had a difficult time (see what Pema tells in chapter 6). The only weapon he relied upon as an infant was his health. By continuously threatening to die he challenged his parents to look for possibilities to heal intensively. His mother Pema would have been ok with giving him to Karmapa but the interests of the male head of family were stronger.

Jamgon goes, Jamgon comes

In reality Topga is fed up with all this talk about death and reincarnation. Of course he has been thinking about why his brother died and he says: "If Jamgon really has been aware and has felt that his death would help Karmapa, I believe that he would not hesitate. Nevertheless this does not change the fact that I have lost my brother." – Situ tries to comfort him: "Yes, it is certain that Rinpoche's death was very sad and a great loss but at the same time we see that he has realized his dream."

CK: *Topga, Jamgon's wish was to support the reincarnation of his mentor, was it not?*

Topga: *Yes, sure. But who is protecting me? I feel totally abandoned*

> ... when I was born, my father died. And then Jamgon went to the monastery and I was alone with my mother. Only when mum married again and I was 15, I got another brother. Owing to the great age difference he was no mate for me and even less could he replace Jamgon. And now that I wanted to create a new link with Jamgon by giving him that car, this very gift brings death to him. This is horrible. Even the driver came to him through me. It was I who recommended him. I do not know how I can ever atone for that.

Others who are not relatives to Jamgon see his death in a more positive way, such as Marlis, an adept of Jamgon, who speaks Tibetan well and has come to assist at the bardo funeral ceremony to Rumtek in Sikkim.

Marlis: *What I have seen is that a lot of negative karma has been built up around Karmapa's reincarnation, just like a pus-filled abscess. I have experienced Rinpoche's death last week as if he had cut into this abscess and now everything comes out, then the wound will be cleansed and will heal so that Karmapa may come again.*

I imagine that Jamgon takes great pleasure in the fact that he has managed to cross the plans of intrigue of his colleague Shamar and at the same time the display of force of the superpower China. It is an immense liberty of spirit when using your body as a cut in an abscess which indeed opens and heals then. The fact that it worked may be a magnificent reason to feel joyful – a joy for the benefit of all. How will his next incarnation be?

Mother Pema says: "I am sure that he will be back soon. I totally believe in reincarnation!" – But where and how? – Her son Topga, however, means: "It is nice to believe in reincarnation but I don't. I will get accustomed to death. I will go back to work again and fulfil my duties. I have three children and I have to feed them. As time goes by the sensation of loss and the mourning will go by too."

Topga already said that he was a Buddhist since birth and believes in reincarnation as such, but it is not a real faith in it, only a tradition, the same as in Christianity where adepts also think that their faith is merely a matter of convention and has little influence on their daily routine.

It is different with Tenzin. He is a monk and was raised with Jamgon. For him there is nothing else than the spiritual life of a monk. His mother died when he was four. From then on he has received a Buddhist training by Jamgon. His biological father died when he was 18. Now he is 22, and his foster father, teacher and guru has also died. How does he cope with the separation? Has he developed his consciousness in such a way that he is not desperate or sinking into mourning? Until now, every day has been organised by Jamgon. Everything went as his master said. He hardly had to decide anything himself.

In no time at all, at such an early age, he has the responsibility for everything for which his master stood all over the world. Everyone asks him how things will go on without his master. Tenzin has no time to fall into apathy or depression. From now, on he is the example for all students of Jamgon of all ages. In order to accept this challenge more easily he is making a magic find on the very day of the accident.

The magic find

After Tenzin brought Jamgon's body to the Buddhist temple of *Salugara* and quenched the effort of the police to confiscate the body with the help of about 300 neighbours in the late afternoon, he hurries to the hospital where the other two bodies of Norbu and Kunga have been taken. In the taxi on the way to the clinic in Siliguri Tenzin has his first moment to relax. He is sitting alone in the back behind the driver and is reaching a state half-way between meditation and drowsiness. His hands lie on his stomach. He wears a T-shirt under his monk robe which is held together around the waist by a strong leather-belt. In his drowsiness he suddenly notes a slight pressure on his left side between his undershirt and T-shirt. He pulls his T-shirt out of the belt and a relatively heavy thing on a chain pops out onto the back bench next to him ... Tenzin is appalled! It is the amulet which he has asked the monks from Salugara temple to search for at the site of the accident this morning. When he had Jamgon's body laid out in the temple, he noticed that the protection amulet that Jamgon used to wear around his neck was gone. Jamgon had received this amulet from Karmapa in 1981, ten months before Karmapa died. At the site of the accident the monks, however, could not find this golden, 2 inches wide, shiny and heavy amulet. Mother Pema reckoned they should burn all grass around the site in order to find it. And now it drops out of Tenzin's shirt! How is this possible? What happens in a person when it is confronted with such a divine moment? Tenzin bursts into tears. How has this amulet found his way to him, under his T-shirt? He does not understand it! Now and then he remembers Karmapa's words which Jamgon has already told him a few times when he was given the amulet: "Wear it until you want to live." And now it is with him and Jamgon is dead ...

When Pema is informed about it, she also feels deeply touched because she knew this amulet well. To her it is also a mystery how it could find its way into Tenzin's hands. "It is incredible", she repeats over and over, "even the chain is ok."

Tenzin starts crying again when he shows Pema the amulet and tells her how and when he has found it. He is brooding about what his surviving the accident could have to do with the amulet? If it had remained with Jamgon, he might still be alive, he thinks. How can this golden, heavy thing change its owner in such a moment?

Tenzin does not have to worry if Jamgon might have given him this amulet surreptitiously without him knowing, even before they had got into the car. At no time was he so "unsound of mind", that such a thing could have been possible. Tenzin had only been unconscious in the seconds after being ejected from the car.

How can the amulet get from Rinpoche's neck to under Tenzin's T-shirt in such a moment? Our all-knowing intellect has no explanation. Do you call this magic? If yes: which consciousness is necessary to use this magic?

Tenzin is crying again without knowing why. "Why me?" he asks. He is only just 22 and completely overwhelmed …

"My husband", said Pema, "calmed Tenzin by saying that it must have been Jamgon's will that he, Tenzin, should survive to continue his work and find his reincarnation. So my husband has explained why this amulet is with Tenzin now. – And I believe it too", she says. "Why else should this amulet have found his way to him? And why has he survived? This is not normal when you see the car. Have you seen it?" Yes, we have seen it all. It really is not normal for someone to survive such a crash unscathed.

This shows again with what incredible forces we are connected when we let go of our ego. The ego is nothing against the infinite levels of consciousness which are lying above us. What can an ego achieve? What aims does it have? Which interests does it follow? They are of low nature. The ego should never rule – ever. It should and is supposed to serve. Then it has a valuable task. In the same way that reason should serve intuition (and not the other way round), so the ego has to carry out the intentions of our cosmic being. But as long as we equate our I with our ego, the access to our infinite being remains shut. Call it as you wish: soul, god, Allah – whichever name is right to describe your continuous spiritual existence without start or end in the cosmic order of love. Yet it is also ok not to give it any name at all. Nevertheless it is not correct to deny this cosmic dimension because you primarily identify with matter: your body and your ego. This produces fear of death and this fear is not a good advisor.

When your cosmic being lets you survive such an "accident" and in this moment the symbol of physical life – the golden amulet – changes its owner, an event for which neither ego nor reason may give any explanation, then you have got the proof that you are well guided and may trust this lead.

Pema: *It is a good thing that Tenzin has survived so that we know what Rinpoche's projects are. If Tenzin had also died, we would have been completely helpless. We will support Tenzin to carry out everything Jamgon has started, so that the moment Jamgon reincarnates again, we may hand everything over to him.*

Intuition has the insight

Even people who do not have a firm belief in the infinity of the soul still have a feeling for this continuity, e.g. they may say out of the blue: "When Jamgon reincarnates, then this will not be in 100 years, but very soon and surely not as a girl." These are karma-related designations which we understand intuitively. In order to make such suppositions we do not have to be clairvoyant, but we only need to know quite well the person who has died. Those who knew Jamgon a little do not find it difficult to sense that he would have a problem with Karmapa if he did not incarnate as a boy. As a girl he could not collaborate so intimately as in his former life.

In the case of the Dalai Lama, who has incarnated as a boy for the 14th time in order to take over the office of the Tibetan head of government each time, it is obvious that he will not incarnate as a girl.

Now that he has declared that he does not wish to adopt the role of the Dalai Lama in his next life, he actually told me that he toys with the idea of being born again as a girl next time.

If you want to figure out where someone will incarnate the next time, you first should feel which way their evolution could go. Only then can you ask which conditions would be fit for this person to be born in this or that place and how. In this way, you drastically limit the area of search in which this person could appear in a new form. (You may also be inspired by the practical instructions in the "personal masterplan for reincarnation" in the annex).

There are not so many possibilities to reincarnate as you might imagine. When you have known a person in his former life, maybe even known him well, then it is not so difficult to make the right guess as to where and how this person will incarnate again. Often there are relatively few places to be considered. And when you examine them, you may soon find out who is the right incarnation or that he is still in bardo, without any form, awaiting a certain evolution in the circle of persons which is apt for him to be reborn in next. You may even sense which is the step of evolution still to be made. What does it take for this step to be made so that the person (soul) concerned may reincarnate again? These and similar questions should be written down and answered in writing too, because it brings you much more certainty than to merely think about them.

I once experienced a sweet story in Lindau, a town on the Lake of Constance. A grand-mother was taking her three-and-a-half-year old grand-child on a walk when the girl broke free from her hand all of a sudden and ran to a yellow telephone booth (this was still in the analogue era, at the end of the last millennium). The grandma had to help the girl to open the heavy door. Then the girl pushed the grandma back because she wanted to be there on her own. She even climbed the box under the phone to reach the receiver and started to speak and listen. The grandma was totally perplex and circled the booth in the hope of understanding something. Finally the small grand-child returned the receiver to its place and grand-ma helped her to open the door again:

Grandma: *What was it?*
Grand-child: *I phoned grandpa.*
Grandma: *But grandpa* (her husband) *died last year.*
Grand-child: *I know.*
Grandma: *What did he say?*

> Grand-child: *That mum should stop taking the pill, grandpa wants to become my brother.*
> Grandma: *The pill?*
> Grand-child: *Yes, he said the pill.*

The grandma tells her daughter, the mother of her grand-child, who declares that she has never talked about the pill with her daughter. But anyway she stops taking the pill and nine and a half months later a baby is born. All signs point to the fact that it is the grandpa.

We should not take children as idiots, instead we should be open to all kinds of miracles. For most adults these things are only wondrous because their own consciousness is not yet sufficiently developed for the cosmic understanding. So we destroy in our children not only their natural comprehension of their own soul continuity, but also of the soul continuity of animals. In plants, spirit and biology are united. Merely on higher levels of consciousness these two are separate and the free will has to unite both again. This can only be mastered by entering the next level of consciousness. And so we go on step by step.

However we do not have endless time to do so, since we can cause a lot of trouble and suffering when we hesitate to do these steps owing to our free will, and may fall back on a former level of consciousness. This goes for the individual as well as for the Earth on which we live. It would not be the first planet to be destroyed by us thanks to our hesitation. Surely Mars also was a planet we once lived on but this was a long time ago. The universe does not mind how much time we humans take to expand our consciousness. It only depends when we want realize the full joy of life. In this matter Jamgon did not leave anything to the so-called "chance or coincidence", instead he created his fate in an extremely active way.

13
Searching for home

In Kathmandu valley in Nepal, Jamgon had received a large piece of land shortly before his death. He worked day and night to finish the plans for building his new main seat far from Tibet. Nobody could imagine that death was the motive for his hurrying.

Two weeks before he passed away he gave all the plans to Tenzin, they contain every kind of instructions up to the form of the door handles, the gutters of the roof, the motives of the frescos, the strength of the cement and so on – everything to grant a qualified training in all areas of life for 150 children and to provide a meeting place for all students of Buddhism from the whole world. Due to the golden protection amulet Tenzin recognizes that he has to continue with this task after Jamgon's death. He cannot be mourning for long.

Naturally we may cry over the loss of the body but at the same moment we have to feel the joy that death results in a great opening for something new. To do so we take off our focus from the past to put it towards the potential of the future. Then our own emotional situation changes instantly, even if it may take some time to digest the separation of body and spirit since we have always experienced the deceased in this physical and spiritual unity.

If we prefer to think in a material way, we primarily mourn and cry over the dead flesh of our beloved. However it seems that the immortal spirit, the soul of our beloved, means less to us, even though it is not dead. This is the consequence of a socially anchored, adopted philosophy of our age. Every death is a task for us to learn to say good-bye to this age even now.

With his 22 years, Tenzin is just mature enough to take over the whole responsibility for the mission and the projects of his dear master, teacher, foster father and guru, and to carry on with it. Just as Jamgon had wished. Moreover Tenzin accepts the responsibility for all that Jamgon has not laid down in writing: e.g. nowhere did he indicate what he wanted to be done with his body. Perhaps it was difficult to calculate what would be left of it after the car crashed into the tree with 120 mph. The fact that Tenzin had managed to merely have a small scratch on his head in this accident is another miracle or – to put in other words – another performance of consciousness in the highest degree.

Due to this I assume that Tenzin has agreed with all the involved people that this perfectly preserved young body should be mummified. Apart from that it is the most practical form for all that is to come in the future.

By putting down in writing that *Pullahari* in Nepal will become his new headquarters in his next life, Jamgon's body cannot stay in India/Sikkim forever. Since these headquarters have still to be built, a preservation is needed to make time. A mummy is easy to transport and to this effect is put into a stout box of about 4 feet by 4 feet and 4 feet high which is called *Kudung* by the Tibetans. For this Kudung, so Tenzin decided, a golden Stupa is to be set up in Pullahari on the other side of the main building. The move from India to Nepal will take place when everything is ready there.

With the mummification not only the body is preserved, but there will also be a relic. A relic is a timeless symbol to call forth certain contents of consciousness in humans and to remind them of a certain power. Therefore it is quite common for a relic to be wandering from one place to the next to be displayed to a large quantity of people. To this effect, the transport of the Kudung from Rumtek to Pullahari – about 500 miles through the Southern foothills of the Himalayans – is organized as a three-day procession which will be accompanied by many thousands of revering people along the roads.

For Jamgon the relics of his line had an extremely high significance. The first things for which space was made in Pullahari were the statues of the historical Buddha *Shakyamuni*, who sits in the known Vajra position and touches his forefingers with his thumbs of both hands, in order not to point to others but to himself and the statue of *Manjushri*, who sits on a galloping white horse and cuts the knot of ignorance, thus symbolizing wisdom. Manjushri is the spiritual aspect of Jamgon's origin, such as *Avalokiteshvara*, the goddess of compassion who with her 12 arms is the spiritual aspect of both the Dalai Lama and Karmapa. Next to them are – in almost their original size – the statues of both his former lives as Jamgon Kongtrul the 1st and the 2nd.

Tenzin tells us that Jamgon Rinpoche, shortly before his death, went to Pullahari to decorate and fill these statues with everything they represent: mantras, texts, invocations and different symbols. It took Rinpoche a week to do all that. During his stay in Nepal he also met with his brother Topga and asked him if he would come with him on a holiday to India. However Topga did not have time. So after finishing the work on his most important ancestors and former incarnations Jamgon went to Rumtek without his brother. He got there on April 21st and died there on April 26th.

Jamgon visits his former lives

Only 18 months before his death Jamgon had been to Tibet to visit the monastery of his former two lives in East Tibet. He had to go on horse-back since there were no roads leading there. Of course Tenzin was with him and a lot of adepts accompanied him on their horses, thus forming a large group of horsemen travelling through the wide landscape: a picture of another era. Although Jamgon Rinpoche had been raised in exile since the age of four and merely could visit Tibet for short stays, he is well-known in Tibet.

Many Tibetans know him from his former lives and see the same great personality in him as in Jamgon the 2nd and the 1st. In both former lives he was the spiritual head of the great Kagyü monastery

Tsandra Rinchen Drak and had a large impact far beyond its boundaries. There are photos of him in his former life from 1904 till 1952 like the one we saw in the film. And of his first life as Jamgon Kongtrul the 1st from 1813 till 1900, there are paintings and a statue depicting him.

For his 4th incarnation he now receives a new headquarter in Pullahari / Nepal. It will be a well-organized training and instruction centre for the development of the true character. Most teachings will be held in English, yet the regional tongues Nepali, Hindu, Tibetan and many other languages from Asia and the whole world will also be present.

Nepal – encircled by two superpowers

In Nepal, the multi-religious state, people may display their Buddhist faith without receiving any punishment by the state. This is a specialty of Nepal's situation between the two superpowers China and India, whereas one of them may spit Nepal on the head and the other one may cut its supplies. In this case to spit means to rattle their arms and shoot from above using Tibet as a shooting gallery. And to cut supplies means to lessen or stop the petrol supply coming from India at 100% next to a large amount of other basic goods. Owing to the fact that both superpowers, with their 1.2 and 1.5 billion inhabitants, respectively, do not favour each other and that both could blackmail Nepal at any time, it is difficult to rule Nepal. So it comes as no surprise that there are strange things happening there, like the fact that the son of the king murders all his family with the Maoists cheering.

This revolt has not affected the Buddhist facilities although Nepal had to sign a treaty for head money: for every Tibetan refugee caught on Nepalese territory and delivered back to China a great bounty is paid. Thus many bus drivers in the border area earn some money on the side if they are willing, and those who are not are tortured. In consequence the refugees have to pay more money than the bounty or they must dress up as a native after an almost deathly escape through the eternal ice. Still the bus drivers know who is foreign on their route anyway. So most refugees avoid the bus and only walk at night without light in the Siberian cold, like Karmapa did, and hide during the day.

For Karmapa things worked out well after he had crossed the border to Nepal with his comrades safely and they met with a helicopter in Mustang that had just delivered some tourists to Mustang in this impossible winter time. During their stay the helicopter then flew three times from Mustang to the valley of Kathmandu taking Karmapa and his company. Karmapa got dropped off on a field there. He only found his companions who went on the second flight after they had crossed the border from Nepal to India in a taxi. On this border there is a gigantic movement of people crossing over. So it is possible to pass unchecked if you are shrewd and move inconspicuously.

In India there is no such thing as a refugee deal, although China has claimed one and may throw bombs on Delhi if it wishes to do so. Yet India is a lot stronger than Nepal. China in turn has got an enormous strategic advantage since it has occupied Tibet, because it may now hit India's capital with bombs from the Tibetan-Nepalese border. Yet India may not reach Peking or any other big, important Chinese cities with any one conventional weapon, and it has no other arms, despite having the nuclear bomb, they lack intercontinental carriers.

China promotes its domination with a gigantic military base on the South East coast in Sri Lanka. Without any local infrastructure one of the biggest harbour worldwide is built there, larger than Hong Kong, earning China an additional strategic profit on the Eastern half of the planet between Asia/Australia and Africa/Europe. The small Sri Lanka could not oppose to this. For more than 25 years, from 1983 till 2009, the separatist organization *Liberation Tigers of Tamil Eelam (LITTE)* fought for their independence on this little island state in a bloody civil war with an estimated 80,000 to 100,000 casualties. The arms for the *Tamil Tigers* stemmed from China – the same state that later offered to be a mediator between the *Tigers* and the official government of Sri Lanka and worked out a peace treaty in 2009. By doing so China achieved the right to build this base and when it is finished, China will have shifted the global political and military balance in its favour.

Of course we can and have to protest against the hegemonial endeavours of the superpowers, but our happiness does not depend on it. We may also be happy in a raging war and in an acute famine.

To be sure it is a lot easier to live happily in times of affluence and peace but if happiness really depended on it, all millionaires would be happy. However it is just the other way round. There are a lot more happy poor than happy rich people. And in times of hunger there are more healthy people than in fat years. Sick people make sick politics, no matter if inside an administration or a leading position. It is all about becoming a better person.

Becoming a better person

This is exactly what all these people try hard to do who contribute actively to bring to life the new centre in the spirit of Jamgon Kongtrul with everything he represents. All of them hope that Rinpoche will teach Buddhism in his new life from this centre, as he did in his former life, e.g. like the following extract from one of Jamgon's conferences:

The phase in which spirit and matter are united is called life. In death however matter decomposes into its physical elements. Spirit cannot decompose because it is not made of physical elements. The phase in which spirit lives without matter is called bardo. *Those who identify completely with spirit may continue to evolve spiritually without matter in bardo.*

When we want to have another material expression for our spirit, this is our conception. Thereby our consciousness provides us with a material expression, this means we obtain form again.

How can we understand this sentence: "Those who identify completely with spirit may continue to evolve spiritually without matter in bardo"? Does this mean that the others who do not consider themselves spiritual beings cannot do so? If everybody had continued to develop in bardo, we would already have become better persons. However we have not. Below the surface there is something good in every person, but we lack the tool to put this spirit or attitude into practice.

Therefore I have introduced a sublevel: the above-mentioned *Soul writing*®[19]. By applying this method I create a new reality which is effective but not (yet) true. With this method I help the intuition to reach a superior level and reason is back to its position as intuition's servant. It was the age of Enlightenment which declared reason to be the boss of our thinking as a consequence of our patriarchal power structure based on a male-dominated idea of monotheism. Now this ideology has stopped working and ever more people do realize this. Now intuition is back to the highest rank when creating reality, and reason is submitted to her.

During the change of this paradigm many people have trouble accepting that all they experience without their body is what they think. Some would rather pretend to be unconscious and not think at all. Therefore many notice only in the mother's womb that they have stopped being in their old life. The time in bardo practically does not exist for them – it seems like a dream they do not remember or like being under anaesthetics.

However if I do identify with my immortal spirit and have practised not to cling to my thoughts, I possess some range of decision-making – even if I am not physically bound to a body any longer. These are two completely different ways of life which already become apparent in the physical existence. It is possible to train for that in your lifetime (also see in chapter 12 the paragraph "Addictions are just a nuisance, even in death"), but you need to have a spiritual-emotional

---

[19] More about this in "Personal Masterplan for reincarnation" (see annex).

perspective for it. In order to die in the consciousness that you are a spiritual being it is paramount to have made appropriate experiences in life. Otherwise you feel insecure again when you are in the process of leaving your body and then you are not able to admit to the fact that you are what you think. In my seminars you learn to recognize: *The way I think, is the way I am.* And so is my body and my personal surroundings.

All those who work for *Pullahari* do not merely work for money, but because they want to support this spiritual background for which the centre stands. Everybody gives their very best for it. It is not about profit, but about beauty, the highest human expression. All artists with their special capacities work unselfishly for days, weeks and months so that this new international spiritual centre is ready when Jamgon reappears in a new body.

The interesting thing about it is that they cannot be sure to get what they are working for. To consider Jamgon's reincarnation as a deathly sure thing requires a strong consciousness and above all the trust that his reincarnation will be found and that he can continue his mission from here.

The place itself is of stunning beauty with a view to the South over the big valley of Kathmandu. Behind the city the Himalayans rise majestically with their white peaks even in summer. The whole idyllic setting is blessed with lovely, pleasant temperatures all year round, so it is nice to be there. Most places where Buddhism is taught have special and exceptionally beautiful surroundings. Let us hope that this beauty also attracts Jamgon to find his way into his new life here.

Beauty e.g. in a woman is perceived externally. But however eye-catching the form may be: if the consciousness inside of her does not have the maturity to express itself in loving traits of character, all the outer beauty is wasted. Negative emotions like envy, competition, narcissism, egoism, secretiveness, lacking heart, warmth etc. represent the consciousness which is inherent in the form. Beautiful health and healthy beauty are the expression of a beautiful character coming about through a purified consciousness. When dealing with people it is a good exercise of consciousness to continuously ask: *What would love do?*

Pullahari is built in this and for this very spirit. There is the same amount of people working for this beauty as for the building itself. (In Western countries the ratio is 9:1 in the best case owing to maximization of profit.) Everyone involved in creating the centre in Pullahari is directly or indirectly interested in the philosophy with which death can be overcome. The most costly craftsmanship and the most precious gems are just good enough for it. People from all over the world donate money, gems and other materials for this centre. The precious gems are introduced in the construction by hundreds, especially in the stupas and above all in the one stupa that will give shelter to Jamgon's kudung.

Why plenty of gems and jewels? Every human being is a jewel and wants to shine in purity, this is why they become involved in this project in such a special way. Since all who work here are convinced of the continuity of life, they are motivated to create values which will represent a treasure even in all the future incarnations. In Tibet it is quite a tradition to think so.

This trust in a life without beginning or end is exemplified in the question if Jamgon's reincarnation will be found and if he will move here one day. However there is no guarantee that Jamgon´s reincarnation will be discovered and that he will be able to come here. Until now nobody possesses a sign of when, where or with whom he is reborn. Yet the works will go on unabatedly at full speed. After two years, the main building with the prayer hall and the lodgings for the small pupils (60 beds) are ready. When Jamgon's vision is finished, there will be 150 pupils starting at the age of six who will live and learn here.

The apparently irrational feeling is imposed on the onlooker that the more these people do for Jamgon's reincarnation, the surer it gets that he will come.

However this is not irrational, it is even logical energetically speaking. Why? Because every thought in universe leaves a trace and we are all connected inside this universe.

The family of Topga and Pema become especially involved in the whole project of their deceased Rinpoche. They see to everything what is needed. Even Topga's step-father is fully engaged in the project. Topga can hardly understand that he, as a sceptic, is showing so much commitment to Buddhism. First he thought that this may be something for his mum only and he states: "I have always been sceptical, I never had a firm belief. My philosophy is that you live your life without hurting anybody or doing any evil and help others as much as possible. This is my religious faith. I have never received any instructions of His Holiness the Dalai Lama but these are his principles and I think they are very correct."

Yes, this is the message of the Dalai Lama. In the meantime he even says that nowadays no religion is needed any longer; it would be better if all people stuck to the human ethical values which are at the base of all beliefs so that peace may arise. This is quite a remarkable statement, it corresponds with his modern consciousness and his inner attitude to think, feel and act authentically.

If we look around we note that religions in the form of churches mostly serve certain power interests and less the salvation of the human soul. Therefore it is necessary to abolish them and show people instead how they find in themselves the scale for authentic, caring thinking and acting – completely independent of their belief. Yet if we understand the latter as our only truth, this concept is rapidly declining into dogmatism.

In order to live an authentic life free from aggression we must learn how to communicate with our soul. Plenty of people believe that they can do just that, they possess an inner voice representing their soul. And they hear it but sometimes it gets loud and painful because even if they hear it, they do not listen. If they did listen to it, they would have the best advisor and wisest guru.

They would not need to ask anybody what is right and wrong. The soul knows what is best for the benefit of all. The soul does not represent ego interests. It is the personalized intuition.

With intuition I may open up the limits between my different lives. If I have experienced it in myself, I cannot doubt anymore the continuity of life for Jamgon either. However: not everyone obtains this certainty of reincarnation, even if they have already experienced it. As *Voltaire* said: "I have not believed in reincarnation already in my last life."

In a setting which considers life as a singular, physical event it is hard to develop a certainty of the continuity of life. Often we must not even mention it so that we are not marginalized. Even reading this book may get us into trouble. If we go down deeper into the matter, often there is nothing left to do for us than to change our friends, sometimes even our partner.

True love does not tell lies

Once a woman told me she had concealed her husband the fact that she was studying the continuity of spirit and the *KUBYmethod*®. She had read one of my books about the subject and had attended my seminar in Blumenthal mansion. Luckily for her the price of the seminar was moderate because in her marriage, money was a big matter: they always quarreled about whom the money belonged to. However she did tell him the truth about attending a seminar claiming that she would pay it with her own money. Yet on her return she lied to him saying that she had attended a cooking seminar because she knew that the reincarnation business meant nothing to him, that he would be totally against it and would make her life difficult if he figured out what she was studying and that she had spent money on it. When she lied to him about the cooking seminar, she wondered for a moment if he had sensed the lie.

She was glad that when she put the meal on the table he said at least: "It is delicious." – "Thanks", she replied.

Since she had paid the seminar on her own, she reckoned there was no need for justification and she might spare herself more conflicts with this lie, after all she loved him. Nevertheless at night she asked herself in a sleepless moment: "Is it possible to love someone and tell him lies at the same time?" Most people will presumably answer: *By all means*! Not only women lie to their husbands, men also lie to their wives. It is difficult to tell who lies more. Many are of the opinion that lies keep up the relationship – in the certainty that their love would crumble if they did not tell lies.

They justify their doing so with a situation where all started, stating: "I was belittled and humiliated then so I have switched to lying. In the meantime there are a lot of things I do not tell him. Certainly he does the same. Only in doing so our marriage has been able to withstand time. So lying has been worth it. – Naturally I would prefer to stand up and assert myself but now I do it by lying about my interests. This way is more harmonious than confronting him with the truth. To be sure this is not an authentic life but in confronting him it could happen that I find myself in the street. I do not want to risk that. It would only make everything worse." These are the excuses. But can it really be love what is upheld by lying?

This dilemma can only be solved by writing down the whole scene/situation in script-style. Only then repressed stuff can be dissolved and transformed into something authentic. Not merely for your own benefit, but for the benefit of all. With *Soul writing* it is possible to do this in a basic and above all sustained way.[20]

---

20 Find instructions for script style in the annex.

14
Reincarnation versus genetics

Jamgon taught us: "We are born with totally different characters, something that does not depend on our body, but on our consciousness." I believe that he does not tell us anything new. Every person who has already been in contact with a baby could feel that this being was no blank page, on the contrary: a complete and very individual personality. You can also say: a person with a character. The mainstream opinion however pretends that the human character is a product of our surroundings, conditioned by our closest reference persons, the social conditions we are born into and the whole culture to which we belong since birth.

According to this opinion, a new-born being would be something like an empty hard-disk in which the program is written into gradually. However this theory does not coincide with our perception. We perceive that if we deal with this fresh-born being ourselves the complete program is already present! (See chapter 4.) The body is still small and tender but the being inside of it has an individual character. Where does it come from?

Is it all a matter of genes only?

Generally it is said that the character is a mixture of our parents' characters and they would transfer their characters on the child via the genes at conception. In my opinion, it is even more adventurous to believe in such a theory than to believe in reincarnation. Let us have a closer look at the way "genes" are defined scientifically, in the different countries:

According to Wikipedia genes are defined in Switzerland like that: "Genes are chromosomal, monogenic, multifactorial, mitochondrial effects, respectively their underlying predispositions, and their pre- and postnatal (incl. presymptomatic) diagnose and classification by genealogical, clinical, biochemical, molecular genetic and/or cytogenetic examination processes of defined phenomena."

In Austria genes are defined like that: "The principles of biological functions in men, the aetiology and pathogenesis of hereditary diseases, the general human genetics, the cytogenetics, the molecular genetics, the dysmorphology, the clinical genetics including the syndromology, the population genetics and the genetic epidemiology."

In Germany cytogenetics are defined as: "The examination of human chromosomes via fluorescent microscopy with the intention of finding particularities in chromosome sets and assigning them to certain pathologies, syndromes or cancer tumours. Example: caryogram. It is about researching hereditary diseases and preparing expertise of origin. After the human genotype has been largely deciphered in the Human Genome Project, research is now done on the functions of individual genes and their interaction in the frame of proteomics. The whole human genome contains between 20,000 and 25,000 genes."[21]

How does this help me to explain the forming of character? It is very easy to express yourself in a complicated fashion, but what does it mean? My focus is on being happy and healthy. In what way does genetics help me to reach this goal? When e.g. analysing the genes in a person it is discovered that a certain gene is faulty or lacking, then science explains to the progeny of this person that they too have to count on having this defect. If your ancestor dies of this disease which medicine ascribes to this gene defect, the progeny has to part from the idea that they will also fall ill with this defect and die early.

---

21 https://de.wikipedia.org/wiki/Humangenetik#Schweiz and https://de.wikipedia.org/wiki/ Zytogenetik

I know of the case of Beatrice Wessely from Switzerland.[22] According to the theory of genetics she got a death diagnosis from Bern University stating that she would have no chance of surviving because nobody had ever outlived this defect (in her case the lacking gene no. 19). Even her father and her sister had both died from it at an early age. So she also had to believe and accept that she had to die soon. Beatrice made her will at the age of 18 and wanted to enjoy the remaining months of her life by spending her father's inheritance.

Suddenly she had the inspiration not to waste this money but to search for persons who adhere to a different genetically theory, so she visited shamans and healers all over the world after viewing my film *En route towards the next dimension*. She also lived in the country with a Brazilian healer. While these encounters made her get into contact with and adopt other philosophies and perspectives, she had already outlasted her anticipated death for more than a year in completely good health.

As a consequence, she wanted to get examined by the same genetic doctors in Bern again to see if this so-called gene no. 19 had reappeared or formed afresh. Yet since these doctors believe that genes cannot modify nor form afresh, they denied her being examined. They did not want to question their theory and the corresponding statistics. After more than 20 years Beatrice is still alive in best health without any of the so-called genetic fault.

Can genetics overthrow reincarnation? It is all about philosophy and human image: which one does offer me which potential to evolve? No theory or human image or explanation model of life is true or untrue. Every theory is based on an underlying human image which in turn is based on another underlying human image which in turn is based on another underlying human image. In the end I have to ask again: *What would love do?*

---

22 DVD: *Healing in six steps* (see annex/Media shop).

Love is harmony. When I am in harmony, I am in accordance with the universe. Mathematically speaking the universe is in perfect harmony, even – as I mentioned before – at a very low energetic level. Why is this? Simply because harmony requires the least amount of energy.

Since the explanation model of *Global Scaling* disposes of an infinity of proof, there only remains one question to be answered: do I want to make this model the foundation of my life or do I prefer stress owing to a different human image I believe to be truer? However in these fundamental questions all cannot be about true or untrue, right or wrong, but merely about: what do I want? Do I want to be into love or into stress? It is not about theories, it is about the quality of life – even about the one of the researcher.

The quality of life is mainly decided at the time of conception. Even though I want to believe according to the gene theory that my character is the product of my parents' characters, the moment of conception remains the most important moment of my life. If I want to believe in genetics I decide my fate – just as in the case of reincarnation – in the moment I am conceived. Without wanting to get mixed up in scientific quarrels these deterministic theories depend on: who are my parents and which biological, social and character possibilities do they offer me?

This is the question to answer in both human images with one big difference: with genetics we cannot talk of being competent to evolve on our own, yet we can do that with reincarnation. With genetics it is indifferent what parents offer because in this theory we do not have a choice to accept or reject this offer. I only exist as a human being with a body because my parents come together in a sexual union. I do not exist before that. Therefore I do not have any will at all. I am a nothing.

How can I imagine according to the law of cause and effect that I was born out of nothing? For everything that manifests a spiritual impulse is needed, an energy, an intention, an idea or even a will which is condensed, compressed and thereby concretized – and at the end a human being of flesh and bone comes to life. How can genetics explain this spiritual impulse which helps itself to the biological, social and character elements of one's parents during the act of love? According to genetics this impulse is non-existent. This is comprehensible because how are they supposed to recognize something spiritual with their whole perspective of life consisting of material elements? According to this image of the world there are only parents and their parents and so on.

So I am the sum of all these inherited biologically, chemically and physically detectable chromosomes – of the genetic material in the sperm and the ovum. Therefore there must be physical and biological elements in my parents which I take over. Yet this does not even exist according to their theory, it is only conceived during the sexual act. So who provides for the selection? There must be a selection because nobody is the exact image of all the characteristics of their parents and their ancestors.

In a natural manner I can perceive that I have something from my mum here and something from my dad there, maybe also something from my uncle or my grand-ma and so on. Even if according to Darwin's and Mendel's hereditary theory I want to recognize elements in my character which are also present in my biological ancestors, the question still arises: Who has selected these elements? When genetics comes to its limit with this question, it will either reply: with God or with coincidence. Both are jokers for not knowing. But this is no disgrace. It only reveals that the explanation model of genetics does not reach any further in this area. However for our personal evolution it is of greatest interest to get an answer to this elementary question: *Which forces do form the human character?*

No soul without form

Let us admit it: genetics cannot give a reply to the question of who or what determines the character we have because in its theory spirit – we also call *soul* in the reincarnation model – does not exist. The soul is to be understood as individualized spirit. In the reincarnation model we work on this subject with the universal law of cause and effect because, as we said before: the cause for everything manifest, e.g. a human being of flesh and bone, needs a spiritual impulse as cause.

So this spiritual impulse must have been present even *before* the sexual act of the parents, as nobody could have made the genetic selection then. To be sure we do not want to believe in the stork that brings the child to the parents. Anyway it is absurd to tell our children such a nonsense when they ask for these things seriously, even though one might answer in a joke. Why do we shy from transmitting our children the reincarnation model? Because it is not yet recognized in our Western, materialistically oriented culture? (But the stork is part of it, is it not?)

Nowadays the explanation models are changing ever more quickly since the density of events is increasing fast. One has to surrender one's truths ever more often and rapidly. Let us only think of the speedy change from analogue to digital – a similar thing happens from genetics to reincarnation.

Long-time suffering was imposed on mankind (by the Inquisition etc.) every time they wanted to modify their truth (belief concept) before the ruling class did. Imprisonment, torture and burning were the consequences. There will be no such thing when you want to change from genetics to reincarnation now. Although reincarnation may still be a bit new for some people our possibilities of evolution will expand as incredibly as when we changed from analogue to digital. Those who do not want to change now will waste undreamt-of resources inherent in a conscious selection of genetic elements.

Only think of how our children have to struggle at school because their abilities from former lives are not taken into account and remain taboo owing to the ruling model of genetics. So it is a must to teach them the next step of consciousness even if school does not do that at the moment. (See also chapter 10 the paragraph "Remembering since the beginning"). We could make learning a lot easier for our children when learning is transformed into remembering. Genetics cannot recognize our former lives and those of our children because through genetics' glasses people are not able to see the continuity of spirit.

However when I put on the glasses of reincarnation, I immediately recognize who has selected my parents and their model function for me: I myself or rather my soul. Who else? This does not work when you apply the old explanation model. If I do not want to let it go, there is only one possibility left for me: to evade into the irrational. This is no wonder: if I absolutely want to stick to analogue thinking and ask questions to the digital world, I do not receive any logical answers which make sense to me. Then I must say e.g.: "God has made the choice for me, even if I did not exist according to genetics." Yet it is even more adventurous to believe in God – as I mentioned before – than to believe in reincarnation. God has to serve as creator as long as men need him to be the ruler so they can exert power over their wives. Today you may say: *I am the creator myself.*

With the reincarnation theory you are suddenly in the middle of everything without beginning or end with your potential for evolution. There is no limit by conception and death. It is a completely different way of thinking. You take responsibility for having chosen your parents. By doing so you learn to appreciate the very traits of their character which fascinated you so much that you had created your whole next life with them, including the social starting conditions until you could be in charge of yourself.

When your parents carried out their sexual act, they certainly lacked the consciousness for the question of which genetic parts they wanted to transfer to you and which ones not. However you have used this sexual act for incarnating. And maybe they were aware of the fact that in this very moment they could conceive a child. Still they probably lacked the consciousness that right now they were giving you the chance to come into flesh and bone. It was your decision to give yourself a form with this man and this woman and this is why you chose exactly these parents.

Now these two persons have a whole bandwidth of positive and negative qualities. Perhaps you have been raised in difficult social and humane conditions. These are circumstances whose victim you do not want to be anymore, but you long to be free from them. This is possible when you search for the traces of your former lives in a self-responsible way and provide clarity about all your addictions. Thanks to the reincarnation model you may e.g. write down the character aspects of your mum and dad and reflect on this list by asking yourself which of these aspects you have taken over and which not. You may also ask what has fascinated you so much in her and in him that you have chosen these persons as parents – no matter how hard things may have turned out later. There must have been something which attracted you. There is no such thing in universe as coincidence.

When Jamgon said in his bardo teaching: "It all depends on the consciousness with what character we are born", then the genetic aspects we have taken over are also part of our consciousness. Since this choice has been a spiritual decision, we can also correct this decision spiritually. In the reincarnation perspective this is not a biological bind – so it offers us much more possibilities than the materialistic, biochemical human image.

Apart from the fact that with the spiritual-emotional perspective I can create the appearance of my parents in such a way I most like, it reveals another and more essential quality of life which makes life much easier because as Jamgon said: "Death is nothing final and therefore nothing negative. Death is only a phase in which spirit is renewing its material expression."

How can you come to the conclusion that death is nothing negative when you consider that human beings bring their character from where they come from? To answer this question I always part from my own observations and feelings and ask myself: What is it that makes death so negative that even I feel fear when it knocks on my neighbour's or my own door? Essentially it is the thought that everything is over then or it is the thought that the horror is just starting ("Purgatory"). Is it this uncertainty combined with the feeling of being abandoned which most burdens me?

In the view of death the feeling of abandonment is the prevailing emotion in most people – and not with primary respect to themselves (as far as the letting go of the body is concerned) but to the bereaved. Their feeling of abandonment often is the worst thing with death: to be left by a dear soul in a beloved form. Abandoned by their physical presence and familiar gestures and abandoned by everything which constituted their physical being in all their many facets. Yet when we look beyond the form we can recognize and feel that despite all the mourning and pain only the outer conditions have changed, but the contact to the soul of the other being is still alive, not dead.

Let us have another look at the babies: right after birth it is clear that life does not begin at zero. There is something all-comprehensive, very big and strong that cannot be ignored. Even if I want to ignore it, this being cries and does not even get hoarse by doing so. My baby cries so much that I (or others) have to perceive it. I cannot say that this new-born baby is a blank page that does not need special care yet. On the contrary: it needs greatest attention, care, appreciation, time and affection, love and someone who addresses it – simply everything and from the first minute.

This shows me again that we do not come out of nothing, that we bring something with us. The essential thing we bring with us is not the aspect of our body, but something more essential: our character. This is why I have to ask myself: When did this come into being? Did it only emerge shortly before my birth? Then it must have been a soulless piece of flesh inside the womb of the mother. However every mother feels and every ultrasound scan can confirm that this is not so. So: how far do I have to go back to receive a trustworthy explanation for the question when this being has emerged as a so-called new being? At the moment of conception? During the parents' physical act of love? In this act the whole being, i.e. the whole character of this being must have been contained in the sperm and the ovum, if I try as hard as I can to remain a materialist (in this case a biologist).

Dear reader, before we continue to turn around in a circle, one thing is certain: we are struggling again with genetics because it cannot recognize that the character of a child is something unique and individual. Man is not merely the mixture of his biological ancestors. This contradicts his own experience. The individual and unique part must have existed before conception. This cannot be materialistically proven. For the scientist things start to get mysterious. Something is joining the game which he cannot cover with his philosophy based on reason. He is not able to give an answer because he has reached the limits of his explanation model.

With which human image do I look at life and death?

No explanation model can depict life in all of its complexity. It surely is only a certain grid which we project on life in order to recognize structures from which an order can be established. From this order new insights should arise for the development of our consciousness. In the same way I have to replace my old analogue theory with a new and different explanation model for coping with the computer, I have to leave the materialist perspective and use the spiritual-emotional one

when it comes to understanding why human beings are born with an already marked character. If we want to give an answer to which forces there are to determine the human character traits, we require a human image that provides a structure with which we may analyse all processes.

For the ruling thought concept the metaphor of the stork is the admission that it is incapable of giving a viable explanation for the shaping of human character. It does not make us happy though and we cannot tell our children in a credible and convincing way that they are fully mature personalities with an infinitely long past. Yet if we decide to do just that out of love for our children, death has also lost its horror for us.

Or do you think different? You: *No!*
I: *Why not?*
You: *Very simple. I fail to understand the connection between death and conception.*
I: *But you recognize that human beings bring along their personality and do not only receive it at conception!?!*
You: *Of course! But where do I get the certainty that this personality who is born now has died before?*
I: *Where else should it come from?*
You: *I have no idea, maybe from the moon or elsewhere.*
I: *No jokes please. Just look at your baby again: does it not seem familiar somehow?*

At this point, two different answers are possible. Some parents say yes, some say no. A few even presume that their baby has been switched at the hospital. Even some children have this feeling. Everything is about the question: where do human beings get their character from with which they are born? Or: from where do they get the strong features at birth, e.g. a physical or mental handicap? Whichever the answer, we can always state that this child – no matter where it came from and what it experienced before – wanted to be with you, or rather with both of you who are its reference persons. The child or in other words the personality who incarnates with you has to have a special reason for it: not only the parents could be the reason, but also the existing siblings, the grand-parents, uncles, aunts etc. – all close persons may be the cause for incarnation. Coincidences, as we know now, are not part of our philosophy.

In the philosophy of many people the answer at this point is: "This must have been God's will." Does such a reply satisfy you or could you change your philosophy? By citing God they put off their wish for insight (expansion of consciousness) with something irrational because the questioning and reflexion about it may be very tiring. They sense that they have reached the limit of their philosophy and cannot go any further with their truths. These truths are just like cement walls which take too much effort to tear down, so resistance springs up to say good-bye to your philosophy.

In other people we can see the reasons for such a resistance effortlessly, yet when it comes to seeing them in ourselves we are blocked and do not even notice it. We do not even notice it in our own children because they are too close to us. Maybe you ask yourself why your child is so full of problems. What possibilities do you have to help your child to live a happier and healthier life?[23] It would be very helpful if you knew who your child was in a former life.

This answer has nothing to do with knowledge and everything to do with looking sharp and perceiving. It can be compared with the first contact to people of a different race and colour. At first you can hardly distinguish them but when you live with them for a while, you do not even understand the question of how you know who is who anymore. Every human being has their very own and special character, even the animals.

A farmer with 100 cows knows all of them by name and can say which is which without any trouble. For a stranger all cows look the same at first, if they belong to the same race. Only by watching closely and by emotionally perceiving their different characters arises the

---

23 You may look for a lot of different help on my website www.clemenskuby.de

intuitive knowledge of distinction. The same goes for recognizing a person from a former life. This also requires some time of adaption. When I finally have found a connection to their soul and come to know their character better, I can sit down and have a written dialogue with the soul when I am in alpha phase.[24]

Applying the *KUBY method*® I employ *Soul writing*®. It does not help to theoretically explain the results of such a method. However the written answers of such a dialogue with the child are stunning. For example the reply to your question: "Why have you incarnated with me?"

To be sure soul writing requires some practice to trust the answers. Yet if you – the same as most people – are deeply touched by the answers even after the first time, you know that you are right and you can continue the written dialogue until the time before conception and even further until before the last death.

Once you have crossed the materialistic limits, the question may arise: "Who was I in my former life?" In your own case you can even determine more exactly what is correct and what is not. The answer is in the responsibility itself. When I have to confess that I recognize in others a certain continuity from their former life to their present life, I have to part from the idea that I am also a continuum. Due to this hypothesis a responsibility automatically arises in me for my being which may be quite terrifying. I have to acknowledge my parents and the surroundings I have incarnated in – and accept them positively, as an expression of my consciousness.

Without this acknowledgment, I do not know who the person was who has selected them to become the person I am now. I am so I am. My soul is a continuum and before having this form (body) it had another form (body). Just as Jamgon said above: "Spirit cannot decompose into physical elements because it does not consist of physical

---

24   More about this in "Personal Masterplan for reincarnation" (see annex).

elements", I accept that the character with which I came into this world is the same character I left my form (body) with. Therefore I do not have to look for something else than what I was at birth. (In soul writing we always use the present tense). I only have to acknowledge my parents as my own choice, no matter how much I criticize them today from my present perspective. There must have been a good reason for my election and this reason stems from my former life.

"Death is only terrible if you define yourself primarily by material values and less by what you think and feel", says Jamgon.

Belief concepts – life's glue

How do you change your truths or philosophy (finally it is the same thing)? How do you recognize your own belief concept? Are you aware of adhering to a certain belief concept? Atheists are e.g. of the opinion that they do not believe in anything. However they believe in science. Nowadays science is the most wide-spread religion and has overtaken Catholicism followed by Islam which is about to become the biggest religion on Earth. However atheists who believe in science are still the largest group in the world. Whom do you belong to? What belief system do you adhere to? Some people belong to a different group as they are supposed to.

For example I do not count myself among the group under suspicion of being a sect, however people suppose I am part of it because I live in *Blumenthal mansion*, and some think it is the home of a sect (www.schloss-blumenthal.de). Although the Bavarian broadcast (the *Bayerische Rundfunk*) made a film about us to make it clear that we are not a sect but very normal citizens. – Some people are also counted as esoterica's, terrorists, populists, fascists, gurus, charlatans, saviours etc. even if they do not count themselves among them.

Therefore I am in favour of the *transparent person*. Why? There is no such thing as privacy in a world with increasingly technical and electronical surveillance possibilities. It makes no sense to try and stop this. Everything has a positive and a negative side. By data protection we try hard to get a grip on the negative side. But how many possibilities offers the positive side if we become transparent beings?

Let us exaggerate a bit: everybody can determine instantly which type of person I am thanks to the plenty amount of data available. I do not make any effort to keep a secret about anything because it is too stressful. Is it not the nicest thing that other people put yourself in the just category to which you belong? Then the world is in perfect order.

So I only need to become transparent, then in theory there is no more difference between my inner and my outer self. Thanks to *Google, Facebook* and some more of these relentless data collectors, I can part from the idea that there is so much data about me that everybody who has access to these data may categorize me exactly. Of course to my ideal of a transparent person belongs the fact that these data about me must be accessible for everyone, above all for me. This must be a fundamental law, otherwise the ideal of a transparent person cannot be realized.

Naturally the democratic principle of "the same right for everybody" must also be valid for the access to data. I would like to know everything about my girl-friend others know about her too and what she would like to know about me of course. Nobody will have any secrets anymore – this is my ideal.[25] Once this ideal is fulfilled, I can feel absolutely secure because all and everything is transparent.

I surely know that other people feel insecure when it comes to transparency and they may feel too vulnerable as far as despotism of the ruling class is concerned. This feeling has a strong impact on the quality of life, and fear and helplessness may appear. This is the very

---

25 In the new electronical era a law is imperative which not only regulates data protection but also the access of a person to all data gathered on them as well as the availability of data to them.

thing I want to avoid. I also know that I cannot restrain or even stop the appetite of the rulers as to data. It is hard to protest against it.

So I changed my mind by 180 degrees: I am aware again of being connected to all beings I can feel – this is just the basis of the *KUBY method*®. In every systemic constellation, in every kinesiological test, in every soul writing I profit from this cosmic, universal, spiritual connection. I can therefore appreciate the fact that in our materialist time technicians have tried to reconstruct this divine principle and have invented Facebook spreading it all over the world. With no other technology have we come closer to the spiritual slogan "we are all one" than with *Google* and *Facebook*.

Man wants to be God and would like to create himself on his own. This is what he increasingly does with the ruling human image. In consequence he invents things with which he substitutes self-devised techniques for our natural, inherent capacities.

For example every human being possesses telepathic capacities by nature. And what does man do? Instead of trusting and training his ability to communicate without words, he invents the telephone. Yet the phone is by far not as flexible and as all-comprehensive as telepathy but it is man-made. Of course our spiritual potential withers away, though we have the satisfaction that we have put this capacity in a separate physical form according to our materialist period.

The same goes for our sense of orientation and the navigation system in the car.

Before we follow the technology euphoria, let us rather look at the animals which are not as attached to a materialist ideology as we are. It is stunning how they have developed their inherent potential in the course of time. There is the phenomenal sense of orientation in the migratory birds which know their way around the world with a precise goal which can only be familiar to them from a former life.

Or there is the extra-fast and creative swarm of sardines which in seconds forms into a gigantic fish to make a shark or another big attacker escape. In a flash every sardine swims to its special place in the formation in order to simulate the shape of a gigantic fish. There are even a few sardines that know exactly that they have to swim on their back to feign the white eye of the monster fish. These are qualities from which we are still light years of time away!

Nevertheless we will not lose heart: in order to continue developing in this direction we may consider ourselves spiritual-emotional beings because then a whole bounty of possibilities for evolution are open to us which we have so far thought impossible with our materialist orientation. We can use every evolutionary development in a negative or a positive way. No manifestation has only one side. It is our task to make decisions every time. Therefore I have decided to look at the positive side of *Social Media*. The criticism made to me via *Facebook* is considered by me as a challenge which makes me act with growing awareness and carefulness at the time of formulating my messages. This is a good thing for everyone. If I can do this I can become a member of a great community which gives me security thanks to a strong feeling of solidarity.

Naturally I also see the other side of the mass media displaying a general shallowness which does not promote much human empathy.

Yet I concentrate on the positive side, insofar that more can be done for the expansion of consciousness than with any other tool in the history of mankind until now.

Up to this moment it was the task of religions to expand our consciousness. So every religion propagated certain truths we should trust. However truths possess the property to become absolute and to repress other truths which may contradict them. This is a principle which is expressed in character, e.g. in jealous economic competition. It springs up while competing for proof. If you could accept that with your belief concept or religion every proof is always a subjective truth, then you would stop being jealous and also stop competing with other truths. This would have an immediate impact on all your relationships (see also chapter 5 the paragraph "The truth for the benefit of all").

It is pointless to compare two belief systems in order to show which is truer than the other. By doing so you would compare apples with pears. Pears are as true as apples. It only depends on what tastes better in the present situation, meaning: which belief concept serves our aims better in the present moment?

It serves best the mission of this book when I believe (think it is true) that I am an immortal continuum. I want to feel it, apply it and use it. I check for myself what tastes better to me and what serves my present situation in life more: the belief concept of a singular life or the belief concept of a continuum? Which concept offers me a better quality of life and more possibilities to develop? Maybe I realize that there is still a gap between my demands and reality – that on one side I want to believe in an immortal life but see myself as prisoner in an ideology of a singular life. If this is so, I reflect on the question: How do I change my belief concept without entering in a competition struggle with other belief systems?

In order to change something you first have to know what it is. So ask yourself: How much have you secured your material existence? When does the fear of existing catch up with you? Which feeling arises when you think of a crash in stock-markets? Of divorce or insurance failure? Of landslide or disease? How much do you invest in your material safe-guarding (money-safe, alarm system)? If you are male, how much value do you give to the outer image of you masculinity, starting from the stylish business suit up to the sharp hair-cut which makes you look so cool? If you are female, how important is it for you to have a model shape with perfect hair, make-up, fashionable clothes and shoes and all other signs of affluence?

We could go on asking questions endlessly, but we could also ask: How much are you anchored in your spiritual being? What is the percentage of your belief that your body is subordinate to your spirit? 10 percent, 30 or maybe 50 percent and the other half are physical problems? Or even 100 percent according to the principle: *The way I think is the way I am?*

It is about being aware of what is, not of what you would like to have. For example how much pills do I consume? How do I survive economically? And the last question: What happens when I die? As long as the reply is a black hole or an angel sitting on a cloud I do not have any approach to determine my reincarnation. But this is exactly what we are talking about when the reincarnation concept is to provide me with an advantage with respect to my present thinking. Let us hear my conversation with Topga:

> Topga: *In the end all is about believing. However my own thought concept cannot accept this. I always need a correct explanation of why things are so and so. In every religion there is a point where you simply have to believe. I cannot do that. It is against my nature. Perhaps this will change some time, but I am afraid it does not.*
> CK: *Why should this change?*
> T: *I feel I don't belong if I have trouble believing in reincarnation.*
> CK: *Do you want to believe in it?*
> T: *Of course I do but I cannot say that I simply believe in it. I need proof or maybe not proof because it cannot exist, but at least a sign.*
> CK: *Yes, I also wish for that. As a documentary filmmaker I want to see what I am supposed to believe and if I cannot shoot it I do not see it.*
> T: *And what? Have you seen it?*
> CK: *I am into it. I am like you, I need to experience it to believe.*
> T: *OK, let us see what things are about to happen.*
> CK: *With the camera it is not so easy because with most things the camera is not running or I am not present. Then I only learn it from hearsay.*
> T: *So do I. But I wonder if I will ever see my brother again.*
> CK: *If so, then he will have a different form.*
> T: *Yes, of course. This is the difficult part.*
> CK: *Maybe you will get certainty in a different way.*
> T: *How?*

CK: *By a dream for example.*
T: *Dreams are unreal.*
CK: *Perhaps it is not about a certain belief but about what makes you stick to your present belief.*
T: *I am a businessman. I have 500 workers. I have to think in a materialist and economical way.*
CK: *Then the sign has to be in a way that it really has a meaning for your thought system.*
T: *Yes, this is just the point. I do not believe in such a sign because my brother would have to come back the way he was and as I know him.*
CK: *I am sorry but this is nonsense. Even in your thoughts you will never see him again as you saw him before. With time every person changes.*
T: *But not as crassly as in reincarnation.*
CK: *It depends on where you put your focus. If you imagine him as he was the last time you saw him, then you will never meet him again. But if you think of the feeling you had for your brother, then it could be that you will get the same feeling again when you face his reincarnation.*
Topga is close to tears.
CK: *Why are you crying?*
T: *I don't know. Maybe it is the feeling that I have for him.*
CK: *Then this may be a sign when you will meet him in his new form and have this strong feeling again. Wil you believe it then?*
T: *Let us wait and see …*

The question if I am a sentient or a thinking being is paramount for the expansion of your own consciousness. The first reaction, the first feeling when I feel touched, is never deceptive whereas your thinking is often dominated by doubts. When you think, there may always spring up a But. When you feel and you are close to tears, then you cannot question or deny this feeling. This feeling is there and it came up without my doing. Thus it is a truth for me. In a theoretical principle it is always possible that people add or take away something, so there is no relying on it. If I look for proof, I should rather look with the feeling than with the thinking. When something feels completely right, I rely on it. When a thought is merely a theory I may doubt it.

For example the theory that the universe has originated with a big bang. I do not have any feeling about it. Even less a harmonious feeling. The theory does not convince me because it does not say what was before the big bang. There is no internal proof either. The statement that the big bang took place some 13 billion years ago cannot be proven. On the contrary: the Hubble-telescope has the energy to look into space and see what happened 13 billion years ago. Thus it would have to – no matter where it is located since the big bang – discover the edge of this expansion somewhere in space where the star density radically reduces to zero. But this is not the case.

So the adepts of the big bang theory reply that they had miscalculated and the big bang must have taken place some 13.5 billion years ago. And only because the Hubble-telescope cannot see so far, this new statement cannot be refuted – at least not with the pictures sent to the Earth by the telescope.

Why do we develop such a theory in the first place? First it reflects the materialist thinking by setting a starting point to this theory, so it corresponds with all materialist processes of becoming and passing away. All that materializes has a beginning and thus – unavoidably – an end. The end of the universe is even too theoretical for the theorists and therefore not yet fixed – the end of our solar system however can be calculated. Maybe this calculation is even ok. It would be wrong to pretend that the process of becoming and passing away as such has a beginning and an end.

The Earth is not flat and the universe does not have a centre as man would like to prefer with his linear thinking: some instance present there which would rule everything with a global power. However it is more correct to say that every individual is a centre and I do not refer only to a physical human being. Starting from the atom up to the heaps of galaxies: all these individuals in universe harmonize with each other. They do not need a God. Every planet is a god and every star a goddess. Ying and Yang are everywhere, without beginning or end. This is the world image in which we remain free.

Everyone loves everyone. Every being loves every being. Even the antelope loves the lion when it bestows its body on her. Every being evolves in the sense of the universe without ever stopping. We are far from being ideal and we will never be ideal. We evolve from our incorrect notions of values and of the world which sprang from the attachment to our ego.

15
Social games – an inventory

The division in man and woman in our society is a challenge we have not mastered so far. There were times when the female part dominated the male part but then man remembered his physical superiority and biological independence and therefore he did not have to continue evolving spiritually. When he finished robbing what could be robbed in one place, he went to another one. Pregnant women with children invented agriculture and could then remain in one location. Men did not understand that agriculture required keeping stock. They preferred to wander around eluding the demands of Mother Nature and ran before they learnt to submit to her cycles. Storerooms and larders were a bounty that they took away from the women by force and violated them again before they continued their rambles.

Only nowadays does man begin to provide for his progeny and applies for baby time with his boss, although he has been on Earth for a while. With his ego and his monotheistic ruling concept he was able to disrespect Mother Nature, women and mothers in general. Since the extinction of species and the decreasing quality of life have gradually come to his knowledge now, I can voice such a thing and promote a more natural life-style.

This long domination of the male part has already brought forth the corresponding females. This is normal when someone rules over you. Those ruled upon are not allowed to possess a different philosophy than the rulers. The domination would crumble if those ruled upon would not follow the ideology of the rulers. Men see to that owing to a gigantic hierarchy of fear.

Fear is the reason why most women have submitted to the male thinking which leads to warped convictions like: "I have to see to his well-being in the first place, then I will see to mine. "In our civilization this leads to such excesses where men may abuse small girls in the family with impunity as most of the affected mothers agree to it. First because they have lived through this agony themselves and second due to the fear they feel of the male domination.

The work in my seminars shows time and again that only few women may free themselves from their marriage on their own. In most cases a different man is needed. Often they can only liberate themselves in the second or third effort without needing another man. Or a woman who has managed to free herself on her own will quickly submit to a new man's rule, maybe in a milder form but under the same principle. So her self-esteem has not changed decisively. There are only few exceptions who are extremely careful at the time of choosing a partner or completely refrain from taking any at all in order to maintain their autonomy.

Only when woman has freed herself from the monotheistic thinking can she experience her real worth. Of course she is capable of loving several people, men and women. There is no God any more who obliges her to belong to a single man. It is natural that everybody loves many Gods of different characters. It all depends on which agreement people make for their love life.

To be sure every child only requires the sperm of one man and not of several men and it also nests in an ovum of one mother. This is the holy moment that cannot be replaced for the incarnation of a human being when the being to be formed chooses the biological elements and the aspects of character of their parents whom it feels attracted to. And, like it or not, they are taken as a model for the human's next life.

This does not mean that the new being has to be loved and cared for by the parents. Experience shows that the sound affection a human being needs while being raised, may come from different persons, in fact it is even better when it does so. Nowadays this is mostly restricted to the relatives, preferably to the grand-parents' generation. However in stable communities where two people live together without being married or where more than two people live together sharing a house or flat, children may also get affection and care from others who are not their parents or even family. Millions of children are not raised with their biological fathers and have already lived experiences ranging from happiness to horror.

The greatest horror for a child consists in the fact that his living or dead biological father is either marginalized, not talked about or even denied. If the separation of parents did not mean separation of one part of the parents, children would even gain more affection when a stepfather comes into the game. However the adults must see to it that peace be established between all of them where love-matters are concerned. Here we are again with the problem of jealousy and possession which cannot be solved by our socially established standards.

Owing to the materialist, monotheistic era in which we live it is very hard to expand one's consciousness in so far that we are spiritual beings who create their reality and that there is no objective reality. All positive and negative aspects of character and physical states stem from our own way of thinking. Naturally there is a social mainstream thinking but even this is merely man-made and does not have a firm natural cause. Even the predominant materialism is a mental product and does not have a material or physical cause but it is only a certain interpretation of life. The interpretation is a purely mental process by which we can create our reality ourselves – for everything.

To be able to adopt this philosophy, we have to apply it practically. In theory we can discuss it forever without getting anywhere. Only the experience makes you smart. Those who want to abandon the idea of one God and stop living monogamously must have learnt to listen to its soul well, while doing justice to love and hurting nobody. Often it is not possible to do that because our surrounding social field is conditioning our emotions so much that neither men nor women may break loose of them.

Obstinate power systems

The philosophy of ownership and possession is so deeply rooted in our materialist time that our life only consists of having and not of being. Those who have a low self-esteem need to possess because self-esteem is needed as a foundation for being. It is difficult to let go this philosophy in a world where the ruling establishment destroys self-esteem systematically – from the basis – in society, family, at school and in companies, above all the self-esteem of women.

With our self-esteem in ruins we do fall into an abyss if we do not call any belongings, not even a person, our own. Without emotional and economic provisions men and women both feel exposed to the hostile world unprotected. The feeling of being provided for fills the void which arises through lack of self-esteem. Both in men as in women. This feeling of provision can only be trusted if the providing person "belongs to me".

We most strongly feel this sensation of being cared for when it comes to emotional and sexual faithfulness. If our partner commits adultery, we instantly perceive the fear of not being provided for anymore. Viewed in daylight this fear is mostly based on economic grounds because when our partner satisfies his strongest emotions with a different person, our power over him vanishes. Yet this does not necessarily lead to divorce because some tolerate adultery for this very reason. For mere economic stability, a partner relationship is even possible without any love at all. Where economic reasons do not guarantee provision, sexual loyalty is needed for a continuing relationship. Only when women's self-esteem is on the same social level as men's, such distortions of love are no longer required.

For those women who have not managed to get there yet owing to the above-mentioned reasons, I will try as a man to put myself into their dependent position:

Due to the feeling of responsibility for my children who become my reason for being once I have abandoned my professional career,

I feel especially dependent on my provider. Since in our patriarchal era he is said to be the master of creation it does not really matter if he treats me badly or well, he is my staff and sceptre, sugar bread and whip often mixed with sex and beating.

In his opinion, women are just good enough for bearing children and raising them. However we hardly get any recognition for that. In Germany it took us a decade to fight for the years of raising children being counted for pension rights. The large majority of us depend on men, although we possess the greatest creativity – our womb – which does not belong to them. He knows this (at least subconsciously) and it often causes him to feel inferior which makes him think that he has to compensate for it – unfortunately through violence in most cases. Since time immemorial he uses the fact that the womb cleans itself every month for declaring us impure. This is so perverse.

I – as Clemens again – experienced this in person when I shot a film with the *Todas* in Southern India. And since I mentioned this fact in my film *Todas – at the edge of paradise*, the Bavarian film promotion was denied to me in in retrospection with the statement: "The word menstruation is said too often in this film", although I had already received an oral promise to get this promotion after my success with the documentary *Living Buddha* and although in the final credits of this film I had already thanked for this promotion which I have never obtained owing to the a.m. reason. Yes, I lost DM 200.000 (about 100.000 Euro) because menstruation was supposed to remain a taboo and for men to know blood only in injuries not as cleansing.

This lack of experience leads men to compensate for their low self-esteem by marginalizing and humiliating women. It is obvious that they have not understood to this day their equal part in the reproduction of life. Or is it that women do not claim that males fulfil their part? Most women do not really want to change this state of affairs because as long as the children are "theirs" in the first place, they feel that they can balance the power monopoly of men. The power men gains from their physical superiority is made up for by women when it comes to the power over the children. However, this mutual power game is played at the full expense of the children and does not make anyone happy.

If we are mindful of the fact that in every person both female and male aspects are present because we have not always incarnated as one sex only, the gender fight can be settled much more quickly on a private basis than on a political basis. It is amazing what emotions arise when man or woman imagine that they will change gender in their next life. These emotions say a lot about how they perceive the other sex and how the lack of understanding determines the way of our coexistence. However many things in our relationship may be harmonized once we try to see life from our partner's point of view. If we imagine that we do not only do this for a few minutes, but for a whole life-time, we are not the same person anymore.

Brutalized males

In the ruling male system and his claim for power it is more and more difficult for him to identify with the creation of life. This alienation and the present classical role model relegate him to a more or less marginalized position with regard to family and kids. Often both parents think that their baby belongs to the mother because she has given birth to it and could already call it hers for nine months, therefore restricting the role of the family father as the provider causing a certain psychological estrangement in the father's feelings towards the baby. For society as well as for the peace on Earth and in the family this is quite hazardous since men who have not experienced and learnt how to be at the service of an innocent being that cannot be ordered about and love it from the bottom of the heart because they love it, rather let themselves be sent to war. There they do not only massacre other men, but also children, babies and mothers.

Such a brutalization of sentiment is not possible in men who *have to* love their babies and be at their service from the start in a selfless and self-responsible manner. They rather object to do military service or they become deserters before getting into a situation where they are obliged to commit any horrendous acts, no matter what, while in doing so they look into the innocent eyes of their own children.

When men – which is common nowadays – only take over their role as a father when the children are supposed to be "educated" and need to be disciplined, the image of a completely innocent person is not anchored in them. Then it is possible to order them to commit violent deeds which may even involve murder. In these men a mostly rigid attitude of right and wrong, good and evil is inherent – as transmitted values of a social doctrine working from the outside. They praise and reprimand their kids according to this conviction and divide them into good and bad children.

Other fathers who bring their children into new life starting out at birth and considering them as "their" babies, open their heart so much that they are not apt anymore to become so brutalized that they will wage war against another person. They know from their own experience that there is no good and evil. A new-born baby cannot do any evil. These loving beings teach you in their first year of life to say yes to everything and not to criticize anything. If men adopt the role of provider from the start, there is no enemy anymore. These men would break into tears at the moment they receive the draft notice. However when men at large go to war, it is mostly the women who cry, while men try to keep a stiff upper lip and give a good-bye kiss to their wives and children before they plunge into a barbaric, mindless male behaviour with disgusting superficiality and debauchery to violate and defile divine beings in the form of a person.

We only have to take a look at the present wars or remember the Yugoslavian conflicts which took place in our highly-civilized Europe. In all these cruel acts we can see this emotional brutalization. Germany thinks it is still free from war. Yet this is an illusion. Thousands of German soldiers already fight somewhere in Third World countries and the German armed forces advertise in the mass media the brilliant perspectives any soldier may expect in their troops. I am not sure if all who fall for it know that they can be ordered as a soldier to leave for such an armed conflict anywhere on Earth. A good contact to your soul is necessary in order not to be seduced by these paid "temptations". The soul smells the brutalization and warns us when we do *soul writing*. Otherwise man has to disregard his soul to legitimize becoming a criminal himself. To meet violence with counter-violence legitimizes violence. This is the spiral leading directly to war.

Such brutalization continues even in times of peace. Then it is not the "inferior human beings" who may be slaughtered legally in times of war but other "inferior" beings: every year about three million animals are tortured and killed by mostly decent heads of family in Germany alone who legally murder them in the most gruesome possible manner for purely scientific reasons.

This "modern" war against inferior beings needs also to be questioned in the name of a higher truth like all other acts of war. The murderer legitimizes his deeds with ethical values that are superior to those he grants his victims. This is basically what men who rebuke their children and even beat them now have learnt and then pointing out that this has never hurt anybody. These are education methods legitimized by the intention of teaching children manners and in so far they constitute a measure for allegedly a superior ethical value. (It is a fact that women are also perpetrators but this is not the subject of this chapter).

A supposedly superior ethical intention is also the motive for animal testing in the manufacture of cosmetics, weapons, and chemical drugs. These murders are socially permitted and accepted. They are nothing else than what the "superior Aryans" once did to the living Jewish and other children in the concentration camps while carrying out medical experiments for example for diphtheria treatments.

If we continue looking at this attitude, we can comprehend Tolstoy's phrase "As long as there are slaughterhouses, men will be slaughtered in battles". Every man and woman should reflect about switching to vegetarian food. Apart from the fact that meatless nutrition is liberating a lot more energy – because it is a lot of hard work for your body to digest meat – there is also the advantage that vegetarians have been shown to produce a lot less diseases.

This is surely a consequence of their evolution of consciousness. Those who eat meat must inevitably repress the fact that wonderful living beings have been murdered in the cruellest way for their appetite. Such a repression naturally blurs your consciousness in general. This means on the other hand that we all can do plenty for peace in our interior as well as our exterior when we change our eating habits.

The next step in vegetarian nutrition – by which even much bigger and much stronger beings like elephants, whales, bovine animals of all kind and horses live healthy and long – is *vegan food*. Meaning that humans solely receive their mother's milk at the start of life and drink no milk of other species nor do they eat any milk products. The animals also do this. In addition to vegetarian food there are many good and benefitting reasons which may all be found in the corresponding literature[26]. Or by putting it to test, preferably under the instruction of an experienced vegan.

All these life-changing measures promote peace on Earth which is urgently needed if we want to continue the human experiment successfully. Although we know how a dignified life would look like, conditions on this planet are de facto still despicable. Plenty of men do not know yet how to behave humanely when confronted with pregnancy, childbirth, and infant care. They push these things away from them, pretending them to be women's tasks, even when it is their own child. Many men get drunk while their wife carries out this great act

---

26 Rüdiger Dahlke: *Peace food* or the film by Lee Fulkerson *Gabel statt Skalpell (Fork instead of Scalpel)*.

of creation, often in pain. They sit at the bar and let other males tell them stupid stories on the subject. When it comes to accepting the child lovingly, they act clumsily as if they had two left hands. Whenever the baby cries, they give it back to the wife as if they have no competence for parenthood. Men often seem to feel inhibited with babies and when cradling them in their arms caringly, especially in the company of other people.

In this emotionally destitute condition it does not surprise us that millions of men abuse their babies sexually, as if they wanted to compensate for their own shortcomings by doing so. Part of this display of power is the fact that fathers beat their children and issue prohibitions. All this is due to their subconscious compensation behaviour of their ego feeling separated from the universe.

Yet this separation can be overcome with a loving and joyful relationship towards death. Of course this leap of consciousness may still be perverted like anything else when pretending that reincarnation gives you the permission to kill on the basis that according to this teaching, death is only a change of aggregate. People separated from their soul (the universe) may ask why they should not help others change their aggregate and kill them.

For the men not integrated to the universe, murder is always an arousing affair in order to experience power, that way obviously providing them lust and an erect penis with which they violate women brutally even on a daily basis as soon as the circumstances permit it, like e.g. in the above-mentioned Yugoslavian wars, the last great wars in the middle of so-called civilized Europe. If such a thing had happened in Africa, the arrogance of the First World would have said: Well, these people are so primitive still. But no: these heinous wars took place exactly on the very spot where millions of Middle Europeans spend their holidays. Is such a thing not a testimony of absolute ethical poverty for the civilization standard of mankind? This attitude is only acceptable when we take into account the idea of an only God since it is the preliminary stage for being a king, an emperor, a CEO, the Pope, an army general, a president etc. In short: a person who is the boss and orders us about – like Milošević from Belgrade who gave the order to mass violate all non-Serbian women.

If we had uncountable Gods like some of the remaining indigenous people or at least a second God – a Goddess! – we would not let ourselves be pushed into such human abysses by the orders of our superiors. Yet man still defends his perversion with the one-God philosophy and even becomes a murderer when this philosophy is in jeopardy. He considers this emotion to be love because his God is above everything and has to be kept there by all means (even if he's violent).

Jealousy

Jealousy is a socially respected emotion for which many people even kill. Jealousy is poison for mankind because the very emotion causes trouble in most people's couple relationship. On one hand love is slighted by this feeling and on the other hand this very feeling is considered love. Those who do not feel jealous, do not love properly and those who are jealous, suffer. Jealousy is the emotional result of the one-God philosophy. It makes no sense if I ask: could I love several persons at the same time as long as I am not aware of the philosophy on which my reply is based on?

All emotions and attitudes I have towards this topic are not conditioned by nature. They are based upon a patriarchal, socially antiquated philosophy several thousand years old and yet contradicting nature and the universe. The universe – some call it God – loves us all. It does not make any difference. It flirts with everybody. It is so fantastic to experience this connection with universe, it is incomparable to all other feelings. The coincidences that happen then are love services of pure magic. Nevertheless for many they are just coincidences but universe does not know any arbitrary acts.

Jealousy is the dark side of the magical love service and we do not want to acknowledge it although a large number of children are on the receiving end of its impact. Of course we do not want to imagine such a thing, let alone accept it, just because feelings like jealousy are considered as natural, innate human characteristics. That this is not so may be recognized when we take a look beyond our horizon and get to know other societies in which the idea of an only God has not been implemented. Everything is possible there: polygamy, polyandry (one woman married to more than one man) and all types of poly-amorous relationships like in the animal world. That these extraordinary conditions of individuals cannot be simply copied to our society is due to the surroundings by which we are conditioned. However it may be of tragic consequences to ignore it.

Thanks to the view beyond our horizon it gets clear that nobody must consider their feelings of jealousy to be a personal predisposition. Not only in the context with jealousy do we note that it is very hard to free yourself from socially imposed emotional barriers, we also note this with respect to death and children's education. In reality these shortcomings of character are of a social nature. Naturally society will not change unless I change myself. In this respect jealousy is an individual matter, even though it is omnipresent.

To understand the basis of our emotional life we should become aware of the fact that every feeling depends on the philosophy where it arises. Let us take jealousy: if we take it for natural and if monogamy is expected to protect us from it, we will eventually find out that this does not work. Yet if we understand jealousy not to be natural but conditioned by society, this is equivalent to a leap in consciousness, like when cars or the train were introduced. Those who want to keep up with time, just have to accept these things in the end, as the following anecdotes show:

Thanks to their family in Hamburg my grandparents possessed the first car in Bavaria. People used to stop on the road to shout in

Bavarian: "The devil is coming." The horror was even greater because my grandma had knitted a black woollen cap for her three-year-old son (my father) which only left the area around eyes without cover so that the young boy should be protected against the cold wind when he sat near my grandpa in the front. The first cars did not have any front pane because it was a transformed horse carriage with a motor instead of horses.

Another example: doctors warned about getting in the first train running from Fürth to Nuremberg since it would rise to such speed that man could not tolerate it and therefore would fall seriously ill. This then medically sound statement caused the sponsors of the train project to stop financing it for several years.

Next example: The analogue philosophy was considered natural because digital thinking did not exist yet. Nowadays it does and it opens up a completely new world for us, one we cannot explain with the analogue philosophy. Those who do not share this thinking feel excluded from evolution. On the contrary those who have grown with it consider it natural.

What do these examples reveal? There is no natural thinking: not the one represented by conventional medicine, nor what we figure monogamy or jealousy mean, nor with respect to death. Every thinking – and therefore feeling – is linked to the socially accepted thinking. This is what makes it so difficult to dissolve yourself from it individually because you will automatically get into contradiction with the people surrounding you and eventually be marginalized. In order to develop your thinking and with it your consciousness, you have to be mindful of the relativity of these feelings and norms so that women and men may free themselves more easily from set notions and ideas.

The freedom I mean ...

If we want to be free from set thought patterns, this is best done by associative thinking avoiding logical and practised connections and therefore creating gaps in thinking from which something new and unprecedented may rise to the surface. Such chaotic states in thinking must be allowed if we want to reach the contents to which we do not have access to our intellect outside the alpha phase in waking consciousness.

When Jamgon dies at dawn on the 26th April 1992 on an empty street at full speed probing the new electrical windows and the electrical sun-roof with a pulsing Hi-Fi stereo sound in his ears sitting in the brand new BMW 525i at 120 mph and says his last words: "Don't kill the pigeons" ---- and then CRASH! ---- DEAD, DEAD, DEAD while Tenzin is safe and sound – this is an attitude towards death which is considered impossible. It blasts our rational thinking. *This is a kind of freedom which is not in the least restricted by any monotheistic ideology.*

However we do not want to remain stunned by the sheer unattainable height of consciousness others dispose of, we should rather take it as an incentive to continue developing our own consciousness actively. The method I recommend for it is called *Soul writing*®. For this method you do not need anybody. You may apply it completely on your own, for your own. You do not even have to tell your loved ones or drop any hints if you do not want to. With this method you are absolutely free as long as you do not leave your written notes lying around. They are as precious as the most expensive jewels. Hide them on your PC and buy two USB-sticks where you save copies and keep them under lock and key.

When you finish typing your hand-written documents into the PC, destroy them. In case you exclusively write on paper, guard these manuscripts as safely as your diary. Leave a broad margin for future amendments. No matter where you keep these texts: you should always be able to continue working on them. Especially when you have already changed. Your consciousness is constantly evolving, mostly in leaps. As far as the continuity of spirit is concerned, the evolution of your consciousness depends on what you write. Writing offers you a possibility to reflect and reflection triggers consciousness.

Put your projects in good order. Some projects accompany you over many years or even decades. Your parents and your children e.g. are persons who are important to your psychological and physical well-being for quite a while if not all your life. There are always things to be harmonized.

I also call Soul writing *Soul hygiene*. It is at least as essential or even more than body hygiene and you do not wait to apply it until your body is rigid from dirt. Soul writing should become a habit of yours because it is necessary to come clean with your soul on a daily basis. Once you are trained to do so, you project your own future with it. This means that your future is no coincidence anymore, since you create it to the exact word. Soul writing is best learnt as playing the piano, not quite so hard, but on the other hand it is no piece of cake either. Discipline and work are paramount.

It is worth it when you spare the fees for the doctor, never have to go to hospital, create happy relationships, find your mission for your present life, and for the next and second-next. The *KUBY method*® to which the tool *Soul writing*® belongs, is no external service like the one carried out by a healer, naturopath, shamans or medical doctor. These are the persons we used to ask to do something with us in order to ease the pain. As a consequence we get dependent on another person and on external input. Yet the *KUBY method* is all about self-competence: to be capable of healing yourself – only then we start to be free in life, a freedom which corresponds to the human dignity. As long as I still depend on others in the most significant question in life – health – I am not free. The moment you fall into the hands of doctors, you make yourself dependent on them. They often exert such an unnatural authority with their white clothes and their titles that you quickly end up doing just what they tell you. You allow them to feed you with drugs which you have not the slightest idea of what they cause your body to do. Mostly you do not even understand the language in which these things (chemicals) are described. When doctors say that they want to cut you up and do something inside your body, you agree. Sometimes they even tell you that you *have to* get an operation.

There will be a time when you will ask: what was wrong with mankind then? How could a well-off minority rule over the rest in such a way? In one hundred years you will have difficulty to explain this and in one thousand years even more. How could individuals have the very idea that they are mechanical, biochemical and not spiritual-emotional beings? Even today's modern physics will be antiquated in a hundred years and cannot legitimize the crazy materialism of medicine.

Let us continue with this vision: how could this madness seize mankind in the first place and position individuals inside a system of payment in which everybody was forced to be a member and pay in advance for this materialist human image without even being ill? It remains a mystery why the materialist-biochemical human image could gain such power. On the other hand the magical human image of the Middle Ages, legitimizing the burning of hundreds of thousands of women, can be explained more easily than the one of conventional medicine although both stem from male madness. However, with conventional medicine there were not hundreds of thousands, but millions who had to die for this madness.

During the decades its system became ever more inefficient and eventually much too expensive, so that in the end we continued evolving. However this evolution brought revolts in which the "Gods in white", like they called themselves, were driven away and accused of not being interested in curing cancer, AIDS, high blood pressure, depression or diabetes but to make a profit. After several decades people asked how conventional medicine had ever justified its existence. A cancer patient had been traded at the stock exchange with a starting price of 100,000 US$. Sickness care (vs. Health care) became the biggest business in the world. For economic reasons every doctor had to maintain their patients in a solvent state of disease. When mankind finally had finished their materialist phase medicine itself was considered the largest disease of humanity.

This leap of consciousness however only came about due to great catastrophes because the individuals merely evolve when they are in misery. This is something we can even observe in all aspects of life from our perspective today. We only start looking for new concepts when we suffer, mostly when we have pain. Then we are back to Now and this means: as long as the quantic leap in consciousness has not taken place, conventional medicine with its paying system fulfils a life-saving function. Since most people are still prisoners of the materialist-biochemical human image, they have to be treated to this effect by conventional medicine.

The chief doctor of a large Swiss clinic already told me in an interview in 2017:
For me the KUBY method is a way to include the patients with their self-responsibility in order not to load all the responsibility for health on my back, but to help the patients to find their own way. Health can only be sustained when you find the cause by yourself and work on it. This is what I reckon medicine lacks. We require the KUBY method to find the cause. We doctors will continue in the Stone Age for the next 200 years unless we start working with this method. This approach is something new and this makes it so fascinating for me. I want to work with it and I wish that my colleagues be also inspired by it or at least do not reject it. I am sure that in Switzerland and in our hospital we are open for new methods which allow us to get better in our work.

Slowly the consciousness arises that there are not only drugs and surgery but also the soul. Freud and C. G. Jung have published their psychological findings 100 years ago but we still have not found the way to our subconscious. I do not understand why. Yet the KUBY method closes this gap now. The moment for it has come. We now have to convince our students and young doctors that the soul is more important than all the technical stuff. To be sure they belong to our work, but without the soul work there is no healing.

First we need people who have completely internalised the KUBY method and bring our young interns – the generation between 20 and 30 – in contact with this approach. It has been years that I have recommended your books to patients who I found to be open for this subject, and they get more by the hour. However it still takes time. But if the KUBY method goes on spreading, one day we may not need medicine anymore."

Prof. Dr. med. Gabriel Schär, Aarau Hospital, Switzerland

The change of consciousness is already on the way. Maybe it becomes a reality much faster than only in 50, 100 or 1000 years. As an individual I can move ahead of the prevailing consciousness in society. The basis for this is a completely different relationship towards death than the one we were educated to accept. As soon as the old traditional concept in our heads is replaced by the immortality as a spiritual being, the comprehension of healing will also be totally transformed.

If you do not want to wait 50, 100 or 1000 years until mankind has reached a higher consciousness, you may already connect with your soul now. Your soul knows how to solve your present situation, but not your ego. Your soul is the inner wisdom you can access at any time speaking your language as long as you have a pencil or a voice-recording device. Please note that you may also consider your soul as your personalized intuition.

Via intuition, thanks to soul writing, you are linked to your subjective truth. This starts with the thinking, this is why thought control is imperative. Be mindful of the responsibility for everything you think. The whole spectre of human behaviour begins with thinking.

The most exciting thing with *Soul writing* is: you find the *pain image* as the parts of a puzzle and perhaps this is a bit tricky. Please go on looking if your (pain) image does not show clearly in front of your eyes at once. It consists of pieces which come up from the limbic system to the frontal lobe step by step. In order to manage that, we do soul writing. Each piece is a part of your subjective truth – and there are no other truths in this universe. The universe reacts upon every spiritual impulse as long as this impulse is charged with feeling.

This is not only valid for a new past, but also for a longed-for future. However it is about projections, not expectations (very important)! We wait for expectations and we create projections – we do not sit and wait for them to come. They experience their first manifestation when we have written our projections in script-style (see annex), however in a changeable interim step between the old unsatisfied being and the new reality that makes us happy. Reality would be much more difficult to modify than the one I create on paper first (or in a file). If I did not project future, but expect it to happen, I would exert pressure on reality. On paper everything I write is without any pressure, it is completely free and playful, though perceived truthfully and honestly. Paper is patient and tolerates everything, including every detour.

16
The mummy is moved to a new place

The great day has arrived. Plenty of Tibetans and other people have found their way to Pullahari in Nepal to be present when Jamgon's kudung is moved from Rumtek in India/Sikkim to Pullahari after crossing the Southern Himalayans on a 500 mile voyage. From now on this place is Jamgon's headquarters and the place of studies for his adepts.

It is very courageous to make such an open declaration – like in a procession – by moving the kudung publicly, displaying that Jamgon really moves place despite his absence. This has a great impact on the whole Kagyü order. In the exile headquarters, the Kagyü monastery Rumtek in Sikkim/Northern India, there is no seat-holder anymore. To be sure the original crown of the 16th Karmapa is still there, but even if the 17th Karmapa put on this crown on his head again, he is not likely to move in there. In the original headquarters in Tibet, Tsurphu monastery, 50 miles north of Lhasa, people still count on the idea that Karmapa in one of his future incarnations will reside there again but not the 17th. Due to his escape in 1999/2000 he became a refugee, and therefore an illegal person from the Chinese point of view. They will not forgive him this. It is likely that the 17th Karmapa will – no matter what his civic status will be – remain close to the Tibetan exile government. Outside Tibet offers him the greatest identity and hopefully he will one day be able to travel around the whole world as a free Indian citizen. Thanks to Facebook, two journeys to the USA, two trips to Germany and one to Switzerland have made him become an international guru even before his 30th birthday.

In 1994, when he was 10 and 11, all his possibilities to travel were in the hands of Peking, even if he only wanted to leave Tsurphu valley and go on a trip inside Tibet. Therefore Gyaltsap and Situ had to represent him during the welcome ceremony for the kudungs in Pullahari.

Gyaltsap and Situ are 100 % loyal to Karmapa and also to Jamgon, of whom they do not know if he already has a new body.

Inside the kudung there is a mummy which will remind people even in 100 or 1000 years when Jamgon maybe incarnates consciously the 16th or 17th time as Jamgon that life is a continuum and not a unique event.

How to obtain this conviction is what Jamgon taught during all his life and he did not have to write new texts. All this knowledge about the spiritual never-ending life has been formulated precisely in Tibet ages ago. Reincarnation was the popular consciousness. In 700 A. D. it came to Tibet when Buddhism had already been taught for 1200 years on the South side of the Himalayans developing from *Hinajana* to *Mahajana* – from the small to the big vehicle – and via translation by Tilopa, Marpa and other translators it became *Vajrayana Buddhism*, the diamond vehicle.

By doing so the consciousness of the continuity of life had taken a decisive step, especially thanks to Karmapa who in 1110 was the first man to write down exactly his reincarnation. This consciousness seemed to be bound to Tibetan Buddhism. With the eviction of the Tibetan lamas from Tibet, they were spread through the whole world and incarnated in non-Tibetan and even Western bodies, so this consciousness became known to everybody and no longer depends on a certain religion.

Some pretend that we can almost bar the term Buddhism now. Even the Dalai Lama does not value it anymore,[27] although he will of course stay a Buddhist till the end of his life, exactly as Karmapa will until the end of his 21st incarnation. But after that he will certainly

---

27 See the book *Beyond religion – ethics for a whole world* by the Dalai Lama about the general ethics in which he asserts that neither a special Buddhist orientation nor the Tibetan Buddhism is necessary for freeing mankind. If ethics represented in every religion were part of every-day life, this would already be liberation.

not go on as a Buddhist or even as a Buddhist monk. In the same precise way as he now projects the conditions from one life to the next knowing when, where and with whom he will incarnate, he will also know exactly what he will do after ending his 21st incarnation as Karmapa. Until then reincarnation will also be a popular consciousness in the West. I reckon that this was at least the vision Karmapa had in Tsurphu in 1110.

Tenzin and his crew pack all the important books containing the knowledge of the spiritual-emotional human image inside the stupa together with Jamgon's kudung. The stupa is 40 feet high and 14 by 14 feet wide at its base. It is completely covered by gold leaves and richly decorated with precious stones. It does not only contain the kudung with Jamgon's mummy and the books, many more ritual objects and costly treasures are added before it is closed.

The stupas closed hundreds of years ago in Tibet were plundered by Chinese soldiers in their greed for gold. I wonder what is bound to happen to this stupa in the next centuries. Time will tell if and when people have to look into the stupa to remember the wisdom contained there. If people do not know anymore how to enhance human character, it is possible to look things up inside the stupa. At the moment there are copies of all the documents lowered into the stupa in the Buddhist libraries.

Waiting for Jamgon in his new form

Basically everything is prepared for Jamgon to arrive in his new form, his new life is ready to be taken up. He has occupied his place by having the kudung installed here. Only he can become the boss here in his new incarnation. Tenzin is going to great lengths to prepare the whole enterprise for Jamgon in every material and human aspect. Hundreds of sympathizers help him with it.

The other seat-holders of the Kagyü order, Situ and Gyaltsap, have already created their own headquarters: Situ in North India, not too far from the Dalai Lama, Gyaltsap in East India. To reach Pullahari one or two day trips are needed. Situ also feels responsible that everything will be prepared in the best possible way for Jamgon's return. To everybody who will listen, he says:

Situ: *We should go on praying as best as we can for a fast and successful return of Rinpoche. In my opinion Jamgon will be born again soon because two years have already passed since his departure.*

I ignore why Situ says *"already"* in this sentence, but obviously he has a clear notion of how long Jamgon plans to remain in bardo (the phase without form). This can solely be deduced if you are linked in direct love (equivalent to *line*) with the dead. Whereby Situ's love not only refers to his own network of persons – he has also "viewed" reincarnations not directly related to him personally. Like the Dalai Lama he then may issue written certificates confirming the authentic reincarnation of a dead person. For someone like me who has a much lower level of consciousness Situ's consciousness is as unfathomable as Karmapa's.

Nevertheless Shamar has managed to detain him in India so that he cannot comply with his international mission anymore since the division of the Kagyü order: the Indian Home ministry threatened him of not being able to come back to India once he leaves for another trip to Europe because he does not possess an Indian passport. Shamar had issued such a ban on several persons, even on the ex-president of the *European Buddhist Union*, Rosy Findeisen. Since Shamar's death on the 11th June 2015, the blockade he had erected for all his criticizers is crumbling though.

No matter how high the level of consciousness of any individual, society's consciousness only grants a certain margin for it. No matter how enlightened you may be, the political status which you have chosen for your incarnation as a human being here among all the possibilities on Earth sets you certain limits. The position of a refugee is different from the position of a diplomat. And there is an even stronger conditioning made by the country and the circumstances you are born into by which you want to obtain a certain political status, e.g. a Bhutanese diplomat comes up against other limits than a US-diplomat and so on.

When it comes to planning your next life, it is paramount to take into account all these political limits, because if you only think of your private situation, the plan does not work. You have to reflect on what is the best nationality for you to incarnate to fulfil your mission. This is an essential but also difficult question with all the constantly changing political situations. Firstly you should answer the question of whether you want to acquire a political consciousness next to your spiritual one. To think that you could ignore the political side of life when you live your life as consciously as possible, will have a negative effect on your life's task because you will surely come up against disagreeable limits.

Due to Shamar's politics the Kagyü order is virtually divided and there is now a dispute about the question in whose camp the coming incarnation of important Kagyü members will be born. This question is not restricted to Karmapa's incarnation, it also concerns other high dignitaries other than Jamgon himself.

Shamar already intended to use the dead Jamgon for his aims by pretending that before his death Jamgon had doubted the authenticity of Karmapa's prediction letter, same as he himself. However when Shamar affirmed this, he did not know that Jamgon had said in the before-mentioned interview that he considered the letter to be "very precise" and that with it the true Karmapa could be found in any case. If Shamar had pretended that Jamgon would be born again in his camp, this is not very plausible for Jamgon to do when you take into account his high-level consciousness with which he controls his future development.

Yet the question remains: how can he be found? The search for him could start now: Pullahari is ready, Jamgon could move in here with his new form. Mother Pema says: "Jamgon Rinpoche served Karmapa and I am sure that he will serve him again. "

Speculation is rife concerning the questions where, when and with whom Jamgon will be born. Unfortunately Jamgon has not left behind any written or oral address for his reincarnation like Karmapa did. Since it was the task of his life to serve his master Karmapa, he will surely come back to his master – as his mother expressed above.

It would not fit into this collaboration between master and disciple if his reincarnation was looked for and found without informing Karmapa who is the first who must be sure that he has the genuine Jamgon at his side again for his future collaboration and not someone who will turn out to be less connected to him when he gets older. We wonder how this connection will look like.

Everybody wishes for a Jamgon Kongtrul to be born inside their own family, as it may mean a great rise in status and social position. Therefore greatest care is paramount when it comes to looking for Jamgon. It would be irresponsible and senseless to undertake the search on my own. As Jamgon himself, also Tenzin can only count on Karmapa in this important matter and follow the latter's instructions. In this respect a letter from Drupon Dechen, Karmapa's abbot in Tsurphu, had a great impact on Tenzin. It says: "Dear Tenzin, do you want to visit us? There are good news."

So Tenzin calls a meeting with his most intimate colleagues to put up a search group travelling to Tibet. Eight of his confidants meet without announcing anything to the outside and debate who is going. Who feels it is his vocation to go? Much intuition and confidence are needed. Doubts and fears are bad consultants in this delicate matter. Who may take over the responsibility for finding the true Jamgon?

How does one use one's intuition and confidence when searching for a reincarnation? First it is necessary to lower one's expectations without abandoning them or becoming too pessimistic and dubitative – independent from the difficulties which may arise. Thoughts must be calm and in peace.

You may find practical indications for finding a reincarnation and how to prepare your own next incarnation in the "Personal Master plan for Reincarnation" in the annex of this book.

17
Reborn! – Starting the search

To be sure, Tenzin does not do any soul writing, but his Buddhist practice teaches him to gain control over his thoughts until they remain automatically calm and level-headed ensuring peace once they are formulated and expressed. Thus prepared he now starts the search for his fatherly friend and master. Two of his colleagues accompany him: Lama Tsewang Phuntsok, a senior colleague, and Sonam Chopel, a younger colleague. They are only in an intuitive state if all three of them proceed with the greatest attention and care.

After a six week wait for visas they eventually fly the short trip from Kathmandu to Lhasa via the Mount Everest. It is only a one hour flight, but when you land, you have the feeling of having passed the longest journey ever. Once you get off the plane the contrast to the place of departure cannot be greater. It is not so much the landscape – although the Tibetan landscape seems completely extra-terrestrial because of its large horizon. Yet the fascinating thing about the view into far distances is not the distance itself but the pristine air without any moisture (only 4 percent). It is like changing the objective of your camera. However this alone does not make the extreme difference. The essential thing is not the clear air but the *thin* air, i.e. the height. It is because of the height you feel as if you have flown to the moon in one hour.

I ask Topga: *Do you believe that the search group will find your brother now?*
Topga: *I cannot say I actually believe in it. I believe in reincarnation, just as with Karmapa. There were many signs and much proof that it is really him, and many believe in it. Yet some don't. For me as a not very religious person it is hard to give a definite yes or no. I also do not think about it any longer.*

If someone is born a Buddhist in a Buddhist country, this means as little as being a Christian in the West who pays church tax. Both have little to do with a religious conviction. It is a tradition and a habit. Still, now as Topga is personally concerned with the question of whether he wants to remain in mourning his brother and trying to repress his feelings of guilt somehow, the philosophy of his religion may help him to overcome his suffering. Or does it not manage to do this?

The task of religion should be to provide concepts with which one may become happy and joyful. By and large healing is hardly mentioned in religious contexts. The priests and the religious representatives themselves are so sceptical with regard to the healing effect of their belief that they do not send their member to God when these are ill, but to the doctor. Therefore little is left of the healing force of belief and it is not surprising that the Western churches constantly lose members. In Buddhism this does not happen in such a strong way but the tendency for it is growing. The only religion noting an influx is Islam. This is no wonder with all the rituals this belief possesses.

I would like to give an anecdote from the Sudan where I visited for filming work: I sit in a taxi in Khartoum. The traffic-lights turn green but the driver does not move. I wonder why. He opens his door and pulls out a small carpet from the foot space of the passenger's seat. He looks for the right direction towards Mecca and begins to pray. I look behind me. Some cars have passed us but several, above all taxi drivers do the same, no matter whether the traffic-lights change from green to red and to green again. It is the moment to pray towards Mecca, and not only here. Some 430 million men do it now and four more times a day, all oriented towards the black box in Mecca into which everyone may interpret what they want. I figure that nowhere on Earth is there a stronger ritual than this. It grants a power to the individual to which even the street traffic has to bow to, at least in Sudan. Compared to this all other Christian, Jewish and Buddhist rituals seem paltry as far as power demonstration is concerned. Yet it is a different question how this power is used.

It is clear that true power can only be attained if you can determine your next life on your own. Neither Islam has the consciousness for it nor the Judaic or Christian faith. Even in Buddhism it often is solely a theory.

What does Topga do? He could be satisfied that the search for his brother is finally under way but this is no comfort for him. He lacks confidence in his faith. He rather tries hard to focus on his work and so distract himself from his feelings of guilt and loss. This helps him more than to think of his brother's reincarnation.

Topga has enough to do in his two carpet mills where he can successfully repress his pain. To be sure diving into your work seems an appropriate means to do so with both sexes, though even more marked in men. This is helpful when you are confronted with emotions you cannot cope with mentally. This distraction however only works as long as your work really constitutes a challenge for you. But what happens in the breaks and after work? Then the danger to become an alcoholic e.g. is very great. Topga has not become one – his self-love is too great for that. Yet other people with a weaker self-esteem are extremely in danger of escaping into a drug addiction when the mourning phase gets too long.

Tsurphu monastery and its role in my former life

Once we arrive in Tibet Tenzin and his company first go to Tsurphu to ask the abbot what the good news is. From the airport we drive to the local community of Chushur on the Brahmaputra, then in two hours to Tsurphu monastery on 14.000 feet where Karmapa, the *Living Buddha*, has lived for three years by now. Thanks to his presence the reconstruction of the monastery moves forward quickly.

This Tsurphu monastery has been honoured in several of my films. First with *Tibet – resistance of the spirit*, then with *Living Buddha* and with two other documentaries before this one: *Reincarnation – Looking for a Sign*. It came about like this: in 1987 I wanted to make a film about the conflict between materialism and spirituality. First it did not matter to me where, whom with and with which example. I took a great interest in this confrontation since it takes place in every human and wars are waged because of it. If I make this film in Germany, I will land in the monastery of Altötting/Bavaria with spirituality and in the German army with materialism, as the army eventually has to defend our possessions. However all this did not seem very inspiring to me. Due to my research I knew that Tibetans are a very spiritual people – maybe the most spiritual of all – and at the same time we find the most materialist form of existence there in the shape of the Chinese occupation.

As I do not know any people more selfless than the Tibetans who exclude any violent resistance against their suppression and on the other hand I have known no human beings more egoistic than the Chinese who suppress Tibet (with fantastic exceptions, but then they were only exceptions), I had best make my film about this subject there. So I could count on banging into this conflict between spirituality and materialism at every corner.

Six million Tibetans were confronted with twelve million occupying forces in 1987. Under the name of the fifth column the latter followed Mao's troops of 500,000 soldiers to Tibet since the occupation in 1959. Until this year there were exactly two Chinese living in Tibet employed on a constant basis by the Chinese embassy in Lhasa. The 12 million Chinese who arrived later merely came to Tibet for the high material benefits issued by the State and not because of the climate or their love of the country or the people. On the contrary: they consider the Tibetans to be the scum of mankind and the dry climate of the great height makes them all sick.

My film crew and I came to Tibet without any concrete plan and after ten days arrived at Tsurphu monastery. Due to its complete destruction in 1960 and the timid reconstruction started in 1985 without any financial means and despite continuous repression it seemed an ideal example for my film subject. I did not even need any special Chinese permit because Tsurphu lies inside the tourist belt surrounding Lhasa. It only took us two hours by jeep to get there.

Until the end of the film in 1988 I did not attach any particular meaning to the fact that this monastery is Karmapa's headquarters. He was not present anyway and the subject of reincarnation only played a secondary role for me. As far as the film is concerned the monastery could also have belonged to another order with a different leader than just Karmapa of whom nobody knew at the time where and when he could be reborn. It was more important for me to show the degree of destruction from a material point of view and at the same time the spiritual power for the reconstruction. This clear contrast between spirituality and materialism was obvious in Tsurphu.

When I worked on the subject *Living Buddha* in 1990 some five years later, to my great surprise I came back to Tsurphu again. Of course this was a cosmic stroke of fate. In Buddhism they say that this coincidence is due to my karma.

It seems that the mission to make a film about Karmapa's reincarnation has already been imposed on me in my last life. I had a very realistic dream with regard to this matter: I was standing in front of Karmapa in a typical Tibetan Buddhist robe when he shouted at me: "In your next life you will not be given a monastery but a camera." I surely did not know then what a camera was and what he meant, but I said yes. Whatever Karmapa would give me as a mission, I would agree to it because I could never know what it would be good for.

I understood quickly that in order to get hold of a camera, I must not be born again in Tibet. It had to be an industrial country. The Germans had always been held in great esteem concerning technology (and still are, despite Hitler and everything attached to it). Therefore it was natural to choose Germany, if I had to go to the West – Karmapas great objective too. His first journey to the West in 1972 did not take him to the US, but to Berlin. As a Tibetan mountain boy who loves his mountains above all things, I naturally looked for a beautiful place in the mountains for my new existence, preferably with some water or lake before them. Yet it was even more essential to find a family who offered me the prerequisites which I have for my work today. If you believe in coincidence, you could say: Lucky you. And it is true. I was even extremely lucky with the people who became my parents. But luck has also a cause and is no coincidence.

For my reincarnation it was significant that my parents were present when I most needed them: from conception to adolescence. Moreover as I could also choose the time of my reincarnation, I decided not to come back in times of war when I would feel the fear of my mum even as an embryo. Since there was no possibility to pass my childhood in stable and loving family conditions directly before the war in the industrial countries (especially in Germany), I had to wait until after World War II, although I had already died in Tibet in 1937. When my dad came back from war and captivity unharmed, my future parents could live their marriage to the full only then because they had been married just before the outbreak of the war. As soon as they lived their first real honeymoon after the war and captivity, this was the ideal moment for me to incarnate.

I had two elder siblings born in the war times and after me came a couple of twins. However I did not have great affinity with them. My mum said that I was the most affectionate of all the children and it made her love me dearly. Even my father had much time and affection for me. In 1947 there was peace eventually and it did me a lot of good. This gave me a fulfilment in the first years of my life which still benefit me today.

I have already worked for quite a while in order to make my next incarnation as successful as this one. Yet this is hardly possible without a clear intention because in the universe there is the law: *The energy follows the intention.*

To be reborn as a human being and under lucky circumstances requires a lot of good energy. You will not dispose of this energy if your next incarnation is all the same to you.

Karmapa is capable of formulating his intention very precisely: the names of his parents, the place and the time plus several more details so that his new identity cannot be doubted. Since his intention is so clear, he will make it come true precisely. Karmapa made use of the idea that time is only a construct and that this construct can be changed according to one's consciousness. This is also possible in the *Soul writing* – by simply staying in the present tense we can outwit the ruling construct because everything that is in the present can be created and changed by me NOW.

Nowadays life on this planet has certainly some parameters even Karmapa cannot transform. Nevertheless he can control his personal fate in a way that on one hand he remains supportive of his beloved people and is born again in Tibet as a Tibetan in the lowest but freedom-loving class of the nomads. On the other hand he sits on the throne in his cherished monastery at the age of seven. By doing so he is the people and the head of the people united in one person – in the continuity of 900 years. Tsurphu stands for this continuity. In all the weeks I spent shooting there, waiting and being surprised, I never heard a single derogatory word about the Chinese, although their control and arrogance is ever present – maybe just because of it.

Karmapa knows more

When Tenzin, Phuntsok and Sonam are welcomed by the old abbot *Drupon Dechen*, he first teaches them a lesson since he considers these exile Tibetans to be spoiled by the Western culture: "You receive ever more of the great Western technical knowledge about how to send people to space in rockets and make satellites go into orbit around the Earth. Yet this culture does not tell you anything about what to do to reincarnate consciously. Surely the West does not know the first thing about it. Is this not so? Buddhism has the knowledge about how people can determine their future reincarnation. Let us take Karmapa as an example: since 1110 he has already been able 16 times to plan and predict his future reincarnation, although he is only a human being with a human shape. You should take hold of this knowledge."

Yes, but they do not have it yet, especially not as far as Jamgon is concerned. Thus they had come to him because he had announced them good news in his letter. Drupon asks them to go up to Karmapa's room on the roof of the building reconstructed first.

There he lives his very humble and secluded life. His frugal meals are sent to him upstairs and he always eats alone. He also learns on his own with his teacher Tüpten who appears in my film *Living Buddha*. At certain hours he receives guests in his room. There are almost 110 monks in the monastery again, the same number as before the ousting. In former times there were up to 600 monks.

On some days up to 500 guests or pilgrims come here to obtain Karmapa's blessing or just to take a look at him. To do so they undertake a strenuous trip riding in open lorries for days on end during 12 hours a day at freezing temperatures. Westerners would hardly survive such a journey. The babies to the old-aged grand-ma – all huddling together to remain warm and shield themselves against the wind. Yet these lorries are so packed with people that most men have to stay on their feet in the shade with ice-cold temperatures – an extreme weather without moisture.

These transports are death-defying enterprises because they drive full speed on roads unworthy of being called so, so that you already get dizzy when you watch this. Then it can easily happen that suddenly the car is halfway off the road with one tyre hanging above the deepest abyss but the transport continues without anybody batting an eye. It is not possible to stop since the car would get stuck in the mire, snow, gravel etc. Dramatic situations arise when the car gets in an oblique position on slippery ground.

Those lorries are equipped with a rear-wheel drive and undaunted young males sit at the steering-wheel. If possible they drive in convoys because it offers more security. But when a lorry stops rolling for any reason at all, the rest does not stop but send it pushing up the road, all bumpers to bumpers. This is the way difficult terrain is crossed best.

If a pick-up has greater problems and really has to stop, all drivers try to put their cars into such a position that nobody can pass them. Otherwise the Chinese drivers who might come your way do not offer any help. The whole lorry and car traffic is in the hand of the Chinese. There are very few Tibetan drivers. Before the occupation in 1959 the Tibetans did not have any roads. There were merely paths on which the whole goods exchange took place with the help of the yak-herds. To use a lorry for a pilgrims' ride to see Karmapa, the Tibetans have to pay a host of money to the Chinese. I know what I am talking about: when I rented my two Toyota jeeps plus a lorry for my filming equipment to drive to East Tibet, I paid almost twice as much per day as in Munich with *Avis* or *Europcar*. For the last three passes however there were no more roads, so I needed 33 horses for everyone and everything, on a daily basis.

As Tenzin mounts the narrow ladder going up to the roof terrace, he feels much tension because he does not know how to meet Karmapa now. On one hand he is a nine-year-old child in the meantime, on the other hand he is the great enlightened Karmapa and everybody throws themselves on the ground before him. Titi, Karmapa's servant, opens the door. They see him sitting on his bed with Tibetan books and Lego toys around him. Before they can utter a word, they throw themselves on the floor three times at a distance of twenty feet in front of Karmapa. Then they approach in stooped and devote positions, fall to their knees and offer him the habitual white silk kataks with bowed heads. He takes the offered scarves, puts them around their necks and as a blessing gives everyone a quick and cordial slap on the head. Afterwards his focus is back to the Lego toys.

In the Tibetan tradition several polite formulas are required to be expressed before they get to the matter at hand: *Where is Jamgon?* This question is not answered by the boy, he solely asks back if they have already gone to pray in the *gompa* (temple). No, but of course they will go there now.

Very well, they shall go now and recite especially the *Guru-Yoga mantra,* "the call for the lama from afar". Good-bye. The three of them leave the room in a bowing position going backwards. They tell the abbot and cannot mask their disappointment. Yet his answer is only: "Then go to pray."

On the next day Karmapa himself comes down to the gompa for the *puja* (prayers). Tenzin is wavering between doubt and hope. Now and again the phrase comes to his mind: "He is still a child". Not only Tenzin and his company have doubts about the clairvoyance of a nine-year-old kid and this sceptical attitude is very common. Why? Is it necessary to reach a certain age to be clairvoyant? Or is it something innate? Or is every human being basically clairvoyant? How do you judge such a thing?

The gompa is very dark. Tsurphu only has a mid-size fuel generator. The sparse light stems from the candles. Karmapa sits on his high throne. There are many monks and pilgrims present. When there is a break in the prayers Tenzin devoutly asks if His Holiness could give them the address of Jamgon's reincarnation. Karmapa replies: "Do you see the rainbow out there? His other end is exactly on Jamgon's birth-place." Oh dear, Tenzin and his company do not even see a rainbow, albeit the other end of it. "In this case", says Karmapa, "repeat the mantra I gave you another 100.000 times."

So they sit another two days in the gompa to recite the mantra. This does something to them. Those who have not experienced this yet, may not evaluate the effect in any way. After repeating it audibly 20.000 times you practically are in trance but you are still aware of the whole reality. The intellect (the ego) however loses control of you.

Repeating the same sentence over and over again is too daft for the intellect, so it says good-bye and intuition (the soul) takes over. After that you are a different person. The doubts quickly become less and less.

In 2015 during our work on the film about this visit, the news reached me that Karmapa, now 30 years old, would come to Germany for the first time. What an opportunity to ask him how he had "found out" Jamgon's address! We had a spontaneous meeting on the 11th of July 2015 at 4 p.m. in Berlin. Does it matter that in his life as the 17th Karmapa he has never physically known Jamgon? He replied: "I am the Karmapa. I have the responsibility to recognize Jamgon Kongtrul. Jamgon Kongtrul the 3rd had a very close relationship with the 16th Karmapa. Everybody knows this. I have also heard many stories about Jamgon Kongtrul and the 16th Karmapa, maybe this is the reason why I have a special feeling that links me to him."

Do you see? I thought, when I was sitting in front of him in a Berlin hotel room and there were three cameras filming him, this is exactly what matters: "a special feeling that links me to him". Reason or intellect have nothing to do with it. For Westerners who are under the tyranny of reason, it is so much more difficult to rely on our feelings. Those who trust their feelings 100% are clairvoyant. For Karmapa there is no difference between reason and intuition because his reason is wholly at the service of his intuition. Never would reason want to rise above intuition or even pretend it knew things better than intuition. This would be the end of enlightenment or the *full realization*.

Tenzin: "After reciting the 100.000 mantras, we went to see Karmapa again and he gave us a letter. Stated there were eight conditions for recognizing Jamgon's reincarnation": *Jamgon is neither born in the middle nor at the end of the year of the pig, his father is called something with Go, his mother something with Ki, the house has two storeys, the door is oriented to the East and from there you can see three mountain peaks from the middle of which springs a creek.*

"Our problem was that the letter said nothing about where this house was located." Karmapa did not need to repeat that it was at the other end of the rainbow. Tenzin does not take it seriously anyway because he does not see any rainbow. Therefore we continue to ask where and Karmapa replies: "In the south!" Tenzin: "Where in the south? South is too vague a direction. Where am I supposed to look?"

The fact that Karmapa is still so young is what worries Tenzin most. Just as all the others since we grow in the ideology that children first have to learn something before they know how to do things, that they are stupid from the first moment and only with time could they be taught several things. This ideology lets even Tenzin doubt Karmapa's capacities because he is just nine years old in his present body. These doubts are utterly an insult, not only for Karmapa, but for the whole human creature.

When we start to consider this creature as a continuum, every incarnation is a source of wisdom. To be sure this source can also be oppressed as we can see in our school system. Yet there are other systems known as the Russian *Schetinin School*[28] where children promote each other without any feelings of competition. By doing so the wisdom they brought from their former lives opens up and the children are capable of revealing a knowledge we do not even trust an adult professor to have.

I can only repeat: "The way you shout into a forest is how the echo sounds." This means that if I tell people that they are stupid, then they become stupid. Karmapa does not allow such a thing to be said about him. He brought his clairvoyance from his many lives in which he has given proof of this capacity plenty of times. If Tenzin is worried about Karmapa's age, it is his problem and it will only prolong the search for Jamgon's reincarnation.

Since Karmapa's indication to look in the south is of no use to Tenzin, Phuntsok and Sonam, they cannot resist asking him every day

---

28 See www.youtube.com/watch?v=dpHB8kH3yVg

afresh if he can give them any more and precise details. In the end Karmapa points to the notebook that lies on the table in front of him and begins to illustrate his explanations.

Tenzin shows us this notebook: *This is his notebook with his hand-writing. We have kept it here.* (He explains the scribbling): *That is Tsurphu, the mountain before the monastery. He has drawn the rainbow above it. Here are the Tibetan letters:* Ka, Ma, Ta, Ka *and the symbol for the year of the pig. Behind the mountain of Tsurphu, this is where we should look, we see the black mountains which he also mentions in his letter. Here are the mountains and here is the house with the two storeys and here is the creek.*

All these indications were already enumerated in his letter. The search group stills wonders what is meant by the south. The drawing could be interpreted in a way that Jamgon's birth-place is south of Tsurphu. So Tenzin would only have to drive around the mountain to the south slope and look for Jamgon there. But his company and he do not yet combine things in such a way. Of course in the end we are always much smarter than before. Presumably they are not able to do so because they are still sceptical of Karmapa's affirmations. So their free thinking is blocked.

Tenzin is so desperate that he is about to leave empty-handed. He confides in the abbot who can only recommend to visit Karmapa again. But Tenzin is ashamed of doing so and fears to get on Karmapa's nerves since he has already said to look in the south.

Anyway Tenzin controls himself one more time and climbs the stairs to Karmapa's room. In this moment Karmapa is not in his room but jumps around in a boisterous way on the rooftop in front of his room. He jumps from one foot to another throwing his arms into the air and shouting rhythmically: *Chushur* or *Tschu Tschu* or *Churchur*. Tenzin is too shy to interrupt Karmapa in this "dance" and bother him with his same question over again. Resignedly he turns around at the top of the stairs without Karmapa seeming to notice him. He goes back to Drupon Dechen to tell him that he does not know how to approach Karmapa.

Drupon: *What has happened?*
Tenzin: *He is jumping around on the rooftop hilariously and keeps shouting* Tschu Tschu, Tschu Tschu."
D: *What does he shout?*
T: *Well, some kind of sound – Tsch Tsch.*
D: *Precisely what?*
T: *Tschu tschu or so.*
D: *Do you not know what* Chushur *is?*
T: *No.*
D: Chushur *is the name of a local community on the other side of the mountain on the south slope.*
T: *What? Where the airport is?*
D: *Correct. The airport is only in the community of* Chushur.
T: *How big is this community?*
D: *It stretches from the airport in the east towards* Shigatse *in the west, about 50 miles.*
T: *And how many villages are there?*
D: *I do not know.*
T: *Do you think we should look there for such a house Karmapa described?*
D: *Yes, I think this is what it means.*
Tenzin is very excited.
D: *Here you are! You have no confidence in Karmapa.*
T: *Yes!*
D: *You wanted to leave. You were so desperate because you took him for an ill-bred child, you do not see the Buddha in him.*
Tenzin cries tears of humility and shame.

Tenzin is on his way

Every step Tenzin makes in Tibet is followed by Jamgon's adepts via Skype and YouTube. However only a few knew of the concrete plans and Topga is one of them. I ask him: "How do you feel when you hear the news about the search for your brother?" Topga remains completely neutral: "Of course the process continues. Tenzin went to see Karmapa who gave him this vision about Jamgon Rinpoche. In a letter he gave him the name of the family, of the father and the mother and a general direction where to look." Whether they will find him or not is not evident for Topga yet. His motto is: *wait*.

For Tenzin and his company it is clear that they have to look in the Chushur *community*.

They rent a *Toyota Land Cruiser* in Lhasa and drive from the north through the whole community and start looking on the south west border. Since they follow the order "to the south", this is the most Southern part of Chushur and they start searching from there. The community has about 25 villages. Tenzin makes a list with several columns on a big sheet of paper. In the first column they put the address of the house they survey. The following eight columns stand for each of the features that Karmapa told them about Jamgon's identification.

After examining more than 60 houses on the first day, they can see from the list that not a single building fulfilled these eight conditions in the least. The search proceeds tediously. They ask every person they come across if they knew a baby born last year. They ask the children if they have a younger brother of about a year. There seems to be nobody who fits the description.

Rosy Findeisen and her husband are the only foreigners who accompany Tenzin on his search for Jamgon in Tibet. Naturally they do not join him in the search around the villages, this would be far too conspicuous. It already causes enough stir that three monks in red robes are looking for a baby. Of course nobody knows who they search for but in Tibet it is clear that if monks ask around like this, it must be for someone special, otherwise they would not undertake such a systematic search.

Rosy: *When Tenzin Dorjee went to look for Jamgon, we were in Tibet and experienced all this exciting time. Of course we asked for the day's results every night. After they had seen ever more children every day, they got confused and asked Karmapa every morning for ever more detail. Once they had had a look at more than 100 children who were born the year before, Karmapa almost lost his patience with them and made them a drawing where he put the house with all details, even with the tree at the crossroads and wrote that eight persons lived in this house. So they gradually got closer to Jamgon.* This is what Karmapa also confirmed to me in the interview in Berlin in 2015: Karmapa: *Tenzin Dorjee often came to see me and asked me for the reincarnation. Eventually I had to do something and went into meditation. I closed my eyes and suddenly I saw a clear image with Jamgon sitting on a chair. And this image changed into a little boy who was very similar to the 3rd Jamgon. This boy sat on the knees of his father and it is Jamgon the 4th. This image or vision revealed me how the 3rd Jamgon came to be this small boy.*
CK: *And how did you come to know the syllables* Ki *and* Go *for the parents' names?*
Karmapa: *In the same way during meditation.*

From now on Tenzin documents the search with a small video-camera. After two days he and his company have examined 167 houses but in none do all eight conditions match. When they drive back to Tsurphu at night, Karmapa sees them coming up from the valley with their jeep and makes a disappointed gesture with his hand: "They have found nothing still."

This time Tenzin does not even mount the stairs to Karmapa's room, he is completely exhausted and about to abandon the search. A new problem has arisen now: the contract for his rental car will finish tomorrow morning and he has no money left to continue renting the expensive vehicle. But the abbot Drupon Dechen has a solution: he obtains from Karmapa that he will put his own vehicle with driver at the disposition of Tenzin, Phuntsok and Sonam for the next day.

After giving back the rental car in Lhasa, they drive in the direction of Chushur with Karmapa's car and driver when the latter shows them a formidable tree on the edge of the road and tells them that on his last trip to Shigatse Karmapa had eaten his picnic under the very tree. Oh, Tenzin thinks, then let's have picnic there too. When they sit under the tree and eat their little meal, the driver continues recounting that Karmapa was interested in the village over there in the distance at the south slope of the mountain. "He begged me", says the driver, "to find someone and ask the name of this village." I found a farmer woman working on the field and asked her:

Driver: *Please, what is this village over there called?*
Farmer woman: *This is Khyung Tsum.*
D: *Thank you very much. Is it across the river?*
F: *Yes.*
D: *Is there a bridge?*
F: *Yes, but you can only cross on foot.*
D: *... but how do you cross?*
B: *Well, the bridge is in a very bad shape.*
D: *Thank you!*
Tenzin asks the driver: *Does this form part of Chushur?*
D: *Yes, we are in the east of the district.*
T: *And the village over there is also part of Chushur?*
F: *Yes but it should be one of the last villages to form Chushur, further east is an area which does not belong to it anymore.*

Something stirs inside Tenzin: if Karmapa was interested in this village and it belongs to Chushur community, this means something special. They decide unanimously not to drive towards the South of Chushur in order to continue their search where they stopped yesterday. They will rather go on to the village in the North-East of Chushur to look for Jamgon there.

In Berlin I ask Karmapa how he came across this village 21 years ago.

Karmapa: *I believed that Jamgon was born there. So I begged my friend and driver to ask the woman on the field for the name of the village.*

Even for the nine-year-old Karmapa it was a feeling and not a rational reflection. He simply trusts his intuition. The normal humans of today do not do that. We are still dominated by a certain type of superstition, a product of reason. With this it came to the top of our thinking. Science is its material expression, this is why it is not capable of being in harmony with nature. No matter which feeling arises thanks to intuition, reason may always resist with a But, thus unsettling intuition. Yet intuition is always completely sure when producing feelings.

Nevertheless reason has to submit to intuition clearly, so that the feeling may have space. When it is not disturbed by reason, a feeling is a feeling and we perceive immediately which amount of truth and which character it has. We can also call this feeling our all-perceiving soul. To emphasize it again: the soul is our personalized intuition. Reason must not reply with Buts to feeling. Intuition has much better possibilities to find out the (subjective) truth because it may check itself.

This is a problem for reason. To check itself it requires the help of so-called natural laws which do not persist either if we have a closer look at them, since they are purely material: weighing, measuring, counting, using your five senses, but declaring the sixth sense as unscientific. Yet it is the best sense mankind possesses. When the sixth sense perceives something, all the other senses may question it without patronizing it – as reason used to do. Intuition is first.

My first question is: What do you feel? Then there is some answer and it is questioned and looked into. Not questioned with a new thought but exclusively with one that uses the terms mentioned in the answer, in their most literal and exact form, not a modified or synonymous form. Such a term is considered a door leading to a deeper emotional layer. This is why we formulate this term as a question and we will get another answer and in this answer there is another door and so on, until the replying person (your inner voice) has come to its core: to a concrete scene. This scene may be put down in writing to get a clear picture of it and then recognize which kind of conditioning it has triggered.

This is soul research or *feeling research*. This is how you get to the source of a disorder or fear. You then write down all this scene in script-style (see annex). In the end you know exactly what caused your feeling and recognize your subjective truth. It is all about a strong, clear and emotionally true recognition on the basis of which you know that this scene must not remain so, because it has made you ill and / or unhappy with all its repetitions. This will be changed now in the rewriting.

With this method we may find all the problems inside you and bring them to light, i.e. on the paper and thus into your consciousness. After this cleaning up you may trust completely in your feeling, and your intuition works fine. In this state you have the feeling yourself, e.g. you may ask how this village is called because you are in resonance with a beloved person you look for. All this and even more may be looked at in depth.[29]

Is it him or not?

As in an old legend Tenzin, Phuntsok and Sonam have to cross this foolhardy narrow suspension bridge crossing the mighty Brahmaputra River. Almost 100 feet under them roar the masses of water, the wooden boards of the bridge are brittle, full of cracks or wholly

---

29 In "Personal Master plan for Reincarnation" (see annex).

lacking, whereas the bridge moves frighteningly at each step. The three monks in their dark-red robes decidedly move along the bridge clinging courageously to the steel ropes on either side.

As soon as Tenzin has arrived in Khyung Tsum with his company, they split up: two of them start inquiring in the upper part of the village and Tenzin starts in the lower part together with a monk from Tsurphu who accompanies them with the driver. The latter stays with the car and looks for a passage on a bridge made for cars in the surroundings. After they have just split up, a girl of about 13 years appears in front of Tenzin. She has heard that they look for a baby and wants to show them her nephew who was born in the year of the pig.

In the last days the news about monks searching for a tulku was rife in the district. *Tulku* is the Tibetan word for someone whose former life is known. Of course nobody knows who the search group is and even less who they look for exactly and that this someone is such a great personality as His Eminence Jamgon Kongtrul Rinpoche whose name was well-known in all Tibet before the Chinese invasion. The turmoil would be too great and would endanger the search. The girl says that her nephew was born in 1995 and that the house is just over there on the slope.

When Tenzin notices that the house has two storeys and that the door opens to the east, he sends his colleague to the upper part of the village to get the other searchers to this house. Excitement is rising. For the first time in a long while all the hopes and wishes rise to the surface again and Tenzin wonders: "Have we reached our aim?"

Sonam: *Two storeys and the door to the east. It fits.*
Tenzin: *But all eight conditions must be fulfilled.*
Phuntsok: *Who is this?*
S: *This is the grand-mother.*
T: *If there are eight persons living in the house, then we already have three conditions that fit.*
P: *We can also see three mountain peaks from here.*
T: *But is there a baby?*

S: *The young parents are on the field it seems.*
T: *When do the parents come back?*
Grand-mother: *They are working on the field.*
S: *Please ask for the baby,* whispers Sonam in Tenzin's ear in Nepali.
T: *Not so fast. Let us first ask them when the parents get back from the field, maybe they took the child with them.*
S: *Yes, ask them when the parents will be back.*
T: *OK. – When will the parents be back from the field?*
G: *In the evening.*
S: *This is ok. If we ask too much, she will become suspicious. We have to be patient.* – says Sonam in Nepali, a language the grand-mother does not understand.

The family is not suspicious towards the monks, only a bit timid. Nowadays in Tibet the third generation under Chinese rule is not as familiar with reincarnation as in Buddhist times. Some Tibetans already speak better Chinese than Tibetan. At school all students have to speak Chinese. Tibetan is treated as a foreign tongue. You may still speak it at home, but not really openly in the street. Above all it is not allowed to mention the Dalai Lama and everything connected with him because people may be imprisoned and tortured for this.

The monks are respected since they are foreigners, but the family still does not have a clue what is at stake. If Tenzin and his company had informed them that they look for Jamgon, it was as if you would search for a famous politician, inviting people to cheat. Underhand all Tibetans still honour the old Tibetan reincarnation law, although now under Chinese reign for 50 years it is only a nice tale belittled by the younger generation – a tale told by the grand-mas and grand-pas, even if they had also been born under the occupying force. In the exile, independent from the state form of the countries where Tibetans live nowadays, this old reincarnation law is still valid unofficially. Among the brothers of the order in any case. And among the families? We will see right now:

Phuntsok: *Look, it is correct that from the door we can see the three black mountains which belong to the conditions Karmapa has drawn.*

Sonam: *Indeed, and there is the creek Karmapa mentioned.*

Tenzin is getting more excited by the minute. He hopes that the parents with the baby will arrive soon. From the rooftop he suddenly sees them coming towards the house. According to the old patriarchal habit the man walks three steps in front of the woman. He wears a jacket like many poor peasants who have to wear donated clothes, although such a jacket is virtually inconvenient for field work. The same as the fashion of the Chinese men with regard to shoes with 2 inch heels – produced so cheaply that the heels break at the slightest effort. This is how the men shuffle around the country. Most people only have one pair of shoes.

Tenzin says: "But look, there is no baby." – Then the couple disappears between the houses of the village and cannot be observed anymore. It takes some time until they reappear. The village has maybe 600 inhabitants. There is a strange feeling of fear arising – one that stems from the ego. Those who are totally in their intuition do not fear anything, they just have confidence. "But what can intuition trust in?" reason asks. "In the unknown", replies intuition. This makes reason rant and rave since it does not stand the unknown. Reason always needs an explanation. Yet sometimes the explanation is so subtle that reason cannot even perceive it and this causes reason to feel unsafe. However intuition even feels safe with the unknown. How can that be, asks reason. Intuition trusts in its good intention. It does not need to know exactly ***how*** it works, only that it ***does*** work. To find Jamgon's reincarnation is no ego interest of the monks. They merely put themselves at the disposition as a tool as best they can to help Jamgon's and also Karmapa's mission and all the people who are interested in the evolution of human consciousness. Behind it is the Great Spirit of the harmonic universe which is simply and only love. Harmony may also be understood as love. In this confidence they also trust the reincarnation of the 3rd Jamgon since his passing away: and if it happens now – marvellous. To reincarnate is an act of love. We take shape again to make more experiences by which consciousness grows.

Please think of your own conception, it was also an act of love. Some fear that it will become an erotic film when they put it down in script-style. And why ever not? No matter how we term such an act, it is and will remain a physical act so that a body may be created. The soul loves to take shape again in a body. Of course the form cannot be aleatory. It is – as I have already mentioned several times in this book – a mirror of our consciousness and therefore a mirror of the problems with which we have died.

Surely the soul would know how to let the enlightened body shine in pure beauty but the ego is not yet ready for it. It acts from an emotionless, conflict-laden space and this transpires in the shape of the body. It is the body's task to reflect the emotional contents to make them visible and this requires a transformation leading to harmonization and corresponding beauty.

With every incarnation one might ask: what would it need to harmonize everything revealed in a physical, and emotional way so that life may take place in accordance with the principles of the universe? If the soul said to all the molesting feelings: "No problem, we just visualize the perfect beauty even if we have not reached it yet in our innermost", this would still not produce a beautiful and loving character. To be sure the problems would be well kept under lock and key but they would still stink to heaven above. Things only become virulent when we start digging them up. Yet many beauties hide behind a cover to protect themselves from the discovering looks. Nobody is supposed to know what goes on inside of them, yet the soul knows anyway. Intuition shows how much better its perception works than reason's. The latter is easily tricked by external beauty. No matter how lovely the form may be, it all depends on the spirit inside.

Recognition is a feeling

I cannot judge the amount of fear every single person of the search group feels. Certainly it is not the same for everyone. The fact that Tenzin has mysteriously survived the accident uninjured and found the amulet later puts him in a special position to experience a fulfilment now which gives his life a deep meaningfulness leading to happiness. The doubts of the ego which have overwhelmed him in the meantime, even the ones with regard to Karmapa dissolve into nothingness at this moment. These are the moments in life in which all concepts that accompany us fall off and we look into the void. I know this state of mind.

Everything is at stake: to be or not to be. If there is no baby here, everything will crumble. – Or Jamgon is there, then all is perfect. If you feel a void in this moment, then nothing will collapse, even if the parents say: We do not have a baby, or: We had a baby, but it died. – Buddhism called this a "void" and it is something divine. Because everything that is, is a projection into the void, into the emptiness of the three-dimensional space and into time. It is the same as with great pains or when you are dying: you leave the body and take a look from above, completely serene and free from all.

However if the ego is active, its emotion links with the question: Why do the parents not come? We have just seen them coming into the village, why do they not appear here?

Sonam: *Patience Tenzin! It is better they come later as if they came without the baby, is it not?*
Tenzin: *Yeah, you are right.*
S: *Let go of all your expectations.*
T: *Since Rinpoche's death I have been waiting for this moment.*
S: *If he does not show up now, the world will not fall apart either. Don't you know the saying: "In the end, all will be fine. And if it is not fine, it is not the end"?*
T: *Oh, you ...*

S: *Breathe, this is the best exercise for your spirit. Breathe deeply and consciously. Exactly. Don't worry, be happy.*
T: *Every second is like an eternity.*
S: *Look out! The father: -------He is coming!!!! He has a baby in his arms!!! Watch!*

A warm feeling penetrates Tenzin (yet reason is not even sure that this is Jamgon). In Karmapa's case there were incarnations when his first sentence he spoke in life was: "I am Karmapa." This baby is not yet one year old, it will hardly say: "I am Jamgon." Who wins the fight in this moment: reason or intuition?

Reason asks: How do we know that it is really Jamgon? – Intuition says: The very question is wrong because there is no "we" in this moment. Everyone first has to feel in their innermost heart if it is him or not. All depends on the fact if I can trust my feeling and my intuition.

Breathe in and out ... emptiness ... breathe ... do not think ... What do you feel?

The father with the baby in his arms is only at a distance of seven feet from Tenzin. He cannot see the face of the baby yet.

If you trust your soul, you will have a clear feeling now: yes or no – even if you have not seen the baby yet. Nevertheless you know the truth. Such situations abound in everyday life. It's all about training this perception you have in such a moment. It's the premonition innate in every human but often hidden. It is part of the intuition and can also be trained, the same as reason.

However we do not do this as the before-mentioned Kali era, the ego period, had to show us something different than intuitive perception (and mostly still does so). In the Kali era all was about developing the individuality of the human character. Now in the third millennium it will be finished.

After that evolution will not go back to the animal herd consciousness because repetitions are not possible in the cosmos. Now the next step is waiting: the *Sattva era*. This means we do not throw away the individuality we all together have already developed. We recognize that we are all connected with each other despite our individuality – in a spiritual-emotional way, not in a physical way. This level reason cannot comprehend, it is not made for this. It is the business of our right brain hemisphere, intuition. This is where we feel things. In general women perceive more than men, but also men may evolve.

For those who cannot imagine the global connection of all beings, not to mention feel it, it may be easier to imagine how strong they are linked to all other beings on a physical basis, starting with the air we all breathe in and out. Even plants breathe, and what they breathe out, we breathe in. What we breathe out, other beings breathe in. Collectively we breathe the same air. We eat what already passed through countless hands. On our skin we wear clothes made by innumerable hands and often transported around the whole planet: from the cotton fields via the transportation workers, the spinning and weaving mills up to the salesgirl from whose hands we have received the clothes. We are not alone with anything. Every action was also a spiritual act. Our intuition perceives this connection. If someone feels alone, this is only the ego.

Meanwhile Tenzin has inspected about 200 houses in order to see if Jamgon could be inside. Just now as the man climbs up the ladder to the house with the baby in his arms, he is shooting a film. Thanks to the camera he remains at a distance. Sonam is the first to approach the baby which lies completely still in the arms of his father.

Sonam has the same feeling as Tenzin: *It is him!!!* But neither of them utters a word. Those who are commanded by reason, may think now: Where do they take the certainty from? Do they recognize something in the baby which points to Jamgon? – If you want, you could answer with Yes, but surely this would not suffice for reason, since it could ask: What is it that you see?

Although this is a family of peasants and the baby is totally covered with dirt, it is wearing yellow and dark-red lama colours which is quite uncommon under these circumstances. Even if this could be interpreted as a rational sign, the sceptical do not accept it. In their thinking they may discredit intuition with the word "coincidence" any time. Yet intuition simply says without foundation: *I feel it, it is Jamgon*. – All depends on this feeling, if you want to develop your intuition. You need it especially when it comes to dying. And here it is about being reborn. Both phases of life are intimately linked, they are mastered by intuition, not by reason. While Tenzin is watching through the camera, his blood runs cold before the wonder manifested in front of him. Even in Tibet it is still considered a wonder to meet the bodily incarnation of your confidant. He cannot hold back his tears. Phuntsok warns him to suppress his tears (of joy).

Phuntsok: *If we become too euphoric now, then they will know that we have found him without checking. It is too early and too dangerous because it might raise expectations and greed which may hinder the further reincarnation process until Jamgon is back in his old position. It is essential to remain neutral even if in this moment we are overwhelmed by a feeling of joy as strong as a tsunami.*

Once again he whispers in Tenzin's ears: "If you cry so much, they will instantly know that we have found him." – Caution is indeed paramount because once a reincarnation certificate is issued, the holder will inherit everything he possessed in his former life, independent from the fact to which family he belonged in his former life. This is the old reincarnation law in Tibet.

If someone had been such a personality of rank and name as Jamgon Kongtrul Rinpoche the 3rd and this would be let known when searching for him, then plenty of ego-driven people could try to fulfil the conditions of the prediction in hindsight to pretend it was their baby. If this baby inherits everything it possessed in his former life, it will also occupy the same social position. This is not only a chance for the family but the people in general will also be heavily affected. In so far the search group has a great responsibility to find the genuine reincarnation. Even if Tenzin's tears are the spontaneous expression of his intuition, he still looks for signs to prove the correctness of his feelings. – An amazed Sonam approaches slowly towards the waking baby. Its left arm is hanging down. Sonam is softly taking its left hand establishing the first physical contact.

At the beginning there is a red plastic bowl

Now the mother is coming up the ladder too. She is as unprepared as the father. She is surprised to see the men in dark-red robes who stare at her baby and even shoot it. What do these monks want?, she asks: In any case, this is impossible, my child is completely unwashed. So she takes it from the arms of her husband and disappears inside the house. There is the grand-mother waiting. The mother takes off the baby's clothes and the grand-mother prepares the water in a red plastic dish. She takes a tin cup to fill water from the pale and a piece of soap. In the yard she puts the bowl on the ground, the mother places the baby inside and covers it with soap. The baby does not like it and starts shouting at the top of his voice.

Tenzin and his company arrive at the scene and Sonam goes on shooting. Should he really do that? Should he shoot the recently discovered Jamgon in his new form standing in a red plastic bowl protesting noisily because his mother is washing him thoroughly from head to toe?. For Tenzin it is completely embarrassing that his beloved master, friend and father is being shot in such a miserable fashion. Although it is a very normal washing scene, the baby being washed is not just a normal baby but thanks to the reincarnation belief it is the venerable Jamgon Kongtrul Rinpoche in all his personality. For Tenzin this is downright intolerable.

With Karmapa the embarrassment was even greater since he – as he had wished for – has only been searched, found and enthroned at the age of six as the Holy Karmapa. Until then he had been taken by his father as a more or less ordinary child among his other ten children. When this quite cheeky – we could also say self-assured – boy who had not yet been recognized as the great Karmapa, was reprimanded by his father several times, he even received thrashings now and then. How ashamed must his father have felt when he received the news of whom he had beaten then …

If we always knew at once who our child is, which venerable personality, perhaps even a personality we knew as an older human being, we would never be able to beat our children. It would be utterly impossible. Or do you beat your 80-year-old grand-ma?

In Jamgon's case who has not turned one year yet, it is just important that he gets a good image from the start. In the film we still show the washing-scene because it is absolutely not unnatural. Jamgon stands in a red plastic bowl, so small, so naked, protesting so much.

Tenzin: *Stop that, you should not shoot this.*
Sonam (shooting): *Oh, come on!*
Tenzin: *Wait a bit.*

Sonam continues shooting. And we become witnesses of how His Eminence Jamgon Kongtrul Rinpoche is starting his life as Jamgon the 4th with a washing. Is it seemly for someone with such a highly developed consciousness to be displayed in such a manner?

Tenzin and the other monks still take a barrage of nice pictures of the clean and decently clothed baby and then drive to Lhasa quickly. There they have the photos developed in a special fast lab and then drive to Tsurphu with Karmapa's driver on the same evening. Full of joy they ask for an audience with Karmapa, but it is only granted for the next day. Radiant with joy they meet with Karmapa the next morning and first complete the three inflexions. Then they lay the photos on the low table near his bed where he sits as usual.

Karmapa does not seem to show a particular interest in the photos. He does not take them in his hand and only has a quick look at them without batting an eye-lash. The seconds pass as minutes. Eventually he says without looking at Tenzin:

Karmapa: *Are you sure that you have found the right child?*

Tenzin stops breathing, he is at a loss for words. He takes hold of himself and stutters: *It is not for me to be sure, it is for you, my Holiness.*

The nine-year-old Karmapa thinks: "Stop talking in such a pompous way. I want to know if you are sure?"

T: *Ahem ...*

K: *Where is the place you took these photos of the child?*

Tenzin zealously: *Khyung Tsum. Your driver named us the village.*

K: *So ...*

T: *All your eight conditions are fulfilled there.*

K: *Are you totally sure?*

Tenzin is desperate. What is he supposed to say now? This is a typical bardo situation: I need to think and I do not know what to think. The body does not play any role anymore.

T: *My revered Karmapa, please tell us: have we found the right person?*

Tenzin's whole euphoria evaporates. Yesterday and all of last night he had never been so happy in his whole life. He could not wait to get up. He knew from the abbot that the audience would start at 8.30 a.m. He was awake at 5. He did everything a good Buddhist has to do in the morning. He was so excited he could not even drink tea. He swallowed some hot water. I am so happy, I am so happy, I am so happy, said his feeling ... and now this.

T: *Maybe we found the wrong child.*

K: *Have you checked all the houses in Chushur?*

T: *No, my Holiness, we have not.*

K: *Perhaps there is another child which fulfils the same eight conditions?*

T: *Very well, my Holiness, very well. It is possible.*

K: *So go on checking it all so you can be sure.*

Karmapa could have added: "You do not believe me anyway because I am only nine and stupid." – Is this true? Is a person of nine more stupid than at 19? Maybe where reason is concerned, but as far as intuition is concerned? It does not matter what level of consciousness you have reached. The unknown gets larger, not smaller with every expansion of consciousness. It is a matter of nature.

Karmapa: *So go on checking the rest of the houses.*

Karmapa lends them his car again.

Subdued Tenzin and his company leave Karmapa's room. Tenzin remembers wondering when they flew into Tibet, if the nine-year-old child would already have the capacity of telling addresses. At this point – with 9 years – Karmapa had given 30 addresses of reincarnation yet which had been confirmed. – In Berlin he said some 21 years later: "Sometimes I have to guess", to play down his high level of realized consciousness.

The very next day the monks check another 38 houses. Then they return to Karmapa. Tenzin thinks that maybe the day before was not the right day to ask Karmapa – whichever the reasons – and puts the photos of the little boy they consider to be Jamgon on display in front of Karmapa again. This is the question of the leap of evolution: what or whom do they believe now? Their intuition? Their leader? Their intellect?

Karmapa asks again: *When could you be certain?*

Tenzin: *Well, when His Holiness is certain.*

Karmapa laughs for the first time. But he does not laugh genuinely because he knows how serious the whole thing is. He thinks: "Do you trust your intuition or do you need me for this? Am I authority enough for you with my nine years?" – If they need an authority, they only believe in the intuition of another person. This is no self-competence, this is just the old swarm consciousness. Self-competence is individuality. It is all about this self-competence when you are dying, when you recognize your own former life and your next one.

Tenzin: *Please Karmapa, tell us: is it him?*

Karmapa: *This one?* (He points to the photos with his forefinger.)

T (irritated) gives a timid: *Yes.*

K: *Are you sure?* – he repeats the hundredth time.

New horror shows on the face of the monks.

T: *We do not have any right to say that we are sure or not, we ask for a word from you.*

K: *My word, ha, ha, ha …*

T (more horrified): *My Holiness, if you are not sure, how could we be?*

K: *If you are not sure, you have to go on looking.*

Tenzin feels completely destroyed.

K (in a low voice): *I am only a child …*

Tenzin is deeply ashamed, he has been thinking this of Karmapa for the whole time.

T: *Please, please, Holiness, tell us if we have found the right person.*

K: *If you are not sure, how can I be sure? Go on searching. Become certain.*

Tenzin picks up the photos again. He and his company say good-bye with a devote inclination and leave the room walking backwards. A servant closes the door behind them. In front of the door they straighten up again, look at each other and go down the stairs too baffled to speak. They want to talk to the abbot again but Drupon Dechen can merely repeat what Karmapa has said: "Go on searching, until you are certain." Tenzin thinks with regret that they have already been so sure about it all! – What shall we do now? the three of them are wondering. They decide to continue the search. Karmapa is right: as long as they have not checked every house, they cannot say if there are two babies in Chushur who fulfil the eight conditions.

"Oh, rubbish", says Phuntsok.

"We have to be sure", says Tenzin.

And indeed there they go again with their table in hand and check another 75 houses. Ruefully they show the result to Karmapa in the end: no other house fulfils more than one condition. "So", Tenzin begs again, while pointing to the photo: "Is it him?"

Karmapa, the nine-year-old Living Buddha, asks almost impatiently: *Are you still not sure?*

Tenzin: *Yes we are.*

K: *Completely sure? If you are not totally sure, then you will not be sure if I am sure. You have to be sure yourselves.*

T: *Yes, I understand what you are saying. I deeply apologise, I have doubted you.*

K: *... and yourself.*

Karmapa looks up and shows the little smile only he has, even as a child and still today. It has nothing to do with mockery, it is pure love and comprehension combined with something roguish. And then he says: "It does not depend on me."

Light and shadow of an authority

It seems as if the 17th Karmapa has already adapted his behaviour to the end of the Kali era because up to now the belief of Tibetans in authority was very high on the spiritual scale. It has been deeply rooted there for centuries but with the eviction of the Tibetan people into the whole world the control structure prevailing in the monasteries is lacking ever more. At the same time much evil was done with this absolute belief in authority. Not every Rinpoche really is a Rinpoche, even if he is called one.

At the age of 9 Karmapa has no desire to be an authority. Only later will he fully become one when he starts working as a guru in the West and he will certainly need it for his clients to make them listen. In the third millennium he has still four incarnations as a Karmapa before him, this increases his authority from one life to the next.

The Dalai Lama will get out of his chain with his present life. He does not want to be this authority any longer. This is no disgrace. Not everybody has to work on a project for 21 lives. It always depends on the size of the task. In the 13th century the Mongolian Khan passed the power over Tibet to the 5th Dalai Lama. This power ended in 1959 with China's occupation. So the Dalai Lama may consider his mission as fulfilled.

Karmapa was never supposed to nor wanted to act politically. He still does not do it. But if the Dalai Lama is no longer at the disposition for this mission in his next incarnation – as this will be soon –, Karmapa as a global player will meet new challenges on the slippery parquet of politics. He is certainly the one to dominate this challenge. Dalai Lama already seems convinced of it, otherwise he would not have chosen him to be his successor in teaching wisdom to the world.

For me Karmapa is a guiding star giving orientation to the world without becoming an authority which tells me what to think. I have learnt to think for myself. This is why I chose my parents Edith and Erich. Both were strong self-thinkers. As thankful as I feel towards my parents I also want to feel towards my future parents. No matter which culture they stem from, my evolution with Karmapa is not yet over. I am still playing in a district league when it comes to my consciousness level. He is a star I cannot compare with. I can solely marvel at him and evaluate him critically, yet I will go my own way, like every woman and every man. Karmapa also goes his own way and Jamgon as well. Nobody may tell where this leads to … nevertheless everyone helps one another. This help is no doctrine, it is sympathy which leaves the other's freedom intact.

Tenzin was divided. On one hand he looked for Karmapa's help and on the other hand he was sceptical if Karmapa with his nine years could already give the expected help. Now that Karmapa let him run into a wall, he lies awake at night and sleep will not come. Anyway he has professed to his intuition now and may say: "I am sure." In consequence Karmapa tells him: "Very well, then go to Jamgon and bring him my lucky scarf", handing him an almost 7 feet long, heavy scarf in deep orange colours as a greeting for Jamgon. In addition seven white kataks to honour his relatives.

With this new self-acquired feeling of certainty Tenzin drives back to the house of Jamgon the 4th. Now he enlightens the parents and the other five persons living in the household – grand-mother, grand-father, aunts and nieces – about the true identity of the baby. The parents are only 20 and 22, it is their first child. they have never had anything to do with Buddhism, but they consider it a very great honour that such a high personality has been born in their family, although the belief in reincarnation in Tibet has been suppressed almost as strongly as in Europe since 499 – the Council of Constantinople (today: Istanbul). At the emperor's request the reincarnation philosophy was deleted from the Christian liturgy. However we may become a witness of a reincarnation here in a Christian country thanks to a documentary.

After all have been honoured and after they know who their son is, I ask the father: *Have you noticed anything special in your son so far?*
Father: *No, we haven't, but the other people in the village have.*
I also ask the mother and she replies:
Mother: *I am totally surprised. I do not know what to say. I am completely overwhelmed.*

Training intuition

Dear reader, I want to encourage you to start feeling yourself, just as Tenzin did, to be able to trust your feeling. If you cannot trust your intuition yet, train it. There is no other way. It is the same as with every other capacity: train, train, and train. Autonomous thinking – this is what Karmapa asks of Tenzin right now in a ground breaking way.

The greatest obstacle for Sattva era, the successor of Kali era, is the plight of before-mentioned monotheist thinking. With its hierarchy it has also reached Buddhism. The belief in authority is almost as big as in other religions and worldly structures. The ego springs from this pyramid structure with one ruler at the top whom all the others have to follow: Thou shalt not have another Buddha before me, otherwise

… I have experienced this first-hand, not only in this life, in many lives. I always was the henchman of religion. Only when I was travelling in 14 countries on all continents for my film *En route into the next dimension,* I could overcome my belief in authority, because I saw that there are as many paths towards enlightenment (or whatever you want to call it) as there are people on earth. On this planet every person is a centerpoint. A good example for this shows my video with the orange and the tooth-pick.[30]

I want to remind you over and over again: the universe only wants love as it requires the least amount of energy. The disrupting emotions like hatred, jealousy, envy and aggression merely cause stress. And stress is a waste of energy. Since we are part of the cosmos ourselves, it is also our task not to cause disruption nor unnecessary friction in order to avoid wasting energy. Everybody learns this cosmic law firsthand by falling ill owing to stress.

There is nothing left for us but to adapt to the cosmos, no matter how long it takes. There is no end, as little as there was a beginning. Our consciousness is solely a tiny cosmic snapshot, everything else lies in the unconscious. Even the scope of evolutionary development from animal to enlightened is cosmically speaking a blink of the eye lash. The scope in which you may incarnate, e.g. from a fruit-fly to a female Earth or a male sun is only small part of the infinity of possibilities too.

We may probably not be able to foresee our further evolution as little as an ant may anticipate that it will develop from one incarnation to the next in a way that one day it receives a human form. Perhaps these beings we want to become in one or two million years are already surrounding us now (and e.g. create a gigantic corn circle in the next ten minutes). But we perceive them just as an ant perceives a human person.

We have to be aware that of all the things that influence us

---

30 Video: "I am the centerpoint" (www.clemenskuby.de/member-area)

cosmically here on Earth, the sun makes up only 3 % of it. Yet these 3 % already determine our life. Without the sun no life would exist on Earth. The chlorophyll in the plants and the haemoglobin in our arteries are direct emissions from Father Sun. And if these make up only 3 % we may ask: what are the remaining 97 % doing with us?

When training intuition consider that the first contact is decisive. With a trained intuition it is always that. A normally sensitive person feels this clearly, only reason he or she utters a But and adds thoughts of doubt. This difference between a first thought and afterthoughts is paramount for intuition because there are plenty of possible afterthoughts *but there is only one first thought.* This is pure intuition. If you have learnt to mistrust this first thought, the access to your intuition has been made more difficult. You may change this now.

Intuition is such a precious thing! Therefore we have consciously chosen the title of my film *Reincarnation – Looking for a Sign* to gain confidence again into our intuitive capacities. Reason in its scientific shape pretends to be the holder of wisdom in our society, yet it does not have any wisdom at all. Wisdom always stems from intuition.

These signs which make you so sure that you say: "Yes, this is the one I look for", may only be obtained by feeling with your innermost thoughts. Of course this is a habit, as everything in life. When you are used to feeling, you trust your perception. If you have not trained your feeling by clear and unequivocal experiences, there is always a *But* popping up. Then you always have to ask someone else to be sure, just as the monks had to ask Karmapa whether they had felt correctly because reason believes that they might still be wrong …

Most people imagine that the consciousness of the continuity of spirit is hardly possible to reach. Yet this is only a politics of confusion marking this prejudice. Just as natural as it happened with Jamgon, it is for every person to be reborn again and continue the evolution of infinite lives. However if you do not set an intention when dying, then there will not be any energy. What for? The universe is not responsible for our happiness! WE want to be free beings. WE want to think that we may do and not do just as we want. Nobody influences us, is it not?

To emphasize one more time: if you do not set an intention with regard to your reincarnation and expect to fall in the famous Black Hole after death, then you will just receive this. And then you are exposed to your completely unreflected longings bringing you into a corresponding new form (see also chapter 12 the part: "Addictions are just a nuisance, even in death). No matter what your perspective before death was: if you have not practised to control your mind, you are totally lost to it since you have no form. Your cravings, your unfulfilled love wishes but also the contrary: hatred and envy, are the aspects driving you to your next incarnation. Basically every incarnation is fine for you in this chaotic state of mind. At least you are back in a form because your unattached mind makes your life hell without a form.

Just observe how your mind is bouncing around in your normal state now: how much does your mind leap from one thought to the next? Only due to your body you can remain in one place and do not have to take part in this confusion of your mind. Without form, i.e. without anchor, you are the match ball of your thoughts. If you have not learnt in time to control your thoughts, you will hardly be able to direct them once you leave your body (see also chapter 4 the part "Thought control" as well as the practical indications in the annex).

Like a drunk without consciousness you are simply attracted to some place where something is familiar, where you feel an affinity or where you feel a lot of psychic energy, above all certain people. These people are mostly part of your former relatives, thus it is no wonder that most souls incarnate inside their old family again. So then it is not that the grand-child is *like* the grand-father, but he *is* the grand-father. As long as we have not developed a consciousness for the continuity of spirit, we cannot profit from this continuity either.

It is different with children – maybe they suddenly get the idea: "Now I have to start learning everything from scratch again." Due to the overall lack of consciousness with regard to the continuity of spirit, the curtain of oblivion closes on your mind, cutting off the possibility of the further evolution of a certain ability you have already trained for a whole life or more. To be sure, on an unconscious level everything continues anyway but only in a light fashion and with detours. This curtain of oblivion is basically a great waste of resources and energy when you have to learn afresh everything you already knew before (see chap. 4).

Do you really decline the idea of the continuity of spirit because you want to remain a materialist? This is rather stupid. Reincarnation means I go back into matter (flesh= "carne"), with the spirit I bring from my former life I materialize again, i.e. I reincarnate. When I tell myself that my spirit has not survived my last death, I force myself to start over again. Yet if I tell myself from the start that I plan to do this and that in my next life and I incarnate exactly in the place where I find the best conditions to continue my evolution, then this will happen. Owing to this intention the required energy will arise.

18
Life goes on – Karmapa meets Jamgon

The news: "Jamgon is found!" flies over the Himalayas and causes a storm of enthusiasm in Pullahari. I mostly think of Topga because this is maybe the moment when he could overcome mourning his deceased brother.

CK: *Topga, what does this news do to you?*
Topga: *I suppose there are no doubts with regard to his identity.*
CK: *Since you believe in Karmapa's reincarnation …*
T: *… then I should also believe in Jamgon's reincarnation?! Yes, I should. There is nothing wrong with it. It is only more difficult because he was my brother and now I am expected to believe that this little boy takes his place. This is my problem.*

I think: "Wait until you meet him."

On the terrace in front of Karmapa's room Jamgon the 4th is waiting to meet Karmapa the 17th for the first time. The nine-year-old Karmapa walks out of his room and goes straight to Jamgon who is in the arm of Phuntsok at the height of Karmapa's head. Karmapa tenderly touches the one-year-old with both his hands. Then they have to sit down for the compulsory photographs. Right after the shooting Karmapa himself puts Jamgon in his lap. Will they recognize each other? They have not met before in their present form. The scene in this film cannot be described with words. Karmapa is very sure of who is sitting on his lap and smiles contently. But is Jamgon also certain of the person who is holding him?

And then it happens: Jamgon with all his autonomy of a one-year-old baby turns to look at Karmapa's face above him – and this look, this is it! It expresses the happy fulfilment of all wishes that were his motive for the car accident. Death is not only nothing, it is a benefit as we may experience here.

Karmapa comments: "When I look at the face of 4th Jamgon Kongtrul, it is very similar – not on the physical level 100 % the same, but the feeling is the same. The feeling I had in my vision. I see the 3rd Jamgon when I look at the 4th Jamgon. The very same feeling. Do you understand?"

Luckily Jamgon has been reborn in Tibet. It would have been very difficult politically and organizationally speaking and with the lacking consciousness of reincarnation with non-Tibetan parents if Jamgon had incarnated out of China's territory. In order to be accepted in the *Sangha*, as Buddhists call their circle of friends, Karmapa carries out the haircutting ceremony with Jamgon.

In their former lives the relationship between Karmapa the 16th to Jamgon the 3rd was no different than now, when only the age difference was a lot smaller. Before the difference was 30 years, now it is 10. The haircutting ceremony in their former life was also shot, same as the present one. We see the synchronicity and thus the continuity of their relationship from one life to the next. This is a feeling of greatest possible joy.

It is similar to the feeling you have when you lose your loved-one somewhere in a big foreign city and now you are anxious that you cannot get in touch with him and feel great fear of loss. Suddenly he appears out of nowhere in a place you would never have imagined possible. Who has already experienced such a drama on a small or big scale? Or when your dog or cat were lost and all of a sudden when the hope of finding them again has already vanished, your darling is back at your doorstep.

This is the great feeling of joy which also manifests in people when they find each other's reincarnation – only much greater. In the case of Jamgon and Karmapa there is the added difficulty that both have died without any of them in their old form meeting with the other in his new form before dying too. In this case they both have taken a chance as it may seem to some. Both had to establish or better said maintain their relationship towards each other at the pure soul level.

None of them had disposed of a form for their feeling yet with which they could have experienced the relationship to each other. Both had left their body independently of the other and were still sure that they would find one another again.

The haircutting ceremony is at the same time the ritual of taking refuge. It means that you confess to a certain concept of belief, in this case to the Vajrayana *Buddhism*. Fundamentally it is a baptism. It is not only sealed by the symbolic cutting of some hair whereby they submit to the leadership of the spiritual masters, who have no hair on their head, but also by the throwing of rice. This symbolizes the abundance of the universe which comes with the confession to Tibetan Buddhism in all aspects of your life. Thus Jamgon the 4th belongs to the same community of believers as in his previous life.

Since the same goes for Karmapa who also begins every Karmapa life with a haircutting ceremony, both have a common basis for their lasting friendship which excludes any misunderstandings from the start because the philosophy both refer to has an age-old tradition and thus has developed a language penetrating every aspect of their life. As long as this Buddhist life takes place inside the corresponding social frame in every life, there will hardly be any irritations. Both meet again in this life on this very basis. Both are born again in Tibet as Tibetans: whether this remains so must be doubted owing to the current radical, political and global changes.

The shortening of the age difference by 20 years from their former life to this one can only be ascribed to the car accident and will play a great role on Jamgon's evolution as we will see at the end of this book ...

One child – two mothers

Topga has no time to travel to Tibet now in order to welcome his brother in his new form. Since he does not really trust in reincarnation, he rightly fears that it will hardly liberate him from his mourning. However his mother does travel and she does so immediately. For her, reincarnation is something normal and she wants to see and feel how her relationship to her son will be in his new form. Quickly she obtains a visa and with her husband (the stepfather of the 3rd Jamgon and of Topga) they make their way to Lhasa. Due to the large number of guests Karmapa has rented a house in Lhasa for Jamgon's family. This is where the further events take place with Jamgon the 4th.

It is a heart-warming as well as awkward scene when the former mother Pema greets her reborn son while his new mother *Yangki* sits near them. Pema is cautious as she does not want to hurt Yangki's feelings. Yet we can see what a loving relationship she has towards Jamgon, independently of his age and form. It is the human being who is so close to her. And the fact that she can touch him again after a pause of four years transforms any remaining grief in her.

The feelings of the new mother for her one-year-old son are of a wholly different kind. With an almost painful look she observes Pema greeting her son. Yangki has been confronted for only a few weeks with the faith in reincarnation and does not know yet how to handle such a situation. She is disconcerted since Pema is a stranger who virtually has nothing to do with her son nor her son with her.

Sometimes similar feelings may arise when the biological mother meets her child living with adoptive parents. For those who have not yet studied reincarnation and consider their child as a singular creature, it is normal to be confused. However for Pema it is the same feeling she formerly had with her son in his old form. A natural loving relationship which is simply there and has never died.

Of course the biological mum Yangki has a similar loving relationship to her baby but for a shorter time than Pema. Westerners without the conscious experience of reincarnation have trouble with such constellations of love. Two different persons love one and the same baby: will there not arise any feelings of jealousy? It would be understandable if Yangki had a claim of ownership with regard to her son Jamgon because it is impossible that a stranger has an intimate relationship with Yangki's son. Such a thing is incompatible with our materialistic thinking.

As Yangki has been conditioned by a rather materialistic philosophy due to her Chinese socialisation, at first it is not so easy for her to take pleasure in Pema's love for her child. Patriarchy also rules in Tibet but mingles more easily with the consciousness of reincarnation than in the Occident as Jamgon the 4th's grand-parents have still been raised with this spirit. The beautiful thing in such a philosophy is that many persons have a loving relationship towards a new-born child, practically all people who have also cherished this child in its former life. In an adult person who has lived a life to the brim, they are quite a few people. In the case of Jamgon even plenty of people love him, no matter in what form.

For the benefit of the child, for the benefit of all

The person who rejoices the most is Tenzin of course, he now knows why he has survived the car-accident. After the death of his mother – as I mentioned before – his father had given him to the monks at four. Jamgon had promised the father to care for Tenzin during his whole life and to bestow on him the best and free teaching a monk could receive in a Tibetan monastery. Normally the parents pay for their children in the monastery – comparable with boarding-school fees, only much lower. Since the age of 18 Tenzin has travelled non-stop around the globe as an assistant to Jamgon: his boss, master and teacher.

Tenzin is now feeling an overwhelming joy because everything he has longingly wished for all these years has come true and he is holding his beloved foster father and friend in his arms again, this joy is also an authentic challenge for Yangki, the mother of Jamgon the 4th.

If you could see how tenderly Tenzin is holding the little Jamgon on his lap, then there is only one thing amiss: that he could also breastfeed him. Yet the biological mother has a significance that nobody can take away from her. And of course she loves her child, this is something completely natural. She is still very young and it is her first child. She is very proud of her child and at the same time she knows now of her important responsibility towards him. Exactly this is what makes this love by "strangers" for "her" child a great learning opportunity. She notices that owing to this love she cannot possess "her" son on her own.

The same thing happened to Pema with Jamgon the 3rd. She also had to cope with the fact that her son loved Karmapa more than her. Thanks to this difficult lesson her consciousness was opened for the continuity of life and she could explain to herself why she was not the only love for her son. The love of her son for her was certainly something very special as it is for most people towards their mother. Otherwise he would hardly have spent his last day and night before his death with her. With her confidence in reincarnation Pema could emotionally process his sudden death the following morning in a completely different manner than her other son Topga who distrusts this belief. For Topga it was the end, for Pema only a transition.

Both could say that death is nothing. Nevertheless they are divided by two different concepts of faith. Each concept is true. The question is only with which concept do you solve your problems? For Pema her confidence was reinforced while for Topga his grief was deepened. Everybody forges their own destiny by taking responsibility over which concept of belief they embrace. With Topga death led to nothing, with Pema death is nothing.

It is more easily said than done that every person is responsible for the concept of their belief when the generation of their parents see to it that their child is baptised and thus cannot stray far from the concept of its faith. Children are already baptised at such an early age that they cannot protest. Even babies who cry horribly when being baptised, are not spared the procedure.

Every religion does this, even Buddhism. In the Catholic Church the parents even must swear that they will raise their children in the Catholic faith, otherwise they are denied the marital ceremony.

Nowadays all religions and traditional concepts run the risk of not being able to control the information the next generation receives from the Internet about these concepts, later causing the withdrawal from the community of faith. The flock consciousness is eroded by the individual consciousness owing to the Internet. The entire journey must be travelled through the different periods up to the present information era.[31]

At first Yangki cannot feel something different than what her consciousness allows her to. Rather than embracing the reincarnation philosophy it is easier for her to enjoy the privileges her highly esteemed child has all of a sudden provided her and her family. Even if the anti-Buddhist Chinese dominate Tibetan society: in Tibet a Rinpoche still enjoys a very high prestige. And Jamgon Kongtrul was not only some Rinpoche, but he also possessed the added title of an *Eminence*. Rankwise an Eminence comes right after *His Holiness*. His Holiness is the title for the leaders of an order or a faith. We Westerners have church leaders like the Pope. In Roman Catholic hierarchy Jamgon would be a cardinal.

Those who have such a son immediately rise in society. Karmapa's monastery Tsurphu not only bestows his blessing on the parents, but also monetary rewards. This is instantly demonstrated by the new clothes the parents are wearing. We must not imagine the huge amounts of money as in the West. Materially speaking Tibetans are extremely poor people. Almost every Tibetan is worse off than the poorest Chinese in Tibet. Thanks to Rinpoche the family is a bit better off now, but her daily routine remains the same. The social rise is linked to the condition that – if they agree – their son will be raised to by the teachers of his former life. This is no easy decision for Yangki

---

31 See also chap. 4 the part "How to reincarnate optimally".

to make. In his previous life as Jamgon the 3rd his father-in-law and his brother had refused to give Jamgon's education out of hand for six years. The result was that – as I mentioned before – Jamgon fell extremely ill until he entered the monastery. Jamgon's connection to Karmapa permeates all his lives and is becoming as close as ever before. It would not be uncommon for a relationship to only blossom to its full in its 4th continuation. But things may also be completely different …

In many histories of life it becomes evident that there has already been a relationship in former lives when woman and man enter in a close bond again, though not as a couple but as parent and child. Father-daughter or mother-son, but still close. Such a former togetherness is also displayed in love at first sight. Once a person who was doing soul writing in my seminar said: "Totally normal!" Why should the soul be satisfied with a single facet? There are so many aspects in a couple´s bond that a single life can never express. Is there something greater than to be connected to someone else in such a way that you find each other unexpectedly and instantly recognize one another at first sight?

Karmapa and Jamgon recognized each other even without form. To die for your friend or to know the address of his reincarnation are two testimonies of a bond on a high standard of consciousness of different levels. Karmapa says that once he is the disciple and Jamgon is his teacher and then the other way around. This may vary from one life to the next. "Basically", says Karmapa, "we are as closely linked as two drops of water. It is impossible to separate us. This is true love."

Yangki and her husband *Gampo*, the father of Jamgon the 4th, have quickly arrived at the decision to grant their son a life in his continuity. In his former life Topga had to be born first so that Jamgon could come to Karmapa. Topga thought that as a second-born, life would be comfortable because usually the first-born will take over the father's role after his death. Yet since Jamgon already entered in the monastery as a child and his father died early, Topga got the role of the successor. This did not please him at all. However Jamgon the 3rd could finally follow his destiny at the age of six.

For Topga, it was doubly hard to fulfil the role of heir because the profitable business of his father came to an end with the Chinese occupation of Tibet. For several generations they had lived off the trade between India and Tibet. Luckily they had a trading post in India/West Bengal (Kalimpong) which became their exile headquarters in 1959. Yet their income had stopped. His father died when it became obvious that there was no going back to Tibet. So all the expectations were directed towards Topga to provide the family with their habitual standard of living. A formidable task but Topga mastered it with enormous zeal and with great entrepreneurial capability. As mentioned before he became one of the great carpet dealers for an international furniture company and other customers worldwide. He could not deny that he had felt jealous of his brother Jamgon because he had travelled around the globe with Karmapa first and then was invited as a guru in all countries himself. Time and again his thoughts revolved around the idea that Jamgon, the sunny-boy, always got the best out of life, whereas he had received the hard bit. Now the fact that Jamgon had suddenly passed away at 38 changed his perspective about him completely, especially since he felt guilty for his death. However it is still not obvious whether this death has transformed his concept of belief.

At the right moment

Karmapa had decided for himself that his reincarnation should only be identified when he was six, thus making sure that he will have some time out as a child in his 17th incarnation. As a nomad boy with nine sisters and one older brother he enjoyed this time out in a superb way, impossible to imagine it being better and more exciting from a child's perspective. The second reason for it may have been the knowledge that the Chinese could not eliminate him as easily at six as when he would be a baby.

I fathom I am the only Westerner who has moved from the winter valley to the summer valley on horseback with Karmapa's nomad family and their 250 animals and has been cared for in their yak tent. When my crew and I had crossed three mountain passes of about 16.000 feet to reach Ladakh, Karmapa's family already was in their winter quarters at the end of October. Since Karmapa had been born on the 26th June, I begged the whole tribe to move back with me to the summer valley especially for the film documentation. It was a great enterprise with a full day's ride. But then we could pitch the tent exactly at the place where *Laloga* had given birth to her son and in the whole valley the sound of a magic conch had chimed for one and a half hours, an event that Karmapa had announced in his prediction letter.

At the end of my stay Karmapa bestowed on me his three-month-old favourite dog which he could not take with him to the monastery. This dog accompanied me for 13 years and was a golden treasure in every respect. Karmapa had called him *Haba;* he came with me to Germany and accompanied me in every seminar and on every trip.

As far as Karmapa is concerned these six years were the only calm years of his present life as the 17th Karmapa.

Jamgon is not one year old yet. For him it is much too early to leave Tibet. His discovery has transformed the entire life of his family. Mother Yangki wants to learn to read and write now because her family was not able to pay the money for the Chinese-led school when she was young. The only way for her to learn to read and write would have been to become a Buddhist nun. But this was far out of reach for her family. She says: "I may not be able to read and write but my mother taught me how to pray and I do it every day. Yet I have never imagined I could give birth to a Rinpoche. Neither have I dealt with reincarnation before. I was not brought up in a religious way. Nor did I see anything special in my child. But others did."

Jamgon's father Gampo explains the reincarnation of his son in the following way: "Jamgon wanted to be with Karmapa again, but in the monastery no children are conceived. We live on the South side of the mountain near Tsurphu, it would have been difficult to incarnate closer to Karmapa. Behind this mountain lies Tsurphu. (He points to a mountain behind the house. The air distance to Tsurphu is only 10 miles at the most. By car it is about three hours to go around this mountain.) A rainbow could cross this mountain without problems. So it was not a joke when Karmapa told Tenzin: *Jamgon lives just at the end of the rainbow you see there.*"

If Tenzin had not remained sceptical from the start, he would have understood at once where Jamgon had to be searched because Karmapa informed him at the very first visit: "Look for him in the south." Indeed: Khyung Tsum is the first village south of Tsurphu, only that there is a big mountain between them. In order to take up such indication with the right intuition you have to have a deep trust not only in Karmapa but in your own intuition.

The universe is at your service

For Karmapa it is a nice game to produce rainbows. This is one of the reasons why Jamgon loves him more than his mother. With Karmapa, Jamgon could develop his consciousness to the highest level. If he had stayed with this family, he would have never learnt how to influence the weather. For Karmapa this is nothing particular.

When in 1994 I shot my film *Living Buddha* with Karmapa in Tsurphu, he had just turned nine. (According to the Tibetan calendar he had turned 10 because the day of birth is the first birthday for them). As the head of the Kagyü order he sat on a large stone on the most prominent place in the midst of the monastery's ruins when the foundation stone for the reconstruction was laid. With the ceremony over he placed his left hand on the stone to support himself while getting up and left his little child finger prints on the stone as if it was Plasticine.

"These are just jokes", you could say. Yet it is evident that such a spiritual piece of art displays a consciousness which is much more evolved than in our Western spiritual masters. Without his capability to leave such relics Karmapa would surely not have known where Jamgon was reborn. In my book *Living Buddha* I describe the finger imprint scene in every detail. Modern physics determine that matter as such does not exist. There are "merely spaces in between", without any firm connection.

Somehow the seven-year-old Karmapa has already been able to put this recognition into practice. From Karmapa's former life several of his foot-prints are still preserved. Such examples show what an enormous change of outlook is necessary in mankind until we really live our spiritual-emotional identity.

You can only live what you can imagine, otherwise it does not exist as a possibility. Everything begins with the training of intuition. Basically you solely have to sharpen your perception to recognize in what a magic world we live: "Looking for a Sign" is no more searching then but a finding in all places, as if the whole universe would be at your service. The most magnificent thing in our universe it the fact that it is at the disposal of every individual – in a total way.

What man copies from nature or the universe is only a poor copy of what the universe itself is capable of doing in the form of nature. If e.g. Google can provide singular individual publicity for each of its approximately 5 billion users in seconds, it is no magic that the whole universe is at your disposal for your individual evolution in a comprehensive sense. All that happens around and with you is exclusively designed for you. If a bird chirps on your left or if a car with a meaningful license-plate is driving in front of you – all has been made just for you. In every minute of your life you are guided if you develop the attention for it.

What kind of leap of consciousness do you think Jamgon's parents experience now that they know who has chosen them to be reborn in flesh and blood? Your child is also a God who has selected you to come to this planet, so treat it as such. Otherwise you may feel shame if you happen to meet in your next life.

Grandpa says

How has grandpa experienced his grandchild?

Grandpa: *Lots of people who have seen our grandchild have said that he is something special, that we have to keep him pure.*

CK: *Have you not noticed something during the pregnancy of your daughter-in-law or when he was born ten months ago?*

G: *He is our first grandchild and we love him dearly but we do not have any comparison. We accepted him as he was. He was a very easy-going baby and well, we are not wondering about something that seems to be natural. If we had noticed something, it would have been disturbing behaviour, but there was none. I perceived everything in Jamgon as normal, he was calm, content and healthy.*

CK: *And now that you know that he is the reincarnation of Jamgon Kongtrul, how do you see him?*

G: *Just as before. We have not known Jamgon Kongtrul before. By birth we belong to the Gelupa, the order of the Dalai Lama. We have never heard of Jamgon before. His order, the Kagyü, is not represented in the whole area here.*

CK: *From now on he will surely be treated differently than before his discovery?*

G: *I hope not. I do hope he will continue to grow normally as before.*

CK: *This will certainly not be the case. Because of him your son will take his wife and his son to Lhasa.*

G: *This will only be temporarily.*

CK: *Yes, but later on they will surely leave Tibet.*

G: *It may take some time.*

CK: *Does it make you sad when you think that you will not see your grandchild anymore?*

G: *If it is his fate to live as Jamgon Kongtrul, then he will surely not live with us.*
CK: *Can you really accept that in such a sovereign manner?*
O (laughs): *There is nothing we can do, and this is OK.*
CK: *OK?*
O: *Please do not get me wrong. We love our grandchild. My wife has cared for him constantly, but we would never be in his way as far as his evolution is concerned.*

Grandma's wisdom

Later I had a very open conversation with the grandma who was a bit timid with the monks at first:

CK: *How come the monks looked for Jamgon in your house instantly and nowhere else in this area?*
Grandma: *We had heard that some monks were looking for a one-year-old child around here. And in this village there are only two children born in the year of the pig. When my niece saw the monks, she led them here straight away.*
CK: *Have you sent your niece to look out for the monks?*
G: *What do you mean we have sent her? The news that the monks were searching for a reincarnation was known to us for a few days.*
CK: *What did you think then?*
G: *What are we supposed to think? It must be some important person.*
CK: *Are there any differences of importance?*
G: *Sure.*
CK: *Which?*
G: *Well, it is evident. There are human beings who have already been humans for a long time, and there are other humans who have not been humans for a long time.*
CK: *What do you mean by for a long time?*

G: *For ages.*
CK: *I beg your pardon?*
G: *In years or in ages?*
CK: *A good question. How long have there been human beings on Earth?*
G: *Which kind?*
CK: *Our kind, you and I?*
G: *We have not been here for long.*
CK: *And your grandchild?*
G: *He is of a different kind.*
CK: *Please? How long has he been a human being?*
G: *Much longer than I.*
CK: *And I?*
G: *I do not know you.*
CK: *It does not matter. But I would like to know why you believe that your grandchild is of a different type.*
G: *Because the monks were looking for him. This does not happen so often.*
CK: *It never happens in my county.*
G: *Never ever?*
CK: *Not yet. Our people does not believe in reincarnation.*
G: *There are still people with a higher level of consciousness than others?!*
CK: *I have no clue.*
G: *Strange thing ...* (Grandma is silent for a while)
CK: *Maybe there are some ...*
G: *... do you see? There are indeed great differences.*
CK: *I heard you distinguish between 20 different levels of consciousness in your language.*
G: *What do you mean?*
CK: *Well, the various steps of recognition.*
G: *Yes, the monks have a different one than we have.*
CK: *And among the population?*

G: *Yes, and also among the prisoners.*
CK: *In prison?*
G: *And in the camps.*
CK: *How many are they?*
G: *Ohhh … it is very easy to get in there.*
CK: *Do you know anybody who is imprisoned?*
G: *Everybody knows someone who has disappeared in a camp.*
CK: *During the Nazi period millions of people have suffered the same fate.*
G: *Here this regime has ruled for more than 50 years now.*
CK: *Oh, I was very lucky then. I could switch the country at the right moment.*
G: *Did you have to flee?*
CK: *No, I died in the old free Tibet in 1937 and was born again in Germany after the Nazi regime in 1947.*
G: *You did fine. I ignore where Jamgon is going to fulfil his mission. Here in Tibet it seems to be impossible.*
CK: *He has got all prepared in Nepal before he died?*
G: *Yes, but how does he get there?*
CK: *How are things with his departure for Nepal?*
G: *The Chinese authorities do not say a word. We have already applied for leaving the country.*
CK: *How dangerous! Hundreds of thousands who wanted to escape are imprisoned now.*
G *Yes!*
CK: *Is it a question of consciousness or of the type of person you are if you finish in a camp or not?*
G: *Also lamas with very high consciousness are imprisoned.*
CK: *But then they were stupid to let such a thing happen to them.*
G: *You cannot say that. They have chosen this destiny.*
CK: *Why?*
G: *Well, you know Yondu?*
CK: *Yes, Yondu the healer?*

G: *Yes. He could leave the camp a couple of years ago. For 25 years he had been imprisoned in a cement cell of less than 3x3 feet together with Kinso Rinpoche. The cell was so tiny that only one could squat while the other had to stand. It was too small for the two of them to be able to squat.*

CK: *25 years?*

G: *25 years! When Rinpoche died they put Yondu in liberty as they thought that he would die anyway, so weak was he.*

CK: *No, he didn't die, he even came to Germany, to Dortmund.*

G: *Then you know how high his consciousness was.*

CK: *He said he had reached this consciousness owing to torture.*

G: *There you can see what kind of person he was.*

CK: *He made a great impression on me.*

G: *This is what I mean. He said that Kinso Rinpoche could teach him everything he needed to be a human being.*

CK: *In a healing seminar in Dortmund he revealed us what Rinpoche had taught him in the cell.*

G: *How many people participated there?*

CK: *150 participants I believe. Quite a lot in any case.*

G: *With Dalai Lama I heard that there are always thousands of people. With Karmapa too. I think with my grandson there will also be quite a lot.*

CK: *Surely, since he is Jamgon.*

G: *I said to my niece: Go and look if you see the monks.*

CK: *But you did not know who they were looking for?*

O: *No, but there are always rumours. It is enough that someone is looked for.*

CK: *I see, when monks search for someone, it is about a different kind of person?!*

G: *(laughs!!!)*

CK: *The 150 participants in Dortmund were surprised that Yondu laughed so much.*

G: *I see.*

CK: *They stood in a long queue in front of him. Several days passed until everybody had taken his turn.*
G: *What? They were standing in the queue without sleeping?*
CK: *Well, the participants of the seminar did sleep of course, but I think that Yondu did not sleep at all.*
G: *What did all these people want from him?*
CK: *They looked for healing.*
G: *The same as with Karmapa.*
CK: *Yes, people always look for highly developed beings who can help them.*
G: *This is the sort of people I am talking of.*
CK: *Yondu did that by a diagnosis.*
G: *A good diagnosis is half the healing. At least you know what is wrong with you.*
CK: *I think we have two different ways to look at a diagnosis.*
G: *Do you think on a different level than me when you hear diagnosis?*
CK: *Yes.*
G: *If you could talk in Tibetan, it would be clear on which level each of us is talking.*
CK: *I think of the causes of illness.*
G: *… and I ask what the symptom is.*
CK: *Every symptom may be explained on different levels depending on the human image you believe in. We strongly distinguish between science and religion.*
G: *But it is the same thing.*
CK: *Yes, you are right. Perhaps science is also a religion, maybe the biggest we have on earth right now.*
G: *Do you think so?*
CK: *Yes.*
G: *What kind of diagnosis gave Rinpoche?*
CK: *… Rinpoche?*
G: *Yondu! Thanks to Kinso Rinpoche he became a Rinpoche himself.*

CK: *How does one become a Rinpoche?*
G: *This is a title for persons with a highly developed consciousness.*
CK: *How do you get it?*
G: *By dying consciously. Those who once went through death and birth belong to a different kind of people.*
CK: *And those are called Rinpoche?*
G: *Yes. Yondu Rinpoche was one of them. What kind of diagnosis did he apply?*
CK: *In Europe diagnoses are normally made by medical devices and lab results.*
G: *Our Tibetan doctors make pulse diagnoses.*
CK: *Yondu had a very particular method of diagnosis.*
G: *What did he do?*
CK: *I believe in Tibetan it is called "Chenrezi".*
G: *This is the name of the aspect of compassion.*
CK: *Of Jamgon it is said that he is an aspect of wisdom.*
G: *This aspect is named "Manjushri" in Tibetan.*
CK: *Ah yes.*
G: *Why was it the Chenrezi aspect with Yondu?*
CK: *You will not believe it possible.*
G: *I may also believe it not to be possible that Jamgon gives his life to help his master Karmapa to obtain a safe reincarnation.*
CK: *Yes, this is incredible …*
G: *What did Yondu do?*
CK: *Everyone who wanted to receive a diagnosis had to bring some urine and faeces.*
G: *This was the only thing he and Kinso Rinpoche had in the 25 years of their imprisonment.*
CK: *Correct! Yondu said he had learnt everything for a complete diagnosis from Rinpoche. He took a little spoonful of their faeces in his mouth, felt it with his tongue and his palate and swallowed it. Then he did the same with the urine. After that he could tell every participant what his illness was.*

G: *What did he tell them?*
CK: *Mum or dad or girl-friend or boy-friend, child or husband, son or wife. Thanks to these excreta he could taste practically all the problems in relationship which exist in life. Sometimes he also mentioned karmic causes from a former life. But I think he only told it to the persons who could deal with that.*
G: *As long as the unconscious ostracise the conscious persons, there will always be problems with relationships. In extreme situations people are even capable of killing for it. This problem is present in the eternal quarrels which exist everywhere. The quarrels in the families contaminate the children. And even when quarrels are settled by third persons it often happens that the persons with the lower consciousness stand their ground against the ones with a higher consciousness.*
CK: *… because those with the higher consciousness have reached the higher level owing to their compassion?*
G: *Yes. Whether a person has brought along compassion or not already shows at the time of birth and during their first two years of life. It can already be seen then how marked the compassion is in a person.*
CK: *With Yondu it was complete surrender. With all these many people in the yard in Dortmund he was never disgusted for one second by their urine and faeces. He used them for a truly compassionate diagnosis, thus helping everybody to expand his consciousness.*
G: *My parents often talked of such Rinpoches with an immense compassion. But lots of them were arrested or killed and most of them have fled. There are still very few who dare to incarnate here again.*
CK: *This is what I admire in Karmapa, and now in Jamgon too.*
G: *I wonder if both can stay here in Tibet. I do not reckon so. Despite their high degree of consciousness they would not stay in liberty here in Tibet.*
CK: *But in exile they are not free either. With a refugee pass you do not get far in the West. And neither in India.*

G: *I know. But where would they go? There is only India for us.*
CK: *I hope that the level of consciousness rises generally all over the world.*
G: *Why should that take place?*
CK: *Because misery is getting greater.*
G: *I do not think so. The fear of death eats up the soul.*
CK: *I hope so anyway. I think that the evolution of consciousness will get cosmic wind from the back.*
G: *May this not just be an illusion.*
CK: *Well I can feel it, it can be observed anywhere: the degree of consciousness on earth is rising.*
G: *Humour is the most important thing for the expansion of consciousness.*
CK: *If you can laugh dying and come back to earth with a smile then it shows a high degree of consciousness.*
G: *Without humour you will never cross bardo in a good shape. Without humour you lose when it comes to dying. You even lose your consciousness with the slightest accidents since you lack humour. The real question is if you can even laugh at the very end, at death.*
CK: (laughs)
G: (laughs)
CK: *The German TV has taken my little film about laughing off the program pretending that the TV has a mission to promote culture and not do therapy. I took it as a compliment.*
G: *Laughing therapy via TV can only be welcomed.*
CK: *Our comic Karl Valentin had a prominent space in my film. I was right to judge him as a people's therapist. The film was not shown until today.*
G: *When you can laugh about death you cannot be blackmailed anymore.*
CK: *In the West everybody can be blackmailed because they all fear for their existence.*
G: *We in Tibet have to learn not to be blackmailed even by torture.*

CK: *How can you manage to do that?*
G: *In 25 years of torture Yondu has not even complained about it with his torturers.*
CK: *This is the kind of person who has already passed through death consciously once, otherwise he surely could not do such a thing?!*
G: *I am positive that he has done this before.*
CK: *Then he knows that he is immortal? When they torture him, he is not identified with his body?*
G: *The way he has borne his fate in this life so far, he must have borne it in his last incarnation too, otherwise he would not have been able to do such a thing.*
CK: *Was he already a monk in his former life?*
G: *Not only. He also had a family*
CK: *I was also a monk in several former lives but this time I have given space to women in my life, after all a woman gave birth to me.*
G: *Did you miss women when you were a monk?*
CK: *Not much. I quickly got used to the fact that I do not have sex anymore.*
G: *None at all?*
CK: *No.*
G: *Would you like to live a monk's life again?*
CK: *No. I can hardly understand any longer why some people want to aspire to a spiritual life without the other sex.*
G: *… very simple: because it is easier.*
CK: *But the price they pay!*
G: *Better than no spiritual life at all.*
CK: *You are right. But nowadays in the third millennium, on the eve of the Sattva era you do not have to pay this price any longer.*
G: *… and are you happy?*
CK: *… I was not happy as a monk either.*
G: *Where were you happier?*
CK: *Difficult question.*
G: *Mmmmmh???*

CK: *What shall I say? What is happiness?*
G: *Happiness is a lot. Indeed it is everything.*
CK: *True.*
G: *Where did you have more illnesses? As a monk? Or in your family?*
CK: *Definitely there are more problems of relationship thanks to sexual connections and these often cause more illnesses. As a monk you avoid these problems.*
G: *I reckon this is why the monks choose celibacy, is it not?*
CK: *Surely. But then you leave aside half your life.*
G: *… but then you can evolve spiritually.*
CK: *If the evolution of consciousness is merely possible without women, you may practically do without it. The purely male societies avoid living a real life.*
G: *You are right.*
CK: *Then let us stop talking because we could continue like this for hours.*
G: *Good-bye.*
CK: *Good-bye.*

19
Crossing the green border to India

One year passes very fast since the discovery of Jamgon Kongtrul. Phuntsok and Sonam stay in Lhasa for the whole year living with Jamgon and his parents to prepare Jamgon for the separation from his parents which will take place when Jamgon continues his life where he has prepared it in his last life: in Pullahari/ Nepal. As long as the Chinese authorities have not issued an emigration permit yet, the joy in Pullahari about Jamgon's reincarnation is dimmed.

Karmapa sends his abbot to the Chinese at a higher level especially but they decide to remain silent. The parents quickly learn to evaluate the political background and prepare everything to stay away for a longer time.

Shortly before Jamgon turns two, all participants choose to cross the border illegally. Before they say good-bye to their homeland, they take the compulsory picture in front of the *Potala*, the former residence of the Dalai Lama. Then the parents take Rinpoche on their back and march with him to India by crossing the Himalayans. It is doubtful they will ever return.

Topga waits for a sign

I ask Topga: *Is it not funny: you will meet with someone who is your brother on one hand, but on the other hand he is no relative of yours?*
T (laughs): *This is exactly what makes it so hard for me to put these two things together. It is difficult to describe this feeling that you want to feel him to be your brother on one hand, but on the other hand your intellect tells you that this is impossible, and how can you believe in such a thing?*

All time long I hope that when his reincarnation is here I will get a sign and I will have the same feeling I had with my brother.

I always have this hope and this is what I wish for. I also wish that this new incarnation will behave as he did in his former life and tells me straight away: "Look, I have come back, do you have a problem with it? Don't you recognize me?" – Something like that. This would be marvellous.

CK: *This would really be the best. But if it does not happen like that?*

T: *I always imagine that this is a matter of belief. But with me this does not work either. I have to feel. I simply cannot pretend that I believe it because I am supposed to. I would be cheating myself.*

CK: *Yet you were educated in the belief in reincarnation.*

T: *Correct but not in a monastery. Due to the fact that Jamgon was the older one who would normally have taken over the responsibility as a breadwinner, I had to submit to this role model in our family. This was very hard for me. I knew that I had an older brother but I never had real contact with him. He was in a world that was mystical to me. I was not even raised in a religious way as he was. We maybe saw each other in the holidays for a couple of days. But as I am seven years younger than him, we had little in common. This is why I had always wished for us to take a holiday together. And in the moment he asked me to do that and we would have gone to visit our dear mother, I said no to him. I will surely be regretting this for a long time still.*

CK: *But now you will surely see him again soon?*

T: *I want to have him back as he was, as my brother.*

CK: *Mmmh?*

T: *Yes I know, this is impossible. If he were back now, he would be five years older and not the same person I have in my mind. I could cry for hours when I think what a great gift this would have been to spend a week or even 3 days with him in Kalimpong before his death. Simply ... tragic.*

CK: *... and you believe that his reincarnation cannot console you there?*

T: *I am excited about the moment I will see him. I cannot really imagine meeting him.*

After fleeing across the Himalayans the little Jamgon first visits the Dalai Lama in Dharamsala, as all Tibetan refugees do. These are the large Tibetan refugee camps. In 1998 the Dalai Lama is still the leader of all Tibetans and without his certificate the reincarnation would not be legal. No matter if someone has got a sign or not, no matter who says or writes that someone is this or that person. Without the certificate of the Tibetan exile government you do not inherit anything.

This is always the most delicate moment in a Tibetan reincarnation as the high lamas whose former life is identified all know each other from before. Therefore it is doubly important to receive the reincarnation certificate to be able to officially continue your friendships from the former life and move in your old circle of connections. This makes everything easier and you can reconnect with the same trusted persons. This is no arbitrary act. This is a feeling, a perception. If you do not have this perception, you cannot have a say in these matters.

CK: *Who has a say when a certificate for reincarnation is issued? Does the Dalai Lama decide on his own?*
Topga: *Government officials have a say.*
CK: *How many are there?*
T: *I do not know.*
CK: *100 or 10?*
T: *Not 100 – never. The exile government is a small group, very small. In comparison with it the prime minister has a much bigger apparatus. I imagine there may be 8 to 12 persons.*
CK: *Will they take into account any dreams when issuing the certificate?*
T: *Very much!*
CK: *In order to obtain the certificate you depend on the dreams of the officials?*
T: *Yes. In any case they have to agree with each other.*

CK: *Does the Dalai Lama have the final say?*
T: *Everyone has a say.*
CK: *But they have to reach an agreement?*
T: *On this level one takes what is in concordance.*
CK: *Do you also believe it then?*
T (laughs): *It would not be bad to believe it.*
CK: *Would you accept such a thing as a sign or an indication?*
T: *If I had such a dream?*
CK: *Yes?*
T: *I will tell you later.*
CK: *Have you seen the video when Jamgon was visiting His Holiness the Dalai Lama?*
T: *Yes.*
CK: *Was there any sign that Jamgon is Jamgon?*
T: *I considered it strange or exciting that when the 4th Jamgon was sitting in the waiting room he held his hands in the same particular way as on the photos in his former life when he was this age. Do you know this photo?*
CK: *Yes, in the film I also show the moment when the 4th Jamgon is waiting to be admitted.*
T: *But it is not a real sign either.*
CK: *So you prefer the certificate by the Dalai Lama?*
T (laughs again): *The certificate, haha, I apologise for laughing.*
CK: *I see, it does not take away your pain.*
T: *No. I wonder what happens when I meet him.*
CK: *Could Jamgon go back to Tibet if he wanted to?*
T (shakes his head in denial)
CK: *What has the Dalai Lama said?*
T: *He was laughing about Jamgon's big ears.*
CK: *He always laughs so heartily.*
T: *I have never met the Dalai Lama in person, I merely know him by TV, but there he often laughs like that too.*
CK: *This is a unique laughter. It is a kind of trademark.*

T: *He laughs as only he knows how to laugh.*
CK: *Would this not be a sign when someone has already laughed like that in their former life?*
T: *Yes, I would take it as a sign too.*
CK: *The Dalai Lama himself does not rely on one sign only. He includes all his and his secretaries' research and dream.*
T: *This is something I have no access to. I do not get such information. I do not know where they take the certainty from to say: Yes or no. I would like to have this certainty though. I am still waiting for it.*
CK: *I reckon you should not wait for it. It is a decision if you really want to believe in reincarnation.*
T: *To generally believe in reincarnation is no big deal. But in your own family circle? It gives me great trouble.*
CK: *... because you would not get back your brother in the form you have known him.*
T: *This is what makes me so sad. Add to it the fact that I was responsible for his death. If I had not given him the BMW as a gift, he would still be alive now.*
CK: *He is alive again!*
T: *Oh ...*
CK: *Since you do not want to accept that, you go on mourning and torturing yourself with feelings of guilt.*
T: *I cannot believe so easily, I need proof or at least a sign.*
CK: *Perhaps you will get them when you meet Jamgon.*
T: *I do hope so.*
CK: *Did you know that the materialists believe that one's being determines one's consciousness? They look for proof because they think that would change their feelings.*
T: *Yes, when the incarnation tells me: "I am your brother", I will believe it then.*
CK: *And then you will not be sad anymore?*
T: *No, I would think that this is unbelievable.*
CK: *Would you believe it then?*

T: *Yes, if it happened so obviously.*
CK: *Do you see what your happiness depends on?*
T: *On a proof.*
CK: *What kind of proof is this? In the end it is about what you believe. Another person would not give anything for this proof, for a child saying: "I am your brother." They would only consider this a nice affirmation without any biological background and therefore it does not have any value as a proof.*
T: *Yes, sure.*
CK: *So it is still the question of what you want to believe. And the materialists believe that their consciousness is conditioned by the circumstances in which they live. And only if these circumstances change, their consciousness can be transformed – they believe.*
T: *This is pure Marxism.*
CK: *This is what all materialists think, no matter if they are employed or the boss, there is no class difference. Do you also believe this?*
T: *Not completely. But you are right. E.g. biology is something I take for the truth.*
CK: *Biologically Jamgon the 4th cannot be Jamgon the 3rd.*
T: *But he is not that anyway.*
CK: *Biology is only the carrier of a certain character or a certain personality and Jamgon has changed this carrier.*
T: *We turn around in a circle. I know what you are getting at.*
CK: *I want to say that it is the other way round: one's consciousness determines one's being. Because to your being also belong your feelings and your feelings determine whether you are happy or unhappy.*
T: *Yes, sure.*
CK: *Your feelings are not "determined" by your being though.*
T: *By what else then?*
CK: *By how you interpret your being. You may perceive one and the same situation as pleasant or unpleasant. It only depends on how you evaluate it. If you evaluate it biologically, the same situation feels*

completely different as if you evaluate it emotionally by your feelings.
T: *The way I look at or interpret something is determined by being.*
CK: *No, it depends on what you believe. Your belief is a matter of consciousness, and not of being.*
T: *OK. And now? I always thought that the consciousness or the thinking dies with the body.*
CK: *Now we are back to the start: why should it die? It does not consist of physical elements. I have never seen a spirit die. How should this be possible? The human beings would long have invented a ritual for it. Yet there is none in which the death of thought or of mind is celebrated.*
T: *You say: what cannot die, cannot have been born?*
CK: *Naturally not. Jamgon the 4th comes into this world with the spirit of Jamgon the 3rd. However he has to grow into it physically yet. Therefore it is counterproductive to speak of rebirth. Strictly speaking what is supposed to be reborn? Not the body in any case. It has already become a victim of the worms, the flames or the vultures. This makes it 100% sure that this body will never exist again. And the soul (spirit) cannot be reborn either since it has never died anyway. What does not die, cannot be reborn. So strictly speaking the term of rebirth is confusing and wrong, whereas reincarnation is correct.*
T: *I will wait for the reincarnation then and try to recognize the spirit of my brother in it.*
CK: *I too.*
T: *But I need a sign.*
CK: *Who doesn't?*

20
Jamgon the 4th on his way to Pullahari

After the 4th Jamgon obtained the certificate confirming that he is the authentic reincarnation of the 3rd Jamgon, the Dalai Lama executes the hair-cutting ceremony with him, just as he did with Karmapa at the time. With this ceremony Jamgon has taken refuge with the Dalai Lama and has been made a member of the latter's community.

From all over the world the adepts of his former life come to see him, although not as many as for his death ceremony since they part from the idea that it is possible to meet him at another moment in his new life, without any time limit. Tenzin however makes an effort not to diffuse the news of Jamgon's reincarnation as he does not want to snub the Chinese especially as they have Jamgon's parents in their hands. Yet after the return of Jamgon Kongtrul in his new body something very spectacular takes place:

After Jamgon has visited the Dalai Lama on the Western side of the Indian Himalayans, he travels to the far Eastern side to Kalimpong to see his former mother Pema. What will happen when Jamgon in his new form passes the site of the accident?

Various times the young boy drives on the highway between Siliguri and Kalimpong passing the tree which terminated his former life. But his escort does not mention this or even stop there. For most of them it remains a tragic accident. They do not connect it with safeguarding Karmapa's reincarnation. For them death is still the most horrible thing which should have been avoided.

This is the materialistic interpretation of death generating the corresponding feeling of *grief*. Yet if I interpret Jamgon's death as a heroic deed, I could stop at the tree and – instead of mourning – I could remember this feat with flowers and kataks.

Independent from the fact of how to interpret Jamgon's death, he is received with great honours wherever he acted in his former life. In Kalimpong there is a rest home and an eye clinic which he had initiated and constructed as Jamgon the 3rd. The surprising thing happening at each welcoming ceremony is that every time, a rainbow appears above the reception committee as if it was his logo. On his second birthday there was even a gigantic double rainbow which spanned above him and looked as if it sprang straight from his head.

Rosy Findeisen recounts: *During the festivities for his birthday he stood on a hill with Tsültrim and a gigantic rainbow showed above him, it was simply marvellous. On one hand Jamgon Rinpoche was a small child and I was even allowed to feed him now and then. Then he sat on a high stool and I could feed him his soup. He was so hearty and gave me real hugs. On the other hand he could sit very straight when people came to beg his blessing, look at them seriously and bless them. When you looked into his face then, sometimes a fully grown-up man looked back.*

This is something that no words can transmit even if they are well chosen. The movie shows that Jamgon is a very extraordinary child. He has manners which the monks who educate him cannot have taught him: without any bib he eats complicated meals using knife and fork without spilling any food. He sleeps like a mummy on his back without moving a finger. He plays like a boisterous, cheeky little boy. He cares for the welfare of others like a compassionate mother. He guides the ceremonies with the seriousness and tenacity of an old abbot.

The whole passage from North East India to the valley of Kathmandu in Nepal is 500 miles. On the first half, there are many social projects Jamgon the 3rd could finance with his incoming donations and for which he evidently had chosen the right managers. Otherwise these projects would not have survived and even flourished in the four years since his death. Every person working on such a project had the great hope to meet Jamgon the 4th even if he is only two years of age.

This continuity of life documented by him also reinforces the faith in the continuity of their own life. And suddenly the difficulties inherent in every project and life lose their importance. Of course the different project members felt motivated to collaborate with the common task as long as Jamgon the 3rd was standing behind them and helped them actively when necessary. And certainly some projects threatened to break down with Jamgon's sudden and dramatic death. But the faith in his reincarnation generated a strong motivation to continue. To be sure there was no guarantee for his coming back and nobody could have predicted when, where and how – but now he is back.

This is an event of such emotional magnitude wherever the little boy shows up and is carried to the place of the happening by his motherly monks, so much so that many people start crying without there being any external reason. On one hand there is the joy about the continuity of life and on the other hand the liberation of nagging doubts even the most faithful Buddhists are prone to feel although they have been raised in this belief. As a reward or confirmation every one of these meetings is crowned by a rainbow.

Of course nowadays such events are documented by video cameras and even mobile phones lately. In India his arrival is also published in newspapers and this means that his tour from Sikkim to Kathmandu becomes a genuine triumphant march with several thousands of people lining the roads. Often the rainbow appears in the moment when Tenzin and his company show up at the place of celebration and Tenzin displays the little boy to the cheering crowd by lifting him up out of the open car. Naturally his fans cheer ever more when the rainbow appears in the sky – as if on command. Such a thing is moving even for the sceptical journalists to write about this event in their newspapers.

Little Jamgon does not have to say anything at all. It is terrific enough that he may carry out such a tour without becoming weary and at the same time he receives hundreds of wishes of blessings in the form of Kataks and countless gifts.

All these news travel like a straw fire and precede the arrival of the two-year-old at the next station so that the receiving crowd there has already heard and read all the stories. In some places there is even TV coverage – something that Tenzin to his great annoyance cannot avoid. He just prays that there will be no inconveniences for Jamgon's biological parents in Tibet.

> Topga: *You might want to see the rainbows as a sign. Yet you could just avoid looking at them, such as the people who simply ignore them. In Lava there was a giant rainbow, just as in eight other places of his former acting. Everybody was so impressed. Now people expect a rainbow at the end of his trip, when he arrives at his new residence. If he arrives here and there is no rainbow, it will be a disaster – do you understand?*

Jamgon and his crew cover the last 250 miles of the journey by taking a flight inside Nepal. When landing at Kathmandu airport, they are greeted by a large reception committee. On one hand many lamas of high standing, Rinpoches and monks of the order who live in Nepal or have come especially for this purpose have gathered there. On the other hand there is a group of laymen and several fans who somehow were closely linked to the 3rd Jamgon. Among them is Topga. Then there is a third group of honoraries, politicians and journalists who also want to show appreciation. They want to express that they adore a person who lives this continuity of life which they all surely have dealt with in their life before theoretically and which they all have come across in their religious teachings. However it is a great surprise to everyone that such a thing is indeed happening. Standing there with their white silk scarves and welcoming gifts all of them wait for the plane carrying the "Holy Freight". For the lamas he is their master who shows them bodily what a developed consciousness is able to do. Their faces mirror respect, awe, joy and great curiosity.

For Topga he is his brother. Wearing large, dark glasses he is standing in the second row carrying his Katak and a bunch of dark yellow roses, hardly able to conceal his feelings torn between joy and fear. He does not want to act as if he was happy about something he does not believe in. In his heart he is not able to share the euphoria of the surrounding crowd. Still he has come anyway. And he will be the one who drives Jamgon up to Pullahari. Maybe something will happen to make him feel that this is the person he has lost in such a gruesome way.

The plane is landing. At the end of the runway it turns around and taxies slowly towards the waiting crowd. When the cabin door opens, a small gangway is deployed. The first person to exit from this two-motor propeller plane with some 30 seats is one of the honourable old teachers of the 3rd Jamgon. Then Tsultrim, and now comes Tenzin with Jamgon on his arm. He just stops on the highest step of the small stairs. A cheering cry from the crowd as if a president had emerged from the plane. The whole crowd of welcoming guests is hurrying towards the gangway. The security guards obviously have no more say.

Then Tenzin with Jamgon on his arm is in the midst of the crowd and every guest endeavours to put a Katak round the boy's neck. Therefore Tsultrim is assisting him and gives back the Katak to the well-wishers while they are bowing in front of Jamgon and he touches their head in blessing with his little hand. Jamgon seems to have foreseen this scene. He remains completely cool with an adult and serene expression on his face – something absolutely extraordinary for a child who just turned two.

With this stoic but also compassionate attitude he has already mastered all his former receptions during the last ten days. Sometimes several ones a day. This fact alone made the human image of many onlookers falter. Where has the boy got this from? Surely not from his parents who are just simple farmers.

Meanwhile even Topga has worked his way to the front and is able to hand over the roses with the Katak to Jamgon. He salutes him according to the Tibetan habit forehead to forehead but forgets to take off his sun glasses. This first encounter with his brother did not move him, no deep feelings stirred in his heart.

Among brothers – in the car again

After most people have greeted Jamgon in this mix-up, Tsultrim carries him to Topga's car driven by Topga himself. Tsultrim takes his seat next to the driver with Jamgon on his lap. Jamgon obviously has not developed any dislike to cars since his last life. On the contrary: he is watching with great interest how Topga starts the engine and drives out of the airport. Behind them there is a long queue of cars forming which follow them blowing the horn just as after a marriage. Jamgon is almost sitting on the dashboard and observing the ride with utter attention. He does not show any signs of fatigue or being overwrought. All Kathmandu newspapers honour the arrival of the successful reincarnation of Jamgon Kongtrul Rinpoche in their headlines.

Spontaneously many motor bikes and other vehicles join the convoy on its ride through the outskirts of Kathmandu. They drive in the direction of Pullahari on the North slope of the great Kathmandu valley at about 10 miles east of town.

At the foot of the hill in Pullahari there is a school founded by the 3rd Jamgon in his former life with the donations of his adepts. The 4th Jamgon cannot pass by without honouring his welcome reception. The whole school is financed by the worldwide donations. This has worked like that for many years. All boys and girls have put on their smart light and dark blue uniforms singing songs of praise to Jamgon and the director makes a short speech of gratitude.

Now there should appear this rainbow on the very blue sky. Topga does not stop looking to the sky. And indeed there is a small cloud showing up suddenly, shimmering lightly in the colours of the rainbow. The cameras are picked up all over the place and people are clicking away. It is unbelievable how such a thing can happen wherever the little boy appears without him taking any notice of it in the least. Even his company have stopped wondering about this phenomenon and admiring it.

But now they definitely drive up to Pullahari. After four years of waiting, the very thing happens that everybody has hoped for but nobody has been sure if it would really happen. Already on the 200 yard long driveway the monks gather in their magnificent red and yellow clothes and the 6 foot high monstrances on both sides of the narrow path which the convoy drives along to the monastery. On the side of the road bowlfuls of herbs and spices are burned so that there is a holy smell reigning about the great and spectacular welcome ritual. – Finally the drive has come to an end and Tenzin carries Jamgon to the temple with the golden Kudung stupa mounting the stairs in a swaying crowd.

As a materialist you may ask: Why does this event take place in such a conspicuous glory? It is only a small boy who is moving to this place. Before him about 150 small boys have moved here to live, learn and get used to a monk's life here starting at their fifth birthday – a life that will enable them a far-reaching spiritual evolution of consciousness. With none of these 150 little boys there has been a welcome ceremony of such magnitude. What is this about?

Very simple: *Jamgon has overcome death.* The greatest thing achieved by men. And this is honoured and feasted in this special way. Jamgon has superiorly mastered both the entry as well as the exit of life thanks to his selfless wishes. He shows us: with the consciousness for the continuity of life death and birth are one. This is taking away the fear and horror of death and gives it a sense. Those who do not identify with their body but with their spirit, can even carry out his projects across many lives.

Many lives to become a master

With the perspective of a singular life this is much more difficult to achieve since you act a lot more unconsciously and therefore less efficiently. In order to achieve mastership in one thing, one life is much too short. Of course this is unconsciously shown even in people who indeed have reached mastership – such as in Mozart, Bach, Beethoven, Yehudi Menuhin and many more great masters in music. In their biographies it becomes clear that they already brought their capacities with them. Already at an early age, even before someone taught them anything, it became manifest what kind of talent they had.

No matter if we talk about extraordinary faculties in the area of art, science and technology, or even in the simple aspects of daily life: we only understand completely where the talents of these people come from – taking into account all family influences – when we look at the reincarnation concept.

For such mastership three lives or so are not sufficient, often one million years of development are needed for it. And even this was not a beginning. It is difficult to imagine something without it. And there is no end either: we go on incarnating and incarnating and incarnating ... How long am I supposed to repeat this term which stands for life itself without seeming it to be a repetition for only one second? Every idea of standstill is absolutely alien to our galaxy and the whole infinite universe.

Even mathematically speaking a repetition is not possible. The deepest view on the universe is the mathematical one, in a nutshell these are the prime numbers. Everything is on a continuous, infinite ray.[32] One million years are nothing, not even from a perspective of a mayfly because time is relative, it is a construct – or let us call it an artificial structure – which we lay on our earthly existence. Yet life as a whole is without beginning or end, it is something immortal, something spiritual in different forms.

When we try to understand our evolution as infinite, without beginning, we gradually approach the present state. For us as physical beings this is even more difficult to accept than the thought of reincarnation. Infinity is infinitely hard to feel because then the notion of

---

32 See *Global Scaling* in chapter 5 "The cosmos vibrates".

truth dissolves by itself. Truth actually yearns for a beginning and an end, thus accepting death. Basically it is a paradox: what man fears most, he virtually creates with his artificial materialism – death.

Have a look at the way some people torture themselves with death in, let's say, conventional care stations in residence homes. The torture is generated by their way of thinking. The less clear and the more complicated it is, the more torture these people feel and are often calmed down with drugs. Have you seen this painful dying? Have you smelled it? Could you make a joyful song of it or are you just perceiving disgust? When death is so horrible, then life itself must have been so too. – Certainly there is an exception as far as some palliative stations and above all hospices are concerned which thanks to their integrative attention and care support people in finding a peaceful and dignified transition.

In order not to finish your life in torture, change your consciousness from body with soul to *soul with body*. This is all you need to die happily. The body is a tool of spirit. The other way round the relationship does not make sense. It would be fatal to switch forward and back from one outlook on life to the other. This would only lead to a confusion in your mind and would not help you to get an easy exit. You only die well if you do not die at all. This is an attitude which gives you joy and good feelings.

Let us always be aware of the fact that: death is purely about adapting one's new form (one's future conditions of life) to one's evolved consciousness in your present life. It is rather unlikely that you will gain a new consciousness when you are in bardo (the period without form). You then lack your tool to make experiences. In order to develop your consciousness however you require these experiences – and they are only possible with a body because with it you get the experience of three-dimensionality which means that all phenomena happen in polarity: love and hatred, hot and cold, soft and hard, yin and yang etc. Solely on the basis of this polarity are you expected to continually make decisions which are the prerequisite for an evolving consciousness.

Most people will have to face in bardo the very things their consciousness was dominated by until the moment they left their body. If e.g. you have been a materialist before your death, there will be nothing new happening without form since your consciousness considers the spiritual and continuous existence as nonsense anyway. What you cannot or refuse to think, does not exist. Therefore the materialist will continue to have the same consciousness at death and at the next birth.

Look under which circumstances you have entered life this time. This shows with what consciousness you have left life the last time. If you want to enter life under different and maybe better circumstances next time, then work on your consciousness and the way you want to leave life this time. If you manage to modify your human image towards an emotional-spiritual one before death, then completely new areas will open up. It is even possible that this may happen today, perhaps even with this very book.[33]

With this change you provide a possibility not only to select the best possible parents for your next start in life, but really the *best* parents. A whole lot of things depend on your parents, as you might have already seen so far. Your parents represent a certain social environment conditioning your future life. It is rare that people make great leaps from this environment, such as Jamgon did: from a nomad boy to a world teacher. Such leaps are an absolute exception, the same goes for the leap from a dishwasher to a millionaire at the materialistic level. To be sure, these evolutions exist but they are rather uncommon. And if they happen, they are due to karma. If you want to start today with the projection of your new life, you cannot do anything wrong, even if you may still change things a few times. And as I said: be aware that most souls at least select one parent they already know, accepting

---

[33] Or with the movie or in a seminar or with support by phone. There are countless possibilities to develop your consciousness.

the other parent along the way because it is not possible to have only your dad without your mom to materialize.

Yet very few souls have a consciousness like Jamgon who this time has picked completely strangers as parents in order to fulfil his life's mission which remained the same through several lives: to serve Karmapa. Thus he endeavours to be as close to him as possible and so he came to Khyung Tsum. Now two years later he has already managed to do both things. He has re-established the physical contact with Karmapa and in this very moment is coming back to the place he prepared in his former life. To this belongs the symbolic act where Jamgon himself deploys the flag of his *Kagyü* order. In the film you can see that he is blessed by rose-petals falling down from the hoisted flag.

Now at the latest there should be another rainbow showing in the sky. And indeed: everybody turn their heads watching the phenomenon they cannot explain through their intellect. And yes, there is a rainbow! It seems incredible how quickly people ask to get such a gift, only because it has been given a few times before. And that they would be disappointed if they did not get it this time, although they cannot put any claim on it. With whom would they anyway? For the normal human consciousness it is simply a wonder that can merely be confronted with humility.

Topga: *All are looking up to see the rainbow. Me too. It was not a real rainbow, more like a block. Not a normal bow. Very extraordinary.*
CK: *Is this not also a sign for you?*
T: *The foreign students already call Jamgon the rainbow-Rinpoche. This pet name will actually stick. Wherever he goes, there will be a rainbow showing. This is why he is the rainbow-Rinpoche.*
CK: *… and what is he to you?*
T: *Yes, one could understand it as a sign. Those who take it for a sign, just take it for that. But I want my brother.*

21
Finishing the circle of life

Then there is the moment when the circle of life finishes. In the temple Tenzin together with the small 4th Jamgon approaches the Stupa in which his mummified former body is sitting. For identification there is only a tiny passport photo of the 3rd Jamgon standing on the base of the Stupa on which Jamgon is now looking with his new two-year-old form without moving. As a gesture of greeting he is throwing – as best he can – a white silk Katak to his former body. This was it. One may say: death is nothing. Life goes on. Notwithstanding his tender age Jamgon has to immediately start fulfilling great representative tasks. Obviously he has no problems doing so. You can only attain mastership if you have carried out your tasks in several lives.

Rosy Findeisen: *He sat for hours in those pujas without batting an eye. It was totally incomprehensible to me. My three-year-old grand-daughter Karly would not have lasted fifteen minutes. Yes! Incredible! He could even manage to work the bell and the dorje* (energetic ritual object with double sceptre) *and actually knew the puja texts. Well, it was really impressive.*

With this child we literally wonder how he is able to do this. From the first day his behaviour is so delicate on the whole; he never makes crude gestures, cries or shouts. Not even when he goes to sleep. There is no excitement in a disturbing sense. Jamgon goes to bed or goes in the garden. It has the same vibration. How many parents complain about difficulties bringing their children to bed and making them sleep. Nothing whatsoever in Jamgon's case.

Many children cannot imagine going to bed without any excitement like jumping around or complaining and later as adults without a who-dunnit, alcohol or sex. With Jamgon there is always joy, no matter if he *goes in the garden* or if he *goes to bed*. No excitement does not mean that you make something last longer. Just imagine you would make going-in-the-garden last longer than going-to-bed. It would just irritate you.

So why should going-in-the-garden cause you problems? It is good weather, so you go in the garden. The bed is ready and you go to sleep. So what?

Garden and bed have very different emotions that can be examined. In the garden you are awake and carefree. In bed you go to your unconscious. In bed the children expect attention, a good-night story, a prayer, a hug, and even that the parents go to sleep with them. If there is no loving attention, then going-to-bed is an uncomfortable act the child wants to make last as long as possible. If you notice that your child does not like to go to bed as much and as normally as it goes in the garden, you should ask yourself what is not correct with your kind of loving care. In the crassest case the topic of abuse may arise.

One of the results of the interim report of the Independent Commission for Studying Sexual Abuse in Children from June 2017 is that in every school class probably one or two children are involved in it. The testimonies show that about 70 % of the abuse cases are committed directly in the family or in the near social surroundings. What is happening with our children? And it is happening in such dimensions that they are termed "enormous social phenomenon of violence". This is why in Germany "a lot more things have to be done in the future than which are done now" to make the protection of children against sexual violence more efficient. It would require a stronger education, prevention and sensitization including the dangers of digital media.[34]

---

34 Study from May 2016 till June 2017 commissioned by the Federal Republic of Germany: "Independent representative for questions of sexual abuse in children". Member of the commission among others Dr. Christine Bergmann (former German Family Minister).

Children are a mirror of our society. Especially in the Western societies violence and brutalization already begins with the ambitious social requirements, the speed and the pressure to perform we as adults often place higher and higher demands without even noticing. The consequences for children are multiple stresses that manifest in lacking concentration, calm and mindfulness.

In Tibetan monasteries however I have experienced a hoard of happy little monks between six and twelve years coming into the *Gompa* (prayer room). Without running or jostling they come in and sit on their cushion cross-legged and completely quiet – often for hours on end. If in contrast I have a look at a Western kindergarten or primary school, the difference is vast. Why is this?

It is not a question of physical condition. The Tibetan children do not do more sports than Western children, rather the opposite. So why can they sit contently and calmly for such a long time? With our consciousness we would say: they are occupied with stupid tasks – reciting day in day out the same long texts until they can declaim them by heart during hours. Western teachers would say that this is no means to make a child sit down quietly. They need change and compensation to behave half-way decently.

One may surely interpret this in one way or another and certainly there are some convincing examples. But for the great majority we may say that it does not depend on these physical aspects. The body is 100% subordinate to spirit. It is all about the contents with which the children are being occupied. In Tibetan classes the main aspect of the contents lies in the compassion for every being. Out of this spirit of compassion reigning in the monasteries which I can perceive there, I cannot imagine that there is sexual violence such as in Germany and the USA where between 2008 and 2012 the papers were full of articles about massive child abuse inside the Catholic Church.

To be sure I might complain about a very restrictive and incalculable administration making life very difficult for me as far as filming in the monasteries was concerned. But this is mainly due to the power we attribute to a camera. Especially if a Westerner is arriving with a complete film team and wants to shoot what nobody else has so far been allowed to shoot.

The administration mistrusted my motivation. Should I not first become a convinced Buddhist before I was supposed to receive a permit? I had comprehension for such doubts and insecurities and it was not easy for me to obtain this trust in a short lapse of time. Because way back then every day cost me 5,000 US$, whether I was filming or not. Today with the small mobile phone cameras everything is different, but then we were still shooting with celluloid film for the cinema. Yet the monasteries showed little understanding for this. They asked for my humility and submission to their rules which have no comprehension for the requirements for shooting. They rather considered them a threat, above all when I had to insist on repeating some scenes due to technical reasons, be it direction or camera considerations. And often repetition was not only necessary once, but several times so that the scenes I filmed could at least partly be used.

In the film academy and in TV the ratio of usable to unusable material is 1:8. Under the circumstances of my shooting it grew to a ratio of 1:40 since I never knew what would happen when the camera started shooting, producing costs of life-threatening dimensions per minute. Of course I tried to convey a rough idea to the cameraman about what was to come but in most cases things turned out different since we did not deal with actors who do exactly what is in the script. In documentary-shooting everything is live and we are lucky to catch something that promotes history.

Documentary-filming is an incredibly complicated business and this is why I often had a hard time with the authorities who wanted to decide about my working method for economic reasons. But I hardly had any trouble with those who acted in my films.

I surely understood the requirements administration and Security have to comply with in India, Nepal and China (Tibet), but I could not accept them for my purposes. In the end I almost always could put my foot down. Still I can live without this stress and strain. Such obstacles simply take too much energy. Today all this is not necessary any longer as the spiritually trained and developed Tibetan themselves bring their consciousness to the West. Insofar this was my last film with the Tibetan monks. Even here in the West, islands of higher consciousness have formed lately. It is good to have a look at these islands. As I mentioned before, I live on one of those islands today: www.schloss-blumenthal.de.

Islands of consciousness

In every community a contribution for evolution can be made because everything there is about *swarm consciousness vs. individuality*. One may wonder if in this leap of evolution the challenge leads you towards ego or into solidarity. In *Blumenthal mansion* we have not come together as a community because we yearn for the security of a swarm, but because we want to support each other in our individual paths towards happiness.

This is easier said than done. Nobody in our community is willing to dispense with their individuality. A proof for this is that there are no joint meals. Everyone has their special taste and thus has invested in an individual kitchen. The only meal we eat together is our Christmas dinner we have cooked for us by the employees of our restaurant.

Our similarities and our solidarity are rather more present in our common debts which we have taken up to design our individual apartments on one hand and to create an interesting common source of income on the other hand: a special, individual hotel with 42 completely differently designed rooms. Moreover we operate our guest-house with big events throughout the year such as seminars, weddings, large birthday parties and other important functions for our clients who love to come here because this venue offers such a special ambiance.

All this and much more is owned by every one of us. At the moment we are 42 partners with one voice each, independent of the size of their investment in the limited partnership holding us together as owners. For me the most interesting thing in our community is the process of decision making because we have noted that democracy does not work anymore, it became outdated since there are always winners and losers, so this does not create any good atmosphere. Yet we endeavour to manage that every voice in the community is heard and honoured so that really everybody has got the feeling that they are taken seriously. One of the structural models we experiment with is sociocracy.[35] With its help the evolutionary leap from the swarm animal with an alpha animal towards individuality without any ego-fighting can be attained. In Blumenthal we have already gone a long way on this model path even if we are never satisfied with the achievements and always try to improve any further.

For society as a whole this leap of consciousness can merely work if the fear of the future is minimized because fear demands control and this control requires power structures that challenge individuality. Since the future is never safe and may even become dramatically unsafe, there is continual danger to fall back into the swarm consciousness where we come from. Such a social structure cannot work any longer, not even with the "best" alpha animal as evolution has already progressed too much. The will of individualization has expanded so much that it is becoming increasingly difficult to install such strong controls.

Those who understand individualization as pure ego-realization do not shy away from any effort to be able to exert their egoistical struggle for power over the lives of other beings with the help of the old swarm consciousness. They solely have to induce fear to a minority, then the whole swarm automatically follows – an ancient

---

35   www.thesociocracygroup.com

reflex from our animal time. Without this old swarm consciousness it is inconceivable that a majority is controlled and subjugated by so small a minority. Yet persons who have developed their individuality on the basis of freedom from fear cannot be subjugated just like that.

It is clear that the one who indulges in ego and the one who has withdrawn into swarm consciousness both go this path because of fear. For the first one power provides the longed-for safety and so does well-behaving for the latter one. However many people only go on the paved streets swimming with the swarm and avoid new individual and creative thinking only in order not to offend. If you do not want to compensate your fear neither by the egoistical way nor by adjusting to the mainstream road, you have to reach the source of fear to make it stop from flowing from there.

Here the circle closes again and we have reached the origin of all fear: the fear of death. This fear is only possible if you identify with your body. Yet if I consider myself a continuum, I stop nurturing this fear of existence which is the fear of death in its daily expression. But when you have the consciousness that you live forever anyway, the fear of existence cannot make you feel small anymore. Once you have lost one form (your tool for making experiences) you may create a new form (a new tool) – so what can cause you any fear? This is only possible if you do it yourself. But the things you do yourself can be changed by you personally. Therefore you are free, from the moment you drop the materialistic-biochemical consciousness.

The fear may go away

Until 1985 I did not know the term "spiritual continuum". For the first time I heard it in September 1985 in an English translation of the Tibetan words uttered by the Dalai Lama in Temisgam, and then another time when I was in Choglamsar with him, both are places in Ladakh. With the idea to be a spiritual continuum, the change was made which was required by my fall from the roof to become healthy again. This term took away my fear. Certainly the adequate challenge for this was to feel the Damocles' sword of the diagnosis "wheelchair for life" hanging over me every day.

This challenge had not yet gone when I was dismissed from the clinic walking on my own legs. It remained with me one more year since I left the clinic with a steel corset and I was told I had to wear it for the rest of my life in any case. In order not to forget this I felt a strong electric shock of at least 220 V passing through my body every time I took a step too fast. I was a long way from being able to travel to Ladakh. I did not have the money for it either. This plight dragged on from April 1982 to September 1985, the moment my second child was under way.

However one day I was in Ladakh without any guide and wanted to meet some "uncivilized" persons and shoot them – motivation enough for me to get healthy. The first person I met was the Dalai Lama. In the middle of the desert in Ladakh the cooler of his jeep went bust. His driver and his bodyguards were just collecting water from a far-off spring, thus I met His Holiness sitting all alone in the back of the jeep which prevented ours from advancing on the narrow path. Just as the Dalai Lama could stir something in millions of people, he stirred something in me too.

I still needed two more death experiences to obtain the consciousness to make my first spiritual film *The old Ladakh* and today – 32 years later – to write this book. I am thankful for this evolution, it gives sense to my life. I am especially glad for this life, even if the former ones have not been bad either. But the present life is a particular challenge thanks to the omission of the old and strong Tibetan traditions guiding me in some of my former lives.

I feel I have the task to express myself in a way that the people among whom I incarnated will understand me. Of course this is extremely difficult because I cannot express on all levels of consciousness at the same time.

Those who read this book from the point of view that all is an unscientific nonsense have surely stopped reading after a few pages or has only just opened it on some pages to confirm their preconceived opinion. Or maybe they jumped to the end pages to see how the story finishes. Unfortunately I cannot prevent this.

If I wanted to make it right for everyone I would have to say the least possible things in order to establish the greatest consensus. But I am not like that. I also love to provoke and I am glad for every single person who takes this as a stimulus to expand their possibilities. Moreover I appreciate all readers who have experienced other impulses for the level of consciousness I am talking about, even before they took this book in hand. In the same way as all my preceding books and films have been welcomed by all those who felt confirmed in their own belief by the contents of these books and films. This is how I fulfil my task and I hope to have expressed myself in such a fashion that we have understood each other well up to this point.

Family meeting – Topga's wishes

Unfortunately Topga has still not had the chance to profit from the continuity of spirit for himself. This is absolutely comprehensible because until now reincarnation has always been an academic subject for him. He simply cannot believe in something he cannot feel. This would be the theory and it would not make him happy.

Now that Jamgon has moved to Pullahari though, in a place only 40 minutes from Topga's house, it is possible for a practical experience to happen for the first time being. Jamgon Rinpoche is visiting Topga's family. He has just arrived when we "coincidentally" are also guests at Topga's. Some of Topga's employees open the entrance and a large blue jeep comes driving onto his grounds. The meanwhile three-year-old Jamgon closely observes the scene at the hand of his "brother". When the car has been parked, he releases the hand, runs towards the jeep with greatest interest and calls to Topga: "Open! Open!" Topga goes towards him, opens the car-door of the co-pilot's side and helps him to climb into the seat. Right away Jamgon crawls to the driver's seat behind the steering-wheel and plays driving a car.

Of course a believer will say instantly: "If this is no sign …" Everybody who was acquainted to Jamgon the 3rd knew how much he loved to drive cars. And Topga knew it too. This is why he gave him the BMW as a gift. Now he is being a witness that Rinpoche still adores cars and did not have a trauma caused by the accident because it was his own wish and plan to die for this good and very useful purpose. Witnessing this scene is dissolving tons of guilt in Topga. I ask him:

CK: *How do you feel now with Rinpoche? Is he like a family member for you now?*

Topga: *Yes, somehow he is. I always enjoy when he is around and plays with my children – so he can behave as a child.*

CK: *Can't he in the monastery?*

T: *Yes, he can. The monks care for him lovingly. But he cannot play with such brazen children as mine.*

CK: *Yet there are several children of his age around in Pullahari.*

T: *Correct, but he hardly plays with them.*

CK: *He is only here for a short time usually.*

T (laughs): *Yes, that is true.*

CK: *Does he really need to romp about with them?*

T: *How can you tell what a Rinpoche needs?*

CK: *Does he still need his parents?*

T: *I do not figure that he misses them. He has us now.*

CK: *I have just visited his parents in Tibet.*

T: *And how are they?*

CK: *She was about to give birth soon.*

T: *Yes, Yangki was pregnant when she went back to Tibet.*

CK: *How long did she stay here?*

T: *She came with him from Tibet and stayed almost a year. Until she was convinced that this is what Jamgon himself wants and that he feels fine here.*

CK: *Surely there is the fact that she and her husband will have another child when they are back home.*

T: *Yes, this is what Mo[36] says too, and it will be another boy.*

CK: *Well, they will be ok then. Rinpoche can stay here and play at your home. Is this not marvellous?*

T: *Sure. It was similar when I was a boy. When my mum was pregnant with me, no this is not correct, only when I was three months old – when my uncle was certain that I would live – Rinpoche entered the monastery.*

CK: *Yes, this is his wish in this life too. And this time he could already realize his wish at the age of two.*

T: *Yes, his present family is much more relaxed about this than our family then.*

CK: *Do you realize that his evolution continues? Do you feel that it is him?*

T: *He does not feel like a stranger to me – that's true.*

CK: *... and you don't seem a stranger to him either?!*

T (laughs): *He is even very familiar with me.*

CK: *Is this sufficient for you?*

T: *It would be much easier for me if he does not have to be my brother.*

CK: *No, because you would still be sitting there with your grief and would feel guilty of his death.*

T: *Probably.*

CK: *This is it, so maybe you just try not to see him in his form, but as a familiar person you feel close to.*

T: *It would have been easier if he was not my brother and I would*

---

36 *Mo* is a Tibetan oracle method. A question is answered when a lama takes his prayer chain in his hand and interrupts the course of the pearls in two places and starts counting the remaining pearls -no on the left and yes on the right. As an oracle (*Mo*) counts which pearl is the last one: Yes or No.

be someone else, then I could see all this from a different angle.
CK: *Other people may wish to be as close with Rinpoche as you.*
T: *If he could just give me some proof and tell me in my face: "I am your brother." Or: "I am back."*
CK: *How could he do that? You relate your feeling for his continuity on his old form, and this form is not there anymore. It became a mummy. If your feeling was related to the continuity of his spirit, you would certainly feel a lot different.*
T: *I am still looking for a sign. For something concrete.*
CK: *You have just been a witness that he still has the same liking for cars as in his former life. This speaks in favour of continuity. What else do you need?*
T: *I have to tell you something: I had a dream and in this dream my brother – such as I knew him – was standing before me. Yet in this dream I was clearly aware that he had died and still he is here. I ask him: "What are you doing here?" And he answers: "I am back!" This was so utterly real as if I had experienced it. He was there in person and completely real. This is what touched me most in this dream.*
CK: *So, you see, there is your sign.*
T: *I told it to my wife. She was fascinated. But I said: "No, no, this is only a dream. In reality it is not possible that he says that he is back." My wife simply replied: "You are mentally blocked. You refuse to accept things you are seeing." (thoughtfully) Perhaps she is right.*
CK: *Mmmmh …*
T: *Another thing: when he was here for the first time he instantly wanted to see the house and go upstairs. My wife took him by the hand and went inside with him. He went straight to the stairs and wanted to climb them, nothing else interested him. He beckoned my wife to go after him. For a three-year-old it is quite a performance to climb these stairs in such a free, decisive and quick way. On the first landing he repeated: "Up, up!". So they also climbed the second stairs to the top floor. There are three doors and all of them were closed. He immediately pointed towards the first door on the right and went*

into this room. It is his old room. We have left it as he once decorated it. He then wanted my wife to open him the drawers of the chest of drawers in which we have kept his things. He did all that without showing any special emotion, completely naturally. After that they went down again and she told me everything. I said: "So what? The boy wanted to go upstairs and see a room. She said: "You are mentally blocked again. You refuse to accept what exists."

CK: *Thank you, may I interview her?* T: Sure, ask her.

I go to his wife immediately and have a look at the room with her.

CK: *So he went up both floors on his own and wanted to see this room?*

She: Yes, he was in the garden and wanted to go up. I went inside with him. When we reached the first floor, I asked where he wanted to go and he pointed upwards saying: "Up, up!"

CK: *And he knew to which door he wanted to go?*

She: Yes. And then he wanted me to open his chest of drawers.

CK: *Did he look at something in particular?*

She: No, he just had a look as if he wanted to be sure that his things were still there.

CK: *This sounds incredible.*

Topga who went upstairs with us: *Obviously I have a mental block. The spirit – my spirit – only sees what it wants to see. This is clear to me now. Sometimes there is something right in front of you, but you cannot see it because your spirit does not want to see it. You may be sitting on Buddha's lap, but if you do not believe in him, you do not notice it.*

CK: *Mentally you are completely fit.*

T: *Rationally speaking I understand it all, I just cannot feel it.*

CK: *Yet you could if you wanted to.*

T: *Do you think so?*

CK: *What is it that you fear if you believed in reincarnation?*

T: *Nothing.*

CK: *What is it then?*
T: *I have never thought about it who I was in my last life.*
CK: *Aha, there is the key to the problem.*
T: *Yes, maybe, above all if I started thinking about it. Then I would also have to think about what I expect from my next life.*
CK: *But it is not about your "expectation". You do not want to wait for something because you would feel horribly powerless. The question is only: What do you* **want** *of your new life?*
T: *Oh, this sounds as a lot of work. I have never thought about it.*
CK: *I understand this. It took a while with me too. Years! But today I see myself, my children, and every human being in his continuum. With reincarnation it is all about opening your perspective. Then it seems completely natural that all is a spiritual continuum, that only their forms change in which they evolve.*
T: *I can tell one thing with certainty: since Rinpoche has come here, the atmosphere here and in Pullahari is so much warmer and more lively. Even the most sceptical person cannot overlook this or deny it.*

Jamgon prefers to deal with his peers. However these peers are not the children of his age, but the high lamas who come to visit him a lot. It is great fun for him to laugh, eat and pass his time with them. They are all colleagues and good friends from his former life who are just a bit older than him now but this is of no importance.

Movie scenes: what happened and being in the middle of it

I could recount numberless stories about how the consciousness changed in many persons from the perspective of a singular life to one of an infinite life thanks to Rinpoche. These experiences are so spontaneous, sensitive and personal for every individual that they can hardly be shot.

Once this has been particularly frustrating for me not being able to use spontaneously the then very cumbersome medium of film. As a documentary-filmmaker I am – like I mentioned before – very dependent on what is happening and at the same time I must consider if what is just happening is bringing on my story. However this is very difficult to judge in advance. Thus it is possible that I shoot something which does not advance my story or I just miss the point, something which is often very depressing. Yet I also experience that when I am cutting the pictures that a scene I estimated to have been shot in vain, turns out to be very valuable.

If I decided to put into practice my message via motion pictures with a six million Euro budget, every scene would be constructible. I would have no trouble at all to show what is expected to further the process of consciousness of a Western spectator, all wrapped into a pleasant story for him to relax and feel well entertained. In the end it would still be a motion picture. I would not have taken part in a genuine story like Jamgon's then. It is true that actors could play the story, but the difference would be as great as in a documentary or a motion picture about the little green men from Mars.

You may call me a fanatic when it comes to the point of being able to see what I can believe and what I cannot for my own conscience. In this respect I am the same as Topga. I will also see black on white respectively representing in colour what I can and cannot believe. Things get exciting when something is happening and I am in the middle of it. Then my consciousness is evolving. Just for example in the following event – which I do not have on celluloid due to the before-mentioned cumbersomeness and the famous problems with the batteries:

My cameraman and I are sitting in the living-room of the then five-year-old 4th Jamgon. Earlier he has shot a nice story I will tell later. The door opens to the hallway and one of the monks is putting in his head:

Monk: *May Rinpoche receive a visit? Is it fitting?*

Tenzin is looking at me. I nod my head.

Tenzin: *No problem.*

The monk opens the door completely and says: *Please.*

A woman of maybe 50 years is entering the room, easily recognizable as an American. She greets Tenzin very politely and nods towards us. When she wants to address Jamgon, he runs off.

Tenzin intervenes: *Rinpoche, please say hello.*

Jamgon keeps running out of the door leading to his bedroom. I get up and go after him. My cameraman makes no move. Through the open door I see Jamgon rummaging in his play-box. He gets hold of a small tin box and comes back holding it in his hands. I go back to my seat. Jamgon presents and hands over the small tin box to the visitor from the USA. Completely overwhelmed the woman takes this small tin and observes it attentively. Then her face gets red and tears start falling. – I am perplexed to witness such a strong emotional reaction and whisper to the cameraman:

I: *Shoot!*
He: *You have not asked her permission.*
I: *Shoot!*
He: *Now?*
I: *Now.*
He: *If you want to ...* (as if he felt offended by my harsh order)
He (taking the camera into his hand and putting it on): *The battery is empty.*

I only give a groan. The woman cries heartily. Jamgon has sat down at a distance to her. Tenzin speaks to him in Tibetan.

I: *Where are the other batteries?*
He: *Outside.*

He gets up and has to walk by the American to reach the door where she has entered. At the moment he passes next to her, she gets a grip of herself wiping away the tears and says to him: "Sorry!" But she is still deeply touched. I notice that in fact she would rather go after my cameraman leaving the room instantly. So I approach her saying: "Excuse me please, may I ask what has affected you so much just now? – And she replies: "This small tin box was a present I gave him in his last life."

It seems like an eternity until my cameraman comes back with the fresh battery. I am so frustrated that I make a gesture with my hand saying no because I do not want to shoot anymore how this woman maybe tells us her story other people may believe or not. If I could have shot the witnessed emotional scene happening out of the blue, the whole story could not have been doubted.

As a documentary filmmaker I am used to missing some 80 to 85% of the scenes which could enhance my film. Just because it happens when I am not there. Or I am there, but due to some reason I cannot shoot it. Or – what also happens often – the shootings are not what I wanted them to be, so I cannot use them, thanks to technical reasons or even for reasons of content.

For all that not only the batteries must be loaded, also the light, the sound and nowadays the shooting volume on the chip must be ok. Back then we did not have chips but magnetic tapes and we did not use to walk around with our pockets full of these. And even before that we had rolls of film for 9 minutes at 150 Euro each. However I love to make documentaries. And the things I cannot tell in them are here in this book.

Of course there is the amulet story we could shoot spontaneously a day before: the 3rd Jamgon had been given the amulet by the 16th Karmapa in January 1981, ten months before his death with the words: "Wear it as long you want to live." Since Jamgon the 3rd has been dead, Tenzin – as we know in the meanwhile – wears this golden amulet[37] which he has found on his body under his T-shirt directly after the accident on his way to the hospital. This was some eight years ago. It has never come up in their conversation. But just as we want to shoot the scene in which the little 4th Rinpoche is sitting on the sofa looking at

---

37 see chap. 12 the paragraph "The magic find".

the pictures of his former lives, he discovers the golden chain around Tenzin's neck and pulls at it. Tenzin stops him, takes out the amulet from under his shirt and pulls it over his head so that Rinpoche may take it in his hand and look at it closely.

The little Jamgon takes the heavy gold amulet which is about 2 inches wide into his hands and turns it over. Tenzin has expected him to open it, like a pocket watch. However this does not happen, but Jamgon puts the chain around his head and lets it dangle on his breast, or more like on his belly. He wants to turn away from Tenzin, as if to show that: *This is mine.* Tenzin laughs and says in Tibetan: "This is mine." – Jamgon however keeps turning away from him as if he thinks : "We will see that." Tenzin tugs at his sleeve to stop him from doing so. At some distance Jamgon turns to face Tenzin and plays with the golden, heavy amulet taking it in both hands.

"Tenzin offers his outstretched hand pleading: "Please be a nice boy and give it back to me." Out of respect for the small, great Jamgon he suppressed adding: "This is no toy, this is very precious." Jamgon is indeed so well-behaved that he takes off the chain and puts the amulet very carefully back into Tenzin's open hand. Tenzin is satisfied and pulls it over his head back in its place. – In my opinion it is an impressive scene. Others might not think it so great, as I know. But the exciting question is: to whom belongs this amulet? Has it really fulfilled its intention? Are the original words still relevant: "Wear it as long as you want to live", which were said by the 16th Karmapa when he gave it to Jamgon the 3rd?

Several days later I meet Topga who often drives the 40 minutes from his house to Pullahari, even if he does not have any urgent business to do there, just like that – " … to see Rinpoche". But he does not show it openly. He mainly talks to Tenzin then and to other people who are visiting and spontaneously takes charge of some problem or other.

Only very casually he takes Jamgon by his hand, or sometimes it is the other way round: Jamgon takes Topga for a walk to show him something. Then Topga accompanies him laughingly as if it was his destiny to be led by the child. Now and then it even happens that Jamgon sits on his lap for some minutes.

I look Topga in the eyes and then he indeed says this sentence we happen to shoot:

"There is definitively a feeling that my brother is really back. Something has triggered it." I can see that Topga is fine, even he and many other people have noticed it. His sadness has been overcome. Of course he is very busy with his carpet business and all the other things he has to manage being the head of the family. His life and the evolution of his consciousness are continuing, the same as with all of us.

22
Eternal life

This was the story of Topga. The story of Jamgon 4th is only just beginning. When he fled from Tibet to India at the age of two, the political problems began. He is registered by the Indian authorities as a Tibetan refugee in Dharamsala. His journey from Nepal to his new headquarters is politically speaking only a tourist trip of the refugee. Since Nepal has not signed the extradition treaty with China, Jamgon cannot register as a refugee in Nepal, because as a consequence he would be sent back to Tibet. – The longer he stays in Pullahari, the more critical things will get for him. The Nepalese politicians are too weak where China is concerned, so they cannot hold him for a long time. Finally Jamgon wants to get away from the grasp of the Chinese and go to safety to India but there he feels Shamar's influence.

Rivals

In the meantime it is common knowledge that Karmapa's order, the Kagyü tradition, split in 1992[38] thus permitting the outbreak of a lasting power struggle since the death of the 16th Karmapa. Let us recall that Shamar – after the death of Karmapa – declared himself the interim regent while visiting the US and then never quit again, although the 16th Karmapa had wished for him to do just that. His four seat-holders Shamar, Situ, Gyaltsap and Jamgon should take turns in the regency every three years until Karmapa himself would take over the offices again in his next incarnation.

Yet Shamar never thought of surrendering his power once he had

---

38 see in chapter 9 the paragraph "Karmapa found!".

achieved it. The old secretary general whom the 16th Karmapa had given the mission to provide for the turns in power among these young and so-called "heart sons" died of poisoning during a dinner with Shamar's secretary. This secretary was then named the new secretary general ensuring that Shamar could remain in power uncontested.

When Situ found the letter of prophecy written by the 16th Karmapa, Shamar realized that his days as the head of the Kagyü Order were numbered. If you consider the immense wealth Shamar accumulated during his regency, one might begin to understand why he did everything to avoid stepping down. Therefore he considered of paramount importance his announcement to the Kagyü adepts that the genuine Karmapa was on his side presenting as "his" Karmapa a youngster who would never quarrel about power with Shamar. This means that after 900 years there are suddenly *two Karmapas* for the 17th incarnation. For the worldwide adepts of the Kagyü Order this was quite confusing at first and they had to decide which Karmapa to accept as their leader. This still divides the order until now.

This same strategy was followed by Shamar in Jamgon's case too. As soon as Jamgon had been discovered, Shamar presented a different Jamgon for his part of the Kagyü Order. At the same time he did everything in his power to make life difficult for his rival. With his marked instinct for power he managed that not only Karmapa, but also Jamgon, Situ, Rosy Findeisen and many more people were declared "persona non grata" by the Indian Ministry of the Interior. They would not be allowed to ever enter India again if they left for Nepal for just a single day.

Tenzin tried to solve this problem for Jamgon by finding an Indian woman who adopted him. Yet this adoption was not recognized by the Indian state on Shamar's behalf. To be sure Jamgon respectively his foster mother are conducting a protest procedure, but the outcome has not been sure up to now.

For my Karmapa movie Living Buddha I also got to feel Shamar's power since I did not venture on his side.

He managed to take *Living Buddha* out of the competition for the Oscar nomination of the *Academy* in Los Angeles and also out of the TV-programs of six other countries which had already signed licence contracts with my Swiss worldwide distribution.

Shamar achieved this by having one of his super rich adepts sue me in *the US Federal Court* in Dallas for fake copyright violations. Due to this trial the movie was blocked for three years for a pending process thus preventing its utilization on an international basis. This meant I was bankrupt and when the trial was won after I reached an out-of-court settlement, the movie was outdated and could not be exploited any more.

This meant that the movie could not been shown in the official TV-programs but the new media developed a very different dynamic: in the meantime the movie *Living Buddha* has been watched by millions of people for free on YouTube.

On the throne, but as a refugee

Naturally Jamgon could also have been reborn as a Nepalese or an Indian in a Tibetan family. Yet since Karmapa lived in Tsurphu, he may have favoured a solution which made sure that he would be recognized and identified by him by reincarnating at a short distance from him. Karmapa would not have been able to help Tenzin to search for Jamgon in a foreign country as much as he did in Tibet.

As Jamgon the 3rd had chosen Nepal as the headquarters for the mission in his next life establishing his centre Pullahari there, it was only a matter of time when he would leave Tibet in his new incarnation, because he would hardly ever get a chance to do his worldwide work with Tibet as a base just as in his previous life. The same goes for Karmapa. When Karmapa was in favour of Jamgon the 4th leaving Tibet in 1988 at the age of two, he might well have had his own flight plans in mind.

It is true that China, to her great shame, had completely misjudged the little Karmapa. When the Chinese government announced him that on April of 2000 at the age of 15 he would have to condemn the Dalai Lama in front of the Chinese People's Congress in a nation-wide TV program, Karmapa fled from Tibet between 27.12.1999 and 5.1.2000 on foot with his old teacher on his back during the hard winter when you could only cross the Himalayans at night to Mustang/Nepal. From there he managed to reach India incognito where he first identified himself to the Dalai Lama.

All Tibetan refugees must know that after crossing the Himalayans and on reaching Nepal without being caught by the Chinese, they have to continue fleeing to India. Otherwise they will be sent back to Tibet to be tortured. The Tibetans who live in Nepal have been there since before 1990 when the refugee treaty with China was agreed upon.

Jamgon, whose arrival at Pullahari was greatly celebrated – as my movie shows and as you may have read in this book –, does not find shelter there since China has asked the Nepalese authorities to surrender Jamgon. After five years Nepal reached a point where it could not give a home to Jamgon any longer and he had to escape to India.

So both, Jamgon and Karmapa, have been trapped in the Indian exile as stateless refugees without passports since 2000. – This changed when Shamar died in June 2014.

Surprising changes

With Jamgon's adoption and thus his nationality being still dealt with in Indian courts, Jamgon came of age. Meanwhile he is capable of defending himself. As long as the trial about his status is under way he cannot leave India. To be sure he can meet Karmapa there, but he has to renounce having his own residence in Pullahari in Nepal where Tenzin represents him. However he cannot meet Topga and others any more for whom he had built the centre in the first place.

The place where he lives in India, near the border to Bhutan, is so far off the usable traffic roads that he spends a quite isolated life.

When Jamgon the 4th came of age, a big event was celebrated in May 2014 on the highest Buddhist holiday in *Bodh Gaya* – the place where Buddha got enlightened – with Karmapa demonstrating his profound connection towards Buddha before many thousand Buddhist monks of all orders. For a whole day Karmapa showed himself exclusively with Jamgon on a high platform for which a tent of gigantic proportions was erected in Bodh Gaya especially. His former incarnations Jamgon 1st to 3rd painted in three giant portraits one above the other decorated the wall so that everyone was aware of who was the young man of 18 sitting up there next to Karmapa.

Both teach again side by side the philosophy of love to the people who have gathered there from all over the world – just as in their last life, only not with a difference in age like father and son now, but more as friends with an age difference of ten years.

Jamgon comments: *The relationship between me and Karmapa is not a normal friendship like the one people have. Karmapa is my teacher and I am his disciple*

And Karmapa adds: *The spirit of disciple and teacher is inseparable and will be one in the end. It is as if you poured water into water, every atom is so close that nobody can ever separate us or delimit us from one another.*

Jamgon continues: *The most important thing for me is to fulfil Karmapa's wishes. I hope and pray that I will manage to do so. As his student it is paramount that I learn from his qualities, his good qualities which I need and which I can help to spread. I want to support him in all his activities, not only in this life, but from one life to another.*

What makes those people from all over the world honour this young man? I have not asked anyone but I have sensed the atmosphere and seen countless faces. What I have felt was neither glorification nor guru admiration, and no mysticism either, but rather a very pragmatic esteem which consists in recognizing the following:

Jamgon proved in his former life that he had developed his character in various lives so that he would not abuse his power and would merely give love.

The most essential thing is that next to Karmapa he represents the greatest good in humanity: *He has integrated death,* instead of demonizing or mystifying it. He showed that death may be performed as a meaningful act in order to work for the liberation of humanity from one life to the next without being restricted by fear of existence.

So eternal life has been achieved and it is celebrated here. It is not tied to a robe or gown.

23
What a crazy thing!

One year later something marvellous happened, a catharsis like you say: a jump in consciousness through suffering. I had to evolve in the same way, genuinely, just like most people. Some are luckier than others. I had to fall from the roof and be paraplegic in order to expand my consciousness. Jamgon had to pass a profound crisis so that in his present incarnation as Jamgon Kongtrul Rinpoche the 4th he could open himself to a new dimension of consciousness. For Buddhism this has far-reaching consequences:

On 14th of April 2016, at the age of 19, he announced on Facebook that he has taken off his robe and left the monastery *Lava* in East-India. There, close to Kalimpong, he had been stuck since he was four because his status as a refugee could not be decided upon.

After leaving secretly, Jamgon posted a bitter accusation against his mentors because he had felt at their mercy. In Internet he was endorsed by other tulkus (reincarnated masters) stating that the traditional, restrictive education suffered by the monks, especially the high-born ones, was not up-to-date anymore. Since the moment the Tibetans have been living abroad disposing of the Internet, they have been exposed to an impact which makes them often doubt their old rigid monastery life. The conditions in exile have changed their outlook quite a bit.

As mentioned before, the Dalai Lama announced that he will incarnate as a "beautiful woman" in his next life. Shamar's "Karmapa" also took off his robe in February 2017 and presented his girl-friend on Facebook. In the meanwhile he got married to her and published his wedding-photos of his in-laws. All this is directed towards a development with which spirituality is becoming sustainably secularized.

Jamgon, with his many representative tasks and the high expectation other people have towards him had more and more difficulty in behaving as tradition demanded of him. The conflicts which arose from the traditional behaviour such a high bearer of dignities was supposed to display, drove Jamgon crazy. He was toying with the idea of suicide and inflicted physical pain on himself until he summoned up the courage to leave everything behind and leave the monastery secretly. This reveals the full drama in times of change which obviously is not possible to bring about without suffering. We learn from errors, not from the good.

Due to the high pressure built on Jamgon he broke with tradition, went into a big city, put on blue jeans, found new friends and got involved with a young woman. By all his doing he revolutionized the image of spirituality represented by him as Jamgon Kongtrul the 4th. I rejoice in seeing that eventually a spiritual leader gets involved with sexuality and all that it implies.

In doing so Jamgon puts himself on the same step as his adepts. They might find that his spiritual life appears more real than before. Tens of thousands of Jamgon's adepts do not lead a monastic life but are in relationships in which sexuality often plays a great role. As Jamgon has led a secular life with a relationship in his 4th incarnation since April 2015, he will be much more competent in his teachings about self-realisation.

With this begins a new era: the mountain moves towards the water. We will keep watching with great interest what he will say in his teachings when he has passed his first crisis in his relationship with women. He will be someone who could give important advice because in real-life love experiences, many people experience great shortcomings. As long as we are living in a retreat promoting our spiritual growth without practising sexuality, it is easy to follow Buddha's teachings. But at the point where the daily routine gets at us inside the family we often feel lost. All the drama inside a partner relationship is a spiritual exercise of the highest degree. Illumination with your partner is completely different from illumination alone.

Jamgon is the first Rinpoche of high standing in Tibetan Buddhism who gathers experiences which represent a strange new challenge. Time will tell which consequences his pioneer deed is having on spiritual growth in general.

This book will require a sequel. Maybe not only in 25 years like this time but at the latest when Jamgon is on his way as a spiritual teacher again. Perhaps not on his own, but together with a woman. We will see …

Epilogue

The evolution Jamgon will take is still unknown. We do not wait for what will happen to him. We will get started on ourselves now, this is the most important thing. You do not need anybody to tell you where to go. If you have got somebody with whom you can reflect and talk over your way, it is fine. If you have got somebody who wants to lead your way, this is not good, even though you would like it to be this way.

You would lose your self-competence which you need for a favourable reincarnation. Because when you die you have to rely on your own power, intuition and your own thinking. No-one will lead your way then. Your imagination which is your own is always leading your way and your experience is always behind you.

Unfortunately imagination in many people is limited to thinking. Imagination however means projection and this requires a strong and precise concentration. This is a higher form of thinking. It must be practised while you are alive, otherwise normal thinking will prevail, thinking in terms of normality: we *normally* see each other as physical, biochemical beings and believe the theory of lineage. This is why most souls reincarnate within their family again. Yet if we learn to concentrate on our own projection, we set an intention. It is followed by the energy with which we preserve the life imagined by us. This is not necessarily a life within the old family, this depends on the soul family who looks out for the degree of consciousness with which we leave our body.

The consciousness – as we do it in this book – can be developed from a singular to a continuous life concept. With this step you will find new resources from which to draw energy in order to go your own way. Because you can connect (again) with faculties which you have acquired in one or several former lives. Therefore you must not limit yourself by obeying traditions and sects. Learn to think independently and be ready to cross-walk your life. This requires courage, but brings great freedom.

Every time you read this book, I recommend you to take something from it that you want to try for yourself. After each of your steps which advance your consciousness you will read the pages with different eyes. Surely you may want to dedicate yourself to your "personal master-plan for reincarnation" which you find in the annex of this book. Life is an experiment. Lots of them have gone awry but this is a general experience. Yet we do not stop experimenting – on the contrary.

Self-responsibility is booming right now since running after gurus has not enhanced the planet. Poverty and hunger have never been so widespread and our environment has never been so polluted as right now. However your own competence achieved by trained intuition promises a better world, if reason starts serving intuition. I am afraid that most people do not know what "to serve" means: to be mindful, to listen, to subordinate oneself, to help, to execute, to listen to the voice of intuition and follow it absolutely, to serve and obey it always. This is only possible if you listen to your own soul and not to someone from outside. This book is destined to serve this intention.

I wish every reader a conscious continuity of their eternal life.
Clemens Kuby, spring 2018

Annex

Personal masterplan for reincarnation

Dear reader! In this book you may convince yourself and be amazed by how far the consciousness of His Holiness Gyalwa Karmapa the 16th and 17th and of His Eminence Jamgon Kongtrul the 3rd and the 4th have progressed. Due to such insights and knowledge your own consciousness will expand and – that is the law – this process never stops.

How is your personal opinion towards the idea of getting to know more about your former life? Which questions do arise in you? Who could you have been in a former life? What has driven you to incarnate as you did? And: How can you approach your next incarnation more consciously than your last? Even when you are quite satisfied with your present choice of incarnation, you might be tempted to know what you can do in order to incarnate again in such circumstances or even better ones. In the following I would like to give you some practical instructions.

I wish for everyone who books a reincarnation seminar with me to be familiar with these instructions and even better already have experimented with them. The more profoundly you have plunged into these layers of consciousness **before** *a seminar, the more precious will be a reincarnation seminar for you.*

Should the following instructions seem too difficult for you at some moment, please continue reading or simply read some chapters once again. Or you might want to read other books about reincarnation.[39] Yet the most sustainable way to elevate your mind is with the *Soul writing*®. The challenge to understand yourself as a spiritual and emotional continuity and to act accordingly never ends.

Since there is no unified terminology so far for the science of

---

39 DVD by Ingrid Vallieres, Erika Schäfer (see also "How to continue"/media shop)

reincarnation, you may get more confused by reading other books on the subject than reach clarity on it. We cannot help this. It can only be remedied by creating your own experiences which transport your consciousness beyond the physical limits of your life. Maybe you belong to the group of people who can remember having suddenly stepped out of their body due to a heavy injury or a shock and watching the scene from the outside. Maybe you also belong to the group of people who have noticed clearly when someone of their personal circle has been in danger or when someone was dying before having real information on it. Maybe you belong to the group of people who have thought of someone intensely and then this person has called or even appeared.

Reason-based people also create experiences which cross the material border. These experiences are usually suppressed because they cannot be classified in the socially accepted view. However, if you want to expand your consciousness now in order to dispose of more possibilities in life to be your own creator, just start by making a list of these so-called **super-sensory** experiences.

But what does "super-sensory" really mean? The human being has five known senses: vision, hearing, smell, taste and touch/feeling – all of them are not so sharply defined. For example a blind person hears 100 times more than a seeing person, a deaf person smells 10 times better than a person who has all his five senses. The biggest scale shows feeling. Our senses expand into infinity through feeling. All you can feel in a dream can already be defined as "super-sensory", however this term does not make sense, it rather creates confusion. "Super-sensory" could only be applied to areas which you cannot experience or better: which you cannot experience yet. Naturally there are some situations in which you do not feel at home, for which you lack consciousness, then you do not experience them either. Yet everything I can experience is sensorial and makes sense, although it may not make sense to me personally. But without senses there is no sensorial experience. The term "super-sensory" does not make sense at all.

Other terms that might confuse you are e.g.: *twin soul, old soul, soul parts, soul mates, sick soul*. I do not use any of these. In my terminology the soul is omniscient – without beginning or end, and therefore without age. The soul cannot be sick, just as God cannot be sick. You cannot divide it either into small parts or two parts. And if I am a soul mate to another soul biologically or by choice, this always requires a being with a body. Naturally such a relationship may last over different lives, but there must be a body in order to be a soul mate to someone.

The longer you deal with the continuity of life, the more terms you get to know. They make it obvious that since the Romans we only think about matter and not primarily about spirit. We do have a very precise vocabulary to differentiate matter, yet we still have to work out a vocabulary for spirit. These terms may not be invented theoretically. It would generate a great confusion and adventurous speculation which would not lead to anything but quarrel. We do need experiences.

And this is what you can actively do right now with the following subjects:
- Who was I in a former life?
- How do I recognize in someone else who they have been in a former life?
- How do I invite someone to reincarnate with me?
- How do I project my next reincarnation?

Whichever of these questions you would like to answer, they need a specific working method to be successful. It is paramount to follow the rules of *Soul writing*®. For the better part this has to be done in *script style*. Both methods are precisely explained in the annex. When you are working on your reincarnation questions, please do observe these methods. Believe me you will have more success when you get used to employing *Soul writing* and the *script style*.

Who was I in a former life?

Since we already have problems recording our childhood, a diagram will help us to go back to the beginning of our present life as much as possible. Please take a sheet of paper, draw an inch-sized circle and write ME in the centre. Then take another sheet of paper and calculate your conception date: your birth date + three months – seven days – 12 months. This is your theoretical conception date. We do not take care of pre-term or late births because your conception might still have taken place then in spite of the birth date calculated by the doctors. However you had special reasons to come into this world earlier or later.

You now add your conception date under the circle. Put another two circles for your biological parents on the right and left of this circle with their respective age on your conception date. If there were any brothers and sisters (or half-brothers and half-sisters) in this marriage where you were born into, give them their respective circles with their names and ages above your own circle.

Then reflect who else belonged to your household or the inner family circle. Please note down if these persons (e.g. grand-parents) belong to your mother's or your father's side giving them a place below the respective circles of your parents. Proceed likewise with your aunts, uncles, cousins etc.

When you finished putting down all persons living in your direct environment on this sheet of paper, reflect and – if necessary – investigate where all of this happened then. Write down the name of the place and think about the circumstances reigning then. Imagine how your mum and dad may have looked like then. How was their relationship when they made love then? Just then, during this act of love, you took the biggest decision of your present life: to enter in this life under these circumstances. It requires an enormous amount of energy to create this act and stick it out until you are alive on this planet. Biology says that the relationship between incarnation attempts and a successful incarnation is 1: 1 000 000 000 000 (one to a billion). Just imagine. And you did it! This does not happen either by chance or without intention. You wanted to live, your soul wanted to come back into a physical body. Just imagine the energy you summoned up: you did not incarnate as a dog, cat, cow or horse etc. but as a human being, the most special and the highest developed form we know.

This obliges you to make good use of your time and energy. You must not idle away your time or criticize the circumstances you have chosen. You have to honour your life and your life-span. You must not disregard your incarnation because you could have done it in a much lower form of evolution. (*It is not possible not to incarnate at all!*)

However, you have made it, you have managed to come back as a man or a woman and so far have not slipped out of form yet. So now see to it that you acquire a kind of consciousness until your next exit with which to plan your next incarnation carefully and to select an environment which grants you the best possible circumstances for a happy, healthy and fulfilled life. Please also look in the section "How do I project my next reincarnation?".

First ask yourself: What has brought me into this compound of persons in which I entered this time? Please draw the most important lines connecting the person or persons who have attracted you most on your sheet of paper with the circles. Who was it in the first place? Not always must it have been your mum or dad. It can also be a different person from your network of people who nevertheless could not have had children at that time or had not wanted any.

When you have selected this person on your sheet of paper, feel just how strong the attraction is. This force just could not have emerged in the second in which you have entered the ovum of your mum in this act of love!?! This attractive force was needed for you to incarnate, this means you must have already had a relationship with this person, otherwise there would not have been this force of attraction. Let yourself feel the relationship to this person. What kind of relationship was it? Have you already been his child (for the sake of simplicity

I use a male form, but this is completely aleatory- note of translator), his son or daughter once? Have you been a parent to him? Have you been siblings? Have you both been intimately connected otherwise? As a couple? There must forcibly have been a relationship with this person, otherwise you would not have incarnated there. The universe is not prone to coincidence. Do you notice something now? Just remember how insurmountable the border to your former life has appeared to you until now. With the feeling for this person you have just crossed this border. With all your thoughts that you are thinking right now you are beyond your present life without it being a big deal.

As soon as you consciously feel the relationship you had with your favourite person for the incarnation in this life, you will know if you were man or woman in your former life as well as the type of culture you lived in and many more things. Put it all down on a sheet of paper applying the *Soul writing*® method (see a special chapter in the annex), then you can reflect on it (every time you want to). This reflecting on it leads to the expansion of your consciousness.

In the seminar we do the very same thing – and for so long until you get a clear picture of who you were in your former life. With this method you learn to take seriously all your intuitive pictures, feelings, smells and sounds. You learn to observe your dreams and to question everything that appears, i.e. to associate it more intimately.

How do I recognize who someone else was in a former life?

If you want to take a look at the reincarnation of another person please take into account: How big is your confidence in the deceased person you want to meet again? How intimately have you been connected to him? Have you known him well? Have you loved each other in one way or another? In which phase of his life have you been close to him? How well do you know his character with which he has left the body?

When you understand such a human being with all his personality, you will feel wherein his attraction lies. Just take a look at how this person lived, what his dearest hobbies were, his loved ones and his favourite plants and animals. These features will partly appear in his next life too. However his weaknesses will also go on as a continuum. It would be incomprehensible if his upsides and downsides continue in different ways, if the two sides of a medal – Ying and Yang – would fall apart. Get a clear picture of the following parameters of this person of whom you want to know where he may have incarnated writing down these questions: which features are so strong that they will be kept up regardless of his choice of parents.

- Positive and loving experiences? Which?
- Stressful experiences? Which?
- Relationship to persons? Which persons and what kind of relationship?
- Experiences of fear? Which?
- Love affairs? Which?
- Female role behaviour? Which?
- Male role behaviour? Which?
- Readiness for violence? If yes, in what measure?
- Bossiness? If yes, in what measure?
- Acceptance, apathy? In which area?
- Sadness? Why?
- Submissiveness? To whom?
- Compulsive, strong sexuality? Yes or no?
- The attitude of "take what you can get"? Yes or no?
- Identifications with a nation, race, ethnic group either individual or collectively? Yes or no?
- Identification as a refugee? Yes or no?
- The feeling of home in this person? What place or area?
- Unfulfilled dreams of this person in his life?
  Which ones did he not realize?
- Fulfilled dreams of this person in his life? Which ones did he realize?

There are certainly many more longings and features of his character. Make yourself aware of these things in order to start the search. – You should also take into account that nowadays souls reincarnate a lot quicker than ten thousand years ago (see chapter 4 of this book). In former ages it was well possible to live 250 years in the bardo (the phase with no physical form/body) without missing something in life. If you stayed away for 250 years nowadays, you would not be able to get along in life any more or you would feel like a stranger. You may part from the idea that nowadays souls reincarnate within weeks, months or a few years. (There are ever more people around nowadays.) The distance between the death of a person you look for and his reincarnation may therefore be well within your own life-span. I already know of a case with only two months between death and conception.

Connect yourself with the soul of the deceased person and make a dialogue[40] with him about the places and persons he is attracted to, putting your reason at the service of your intuition, not the other way round! This means that you may pull all the levers if you have got an intuitive picture or insight with this case checking if these may be verified in the real world.

Take care of your dreams as soon as you get really interested in this case. Put them on paper immediately. Do not wait until daylight. After putting them down you may continue with the same dream and control your interest in a light sleep. Keep on writing down the active continuity of your intuitive movie. Such half-awake phases are the best to get profoundly into your intuition. Your souls are intertwined anyway, especially if you answered the above-mentioned questions empathically. This means that the channel to this person is still open, so there may be a lot more things coming. Look around in your environment: maybe this person is already here again. You may well detect it in his eyes or when people talk about his character: "Just as our grand-pa." No, it *is* the grand-pa.

---

40   More about it in the annex in the chapter "Soul writing – in script style".

The reincarnation of a special person may be recognized a lot more easily than you believe with our old consciousness. For example animals have no problem at all doing it. Even if they were accustomed to seeing their master walking with a cane in his former life, they will recognize him in his new form as a baby instantly and may well dance around it or even lick it to greet it. It may certainly take some time until you are completely sure that you have recognized your old love in this new person. Yet this discovery wholly dispels any remaining grief. And you will learn to appreciate and love this new young person as much as you did with the old form. This will change your outlook and the relationship thoroughly. The consciousness of reincarnation promotes a profound sense of humanity.

How do I invite someone to reincarnate with me?

If you as a couple wish to have children, you should talk about the responsibility you want to share, even before the first attempt at conception. Only if both of you are willing to really take over this responsibility, you should stop using contraceptive methods. During this conversation it is paramount that both are aware of the fact that – if the ovule is fertilized – someone will presumably incarnate who already has had a relationship with one of you. However in most cases one of the parents has never known the invited person before and therefore has to completely trust his partner that there will be a caring relationship with the "unknown" without any rivalry or jealousy.

As soon as you invite a soul to incarnate with you, make yourself clear what you and your partner may offer it: that both of you can tell with good conscience that you can provide a caring childhood and on the other hand you ask yourselves (independently of your partner) what this being might wish for. (Such questioning of a soul is usually done most easily with the Soul writing® method.) If both of you agree with the wishes of this being, every phase of excited waiting has ended, even in the case of so-called "infertility". This happens often in contradiction to conventional medicine which might have produced guilt complexes in you or your partner by means of so-called fertility diagnoses. In reality, these are only assumptions based on biochemical facts without any cue of what can be done on the spiritual level and of what humans are capable on this level. Anyway, conventional medicine (and also many alternative methods) are not responsible for fertility. Their concepts of faith correspond with the biochemical or energetic level.

Yet if you approach the matter of childbearing from the perspective of the continuity of the soul, you have to deal directly with the being you want to give life to. Then you will be aware that it not only matters your wanting a child but also if the child fits into the surroundings in which it will grow up. Where and how should the nest, in which the person will be raised in the first few years at least and in which it will discover its environment, be?

Does his father suit him or is he only the one who gives his semen? Does his mum fit him or is she only the one who gives birth to him? To whom, this being you wish to incarnate, would be attracted most and to whom least? Or do you want to carry this child for someone else who is no longer able to do it? Then it would be necessary to include this third person in the family-planning process. This is already the case if both parents are strongly attached to their work and count with a grandparent or two to rear the child mostly on their own.

Nine months for nesting is not much. Especially when the *Soul writing* brings expectations to the surface of your consciousness that might also require a change of place so as to set up a surrounding network in which the child is brought up and looked after. If you as parents only take into account these important parameters when the child arrives, the child-rearing will be arduous and complicated. It is easier to fix most things before.

You may also keep the door open to give service to a being that only wants to use childhood with the corresponding implications (reference person, social status, role models etc.) to continue his mission practised in a former life. This might mean having to accept that this child brings along little sense of family and only uses the family as a steppingstone for the perfection of his mission in life. If you are so unselfish as a parent, then it may occur that a very highly developed personality incarnates with you who will not be held down by family bonds. You can only make things right for this person, but you won't get back the affection you usually wish for as parents. This means letting go of a loved person, to release him without receiving anything in return and to be happy on your own.

When you consider life a spiritual-emotional continuum, it is ideal to do family-planning with the help of *Soul writing* so as to get a clear picture of the attitude of the soul incarnating with you. This is not witchcraft but a challenge that all future parents confront willingly out of love for their child. Instead of just yearning for children blindly, the implications and potential consequences should be reflected before thoroughly and in writing. (Later these notes may be interesting for the child and the research of his former life – so store them away safely.)

Those who approach their family-planning with this awareness will experience pregnancy (also as a father) in a very different way than with the materialistic-biochemical image of a singular life. The relationship "father-child" does not only build up when the child may be disciplined so that the father can practice his role as a family authority, but he may also play a role as a serving or helping partner during the act of conception. Not only the mother, also the father may ask themselves continuously during pregnancy: what does the coming being wish for? If you get an idea of who is to come with *Soul writing,* you may assess the expectation with which this person wants to continue his development from a former life under these new conditions. You do not need to know much, you just have to learn to follow your intuition.

The abdominal wall is so thin that every noise, emotion and touch is penetrating there. This means that the father has multiple and great possibilities to communicate with his new child from the first day after conception and to feel what serves best the personality who is to incarnate.

Since every child is not oriented in a monogamous way, but always loves both parents simultaneously, even if differently, though both at the same time, you have to see to it that it can experience both parents from the beginning.

Naturally it cannot be breast-fed by the father. Yet he may nurse it in a different way by providing calm and security through bodily contact when it is not hungry. Nowadays even breast-feeding is possible for the father with pumped-out breast milk when mother maybe has an important date, provided that he can spend as much time with the child as the mother and making enough money is no problem. This is something to figure out clearly before conception, otherwise you will fall back into the classical role behaviour due to social conventions and other reasons: man is at work and woman is at home with the child. Even nowadays this is a regular scheme and not healthy for anyone.

Breast-feeding is – as long as the child is not primarily considered a physical-biochemical being but a spiritual-emotional being – not a biochemical care but in the first place a spiritual-emotional care. If the spiritual-emotional care is not a top issue, then often the physical-biochemical care will not work either.

When you as parents agree on having a child, speak very clearly with the soul you invite. Address yourselves directly to the concrete person you wish for and formulate a written invitation from the bottom of your heart. This is meant as a clear signal for this soul/person. If in addition your wish is accompanied by beautiful rituals and prayers, then it is often fulfilled quickly. (Even if you may have consulted many doctors before and have been diagnosed with infertility.)

Failed incarnation attempt

Once you have overcome considering life as a singular manifestation, you can hardly keep on thinking: *I wish to have a child* or: *Why can't I have a child?* With the consciousness of incarnation you may rather ask yourself: Who do I want and who may want me? Why does nobody incarnate with me? Who could be waiting at the door? Who might have tried, but then turned back?

If you want to know why the soul turned back, then do *Soul writing*° with it and sort out the reasons why. And then simply accept them, whatever these reasons are. The decision of this soul to end the attempt to incarnate is not in your responsibility. Normally this being has chosen you and not the other way round. In *Soul writing* you can ask the soul of this being why it has changed his opinion.

Speak with the biological father of the child or get at least a clear picture of his situation and his relationship with fatherhood, since the reasons why this being has changed his opinion may not lie with you but with him. It is the global situation in which this being would have incarnated that counts and it is evident that it has discovered things that did not appeal to him at this moment.

When you have another look at the sheet with your own family and loved ones with whom you have incarnated at the beginning of your life, make yourself aware in which situation this being would have incarnated if it had not decided to end the attempt. In this situation you are only one factor out of many for why this soul has decided to end it. It may well have discovered its own reasons in itself which are disadvantageous for a healthy incarnation and has turned back then. You were not responsible for the viability of your child even if you may think so as a mother or as a father. A miscarriage is a miscarriage.

Abortion

If you have aborted your child, also do *Soul writing*® with this being and explain him every single reason that made you do so. A soul who has only been nesting in your womb for a few weeks is not as identified with this home as an older person. Every life is an experiment and not every experiment works out fine.

Apologize sincerely to this soul whose home you have disrupted at base level, whichever your reasons. Then this being might come to the conclusion during *Soul writing*® that it may not have been so advantageous to build a new home just there (in this situation with this network of persons) at this very moment. In consequence you may resolve the mutual conflict of not having given or received an opportunity to stay, because the energy with which this aborted being has undertaken the attempt at reincarnation has not disappeared. With this very energy this being may well start another attempt at reincarnation with you or someone else.

You now may say goodbye to each other in present tense and direct speech (see the chapter *Soul writing*®) or stay friends. Surely this being is now living somewhere, it may even have incarnated successfully in your family at a later moment. You can write down the answers to these questions intuitively when you do *Soul writing*®. You will get a feeling which dissolves your guilt complex. This is very important for you *and* for the aborted (evicted) soul.

Of course an abortion is not easy. And we should do everything we can so that it does not become necessary. However, there may be comprehensible personal reasons for it that do not enable you to act otherwise. In a sincere dialogue with this soul it surely is possible to get rid of your guilt complex. That is what matters: to go on living your own life and the life of the children who are born later in joy and without feeling guilty. Nothing is more stressful for these children than a guilt-ridden mother (or a father).

How do I project my next reincarnation?

With this point we touch the most exciting of the four questions. It affects your future life in the highest possible degree and you will observe that as soon as you have got a clear picture of it, it will have great consequences for your present life. In order to receive a decent next life, you will have to end the present one decently too. What is the best way to do this? In this book there is a lot of advice. Just read it again. It is not about living as long as possible, but about dying purposefully and making sense of your death. Which moment is the best? Certainly not one in which you suffer and need care. A useful moment to die should be one in which you feel good and have your full capacities.

People say: "Too beautiful to die". Or if something has gone especially well, they often say: "I could die now." This means that the people's soul knows what it means to die fearlessly at the right moment. And there are lots of these moments in life. Of course it would be a shame if you chose a moment too soon, and maybe think that some medical measure could have made life worth living again. But how do I know which is really the best moment to die? And which moment is the last one in which it is still fun to live?

In other words: Would it indeed be a catastrophe if I could have had more happy moments worth living and if they had let me die in my last almost-death moment? It would only be a catastrophe if you are of the opinion that after death there is nothing else. With such an attitude it surely is obvious that you would want as much out of this singular and unique life as you can get. Yet if you are an adept of the spiritual-emotional human image, it does not matter whether you have lived your life to the brim, because you will soon receive another new life and a new body. Some people could object that it would be a waste of joy if you do not allow to be resuscitated and then experience more joy with your present body. Nature is always lavish, only the human beings develop an awareness of shortage.

What matters is that: do I believe in a singular or an infinite life? If I believe in infinity, I can leave my body as soon as it gets too uncomfortable to live in it and look forward to having a new fresh body as well as feeling completely free from worrying if there might still be another good moment after this bad one. With these worries the pharmaceutical and medical industries have made a huge business.

So it is paramount to leave your body when you can still dispose completely of your life. Some people might say: But what will you die of then? Most people with a biochemical perspective believe that you have to fall ill in order to die. Yet if you have experienced through your self-healing work that your body is subordinate to your spirit, then dying is also not a physical but a spiritual-emotional matter.

The question you may ask yourself with such an outlook on life is: can and may I die now? Are there any loved ones who I do not want to disappoint with my death? Are there any affairs which I would like to see to? Are there any conflicts with living or deceased persons that are not in harmony yet? These are the essential questions to clarify in order to be free to leave.

Naturally if the physician does not find any physical cause, he will write on the death certificate: "heart failure", because "heart stopped beating" would sound too positive. If he put "cause of death unknown", you might get into trouble. Then the police will show up, impound the corpse and maybe order a post-mortem. For the soul of the deceased this is less than pleasant. It would be best for him to leave his body alone and in a familiar surrounding. The family might want to address him with nice and loving thoughts or words and say goodbye to his body in all awareness that they can still communicate with the deceased on a soul level (best to be done in writing).

Set a clear intention

If you want to die peacefully, it makes sense to set a clear intention for your reincarnation before. How do you proceed? First you take a look at your evolution in this life. It shows you what you need for it to go on optimally. Ask yourself: What can I still do with this body? How and where can I still fulfil useful tasks? Do I want a new body or a walking aid?

What you decide will happen, not what your body decides. Your body does not make any decisions since it is 100% subordinate to your spirit if you have internalized the spiritual-emotional perspective. "Okay", most people will say, "if my spirit determines what my body does, I prefer to go on living and use a walking aid because I will get a new body sometime anyway." Does a walking aid make sense? We have said before that we wanted to die purposefully … will a walking aid encourage my infinite evolution?

Why could I not want to die? Then we are back at the above questions. Most people will answer: "I still want to spend time with my children and grandchildren and great-grandchildren." But feel inside your heart: What advantage do you have or may your progeny have if you are possibly bedridden and cannot enjoy life anymore? Reflect on how you take the best evolution for yourself for the benefit of everybody. Death in itself is nothing. Trying to avoid it means coming to a standstill. This is not in harmony with the universe. The only constant thing is inconstancy. Only death will make you advance.

"Death is nothing" can also be understood that it leads you into nothingness, into a black hole. It only depends on your philosophy in which you say such a thing. With the materialistic outlook death indeed leads you into nothingness since death dissolves everything t matters in materialistic life. Those who believe in it until the end will find themselves sitting in the expected black hole together with your spirit. What you believe is what you project.

Check how strong is your belief. Which other psychological driving forces and emotions are still at work inside you after death? They are decisive for your future. With the philosophy to be a spiritual-emotional being "death is nothing" means that it is of no significance for the spirit because spirit is not affected by death. Therefore the same thought has two diametrically opposed meanings on two different levels of consciousness. In order to make yourself understood you first have to clarify from which outlook you part. Otherwise misunderstandings are rife. Such a misunderstanding may have existential consequences. One meaning is "to die healthy", the other is "infirmity".

With the spiritual-emotional outlook of "death is nothing" you arrive automatically at your never-ending continuity and can project to live in better conditions next time you incarnate. However be aware of the fact that even such a wish is not granted without cause. This means: imagine you just continue your life at the exact point where you were spiritually when you expired. And where is this exact point if you died just now? Have you done everything that you can still accomplish in your present form? What ideas are still in your head wanting to be realized?

Are there – as mentioned above – any unresolved conflicts with living persons or those who have already left their body? Please consider also the persons who have died and with whom you had a conflict are immortal soul beings and you may meet them again in a different form. It is even quite probable that you will meet again because both your souls wish for harmony. Therefore both of you will get a chance of working on it.

There is no escape from making peace. And only because these persons have left their body (or have already incarnated again), peace has not been established. How would you feel if you solved the conflict by *Soul writing* in the remaining time before you also leave your body? The lesser the burden when you leave it, the better it is for a propitious reincarnation.

Whatever you still may want to do in this life, the paramount thing to do is to learn *thought control*. If you see yourself often as a victim of your thoughts (especially with negative, stressful ones, but also with an unfulfilled yearning ache or a hatred still manifest somewhere in your thoughts), then you would be totally at the mercy of these thoughts once you leave your body. As a matter of fact your possibilities of level-headed choice where to reincarnate are rather restricted then because you will not be able to fight these thoughts which will draw you into your pain. These thoughts simply come (just like now) and do something to you that you cannot control.

These unreflected strong emotions with their negative effects are crucial for your next incarnation. In order to control and dissolve these thoughts you better start training in *thought control* right now. (In the second-next chapter about the *Soul writing* you can find more concrete advice about it under "Preparing your own reincarnation".)

Practising thought control

What was your first thought this morning? Was this thought beneficial or stupid, helpful or unnecessary? The best thing to do would be to make a list with two columns: put the helpful ones in the plus column and the stupid or unnecessary ones in the minus column. Are these thoughts familiar ones or new ones not thought yet? Check how you deal with them. Read chapter 4 paragraph "thought control" again. Presumably you will see that the negative column is much longer than the positive column and this is exactly the problem. Therefore thought control is needed. By the written reflection of your thinking you will only just be aware of the warped thoughts you think. However, these warped thoughts do not stop when you die. You have to actively throw them out while you are alive and the first step to do so is making this list.

An essential side-effect with reflecting your thoughts is that you start to think more slowly. Many people speak like they think: much too quickly and without finishing their sentences. If there is confusion in your head, so there will be in your emotions. Yet by slowing down the thought process, you may make less mistakes when thinking and when acting.

How often do you make unnecessary movements with your hands and your feet because you cannot be still and concentrated?. If you only thought of what you are doing right now, there would not be any wrong actions. How often have you put things down which you looked for again immediately? If your thinking was full of disorder, you could not really think of what is needed at the moment because there is too much happening inside. A good example of lacking thought control is the following story:

I just want to wash my car quickly

"So I go to the garage, but on my way I see that the mailbox is full of mail.

I first have a look at the letters, there might be some important one. In order to look through them, I go back to the house.

I put the car keys on the kitchen table, take an invoice out of an envelope and throw the advertisements in the garbage can, but I discover that it is filled to the brim.

I put the invoice back on the table to take the full garbage can to the door so I do not forget to empty it when I go to the garage to wash the car.

I think that the invoice it important because it is a reminder to the payment.

I search the folder with my bank transfers and notice that there aren't any payment forms left.

I look for more payment forms in my study. Next to the keyboard of my computer I see a half-empty juice can.

I leave the payment forms where they are because I first want to drink the juice before there might be an accident and it spills over the keyboard.

Yet the juice is stale and I do not like it any more. I go to the kitchen with it and want to throw it away.

On the way to the kitchen I see that the flowers in the vase do need water urgently.

I put down the juice can on the windowsill where I happen to find my reading glasses which I have missed since yesterday.

Before bringing my glasses to safety, I first want to give the flowers some water, the poor ones are dying.

I put my glasses on the sideboard and fill a jug of water. Then I notice the remote control of the television. Somebody left it there.

I think: if we want to watch TV at night, we will search for the remote control everywhere and nobody knows that it is in the kitchen.

So I take the remote control to the couch table. With the full water jug in one hand and the remote control in the other I walk into the living room. By accident I butt at the door and spill some water on the floor.

I put down the remote control and the jug, go and get a mop and wipe the floor before someone could slip on the puddle.

I then go back to the entrance and try in vain to remember what it is I wanted to do.

In the evening:
- The car has not been washed.
- The invoice has not been paid.
- The old juice is still on the windowsill.
- The flowers have not been watered.
- The full trash can is standing next to the door.
- Where is my folder with the bank transfers?
- I cannot find the remote control any more.
- I do not know where I put my reading glasses.
- I cannot find my car keys any more.

While noticing that I have not done anything properly today, I still cannot figure out why I am so tired since I have been very occupied during the whole day. I have a serious problem and think of getting help somewhere. But first I will check my emails."[41]

---

41 Found in Internet without indication of authors nor copyright.

It does not matter what kind of warped thinking you are doing, if it is due to grief, rage, confusion or yearning. Just try not to reflect on it but immediately look at the next image appearing right after this thought. Remain relaxed as if you sat in a comfortable soft armchair and look at pictures your head shows you on your inner screen. In the moment when you let go of this picture because it is counterproductive for your feelings like for example "I can't do that", you are already curious about the next thought or picture to appear, then the second-next and so on … With this curiosity you create a distance to your own thoughts and an inner flow of pictures is established.

To create the start for it just think of your respiration, it is one thing which you always dispose of. If you follow your respiration with your thoughts and inhale and exhale consciously, at least you do not think anything wrong. However you will soon notice that your brain is quite capable of thinking other things besides the ones following respiration. Of course you now may inhale and exhale stronger so that your thoughts go back to your respiration but this probably will not last long. Yet the good thing about it is that every time you think of your respiration, you do a nice reset for practising thought control. You get aware of what is your present thought (that comes automatically) and let it go again instantly. So you give way to the next thought which is still unknown to you.

As you may notice, your thoughts keep doing as they please and blow themselves up to different scenarios. Therefore it is essential to not let yourself be tempted to hang about these thoughts that appear without being asked to and to lose yourself in the present scenario, because then you will not be free for the next thought which appears. This would be a pity since every scenario has its own value.

Nobody forces you to interpret any thought or scene. You do interpret them anyway because otherwise they would not come into existence for you, yet you try not to give your interpretation any further meaning. When you think: "He has annoyed me", certainly this is just an interpretation because the person who is supposed to have done that has his own interpretation about it. Since you may interpret every experience in this or that way, you force yourself not to give this experience (thought) any more focus/energy by getting all excited and/or believe it to be true. In such a moment you stick to this thought and there is a danger that you may start to justify the interpretation of your truth. This in turn requires so much attention that you are missing out on your next thought. By doing this you do not receive any fresh thoughts coming.

Interpretations use a great amount of energy and care. If you want to confirm that your interpretation (good, bad, stupid, caring, super, cool, uncomfortable, comfortable etc.) is right, then you lose perception of your following thought. This causes you to fall out of the Here and Now and to be mentally occupied with your interpretations only. This means that you will perceive less and less what is happening around you.

Just make yourself aware of the fact that nobody forces you to interpret your thoughts. Let them go and relax. This is the best approach to be in the Here and Now in order to find mental calm in yourself.

In this calm please check the world of your thoughts: What is your favourite movie for the Here and Now, for Today and for Tomorrow? The best should just be good enough for you. Sit down and put your vision into writing. All that is important for you in life is better to be done by writing. However a movie does not consist of words (that would rather be an essay), a movie consists of pictures and scenes. Now watch your vision of the future as a scene.

There is nothing abstract in a scene. It would be a bad movie if the actors had to explain us what they are doing in every scene but we are not to see it clearly. It would be annoying because the main reason for watching a movie is to see, to experience and feel directly what is going on and this is what confers reality to a movie. By writing down the scene in a script style, the scene itself becomes our subjective truth. You take it for real (even if it is completely fictitious), you take it for your reality. Anyway everything is relative, subjective, it is your particular movie, unique in the whole universe.

The difference between your self-imagined movie or the one taken over and accepted from outside could not be greater. The latter is about what you have to do and what you must not do: about what the neighbours think what is decent and what is not, if my hair is ok or not, if he or she is agreeing with my aspect or not – all these things are movies directed from the outside world.

However my soul movie follows other criteria. I ask myself: How do I avoid stress? What do I need, what would be the greatest thing for me, what would make me really happy, how do I remain or become healthy, what is benefitting me for the well-being of all? This movie projected by my own thoughts and written down by me is taken for real by me, it is my truth. This movie is / will be my own personal, subjective and beloved reality.

Soul writing – in script-style

You start *soul writing*® by protocolling in a detailed way a situation in which a conflict or problem is manifest. Please get used to calling a conflict to be clarified a *project* (instead of problem), because then you deal with a challenge which can be handled. Nobody loves disease and problems. But projects – well, there is always something to be learned from and this is what we want.

As soon as you have written the situation on paper (or in the computer), you will work on it some more time until it is increasingly authentic and with full details. (If you write by hand, please do not forget to leave a broad margin for corrections on the right.)

It is essential that you only write in present tense! Otherwise you will not feel the protocolled situation directly. It is decisive that your feeling is authentic, that you completely immerse in the situation so that your emotions in the face of this event are completely present and tangible for you again. You are in the Now. This is why you put down all that happened, all that was said and done – by you and the others – in the first person, that is in *direct speech*.

For every protagonist you start a new line with the short form for his name. For *Mum* and *Dad* you do not use their first names, but M and D, and for you just put "I": Then write down literally what was said, e.g. *I want to* … You put the whole dialogue exactly as a script. This is the best and most efficient form to protocol situations. You proceed as if the situation was filmed or played on stage and you protocol what the documentary shows or the spectators see and what you perceive literally. You abstain from giving comments or explanations.

Between the direct speech you protocol line by line, you jot down the actions of the persons involved and put them in brackets, e. g..: shouts, cries, (in tears) etc. An affirmation such as: *My parents are arguing* does not work. This would be a meta-text generating inner distance. You only immerse into your emotions when you write:

P (shouts): You are always spending too much money!
M (in tears): I do economize with everything.
P: From now on you will get less household money.
M (desperate): Rolf, you cannot do that, the children must be fed.
P (leaves the kitchen): Rubbish … etc.

Do you feel the difference between "My parents are arguing" and the concrete wording in script-style? This way you get the whole pain image belonging to the existing conflict back into your awareness, into the Now. Only in this way the event which is often perceived as traumatic will be recognized and may then be transformed into positive emotions thanks to rewriting the conflict, thus creating a new projection. Rewriting it makes you arrive at a *healing image* with which you sustainably integrate and establish the new and healing reality into your life.

If you want to reach this effect for your projections and rewritings, it has to be a concrete dialogue in script-style portraying the atmosphere in which the scene takes place with unequivocal details. You are not allowed to leave open decisions or open endings. For the movie (your pain image or the rewriting) there is only one possible variety: the one shown in the film. You have to put on paper exactly what you see and hear. Dive into the scene that hurts you, then you feel what makes it so unbearable for you. It does not matter if according to the doubts of your logic the situation has been exactly like you describe it, but subjectively it is felt so, because it is typical.

Maybe you do not finish the writing in one day or one night. It does not matter. Just continue writing. It is important that you find time for it without being disturbed. By no means will you leave this text somewhere or make it accessible for others to see on your PC. These texts are none of their business since they are very personal, you only create them exclusively for yourself. You do not have to and should not explain them to anybody nor justify yourself for them. You solely write them for your own soul work.

The next step consists in rewriting the scene which is in front of you like a movie. This means that you will transform it right at the moment when you fell silent or had to lie down or finally fell asleep in grief. You try to mark on your sheet the last possible moment where you change direction and do exactly the one thing that you never had dared to do "in real life": you venture to appear in your rewriting as you have always wished to do deeply.

This does not only require courage but sometimes also rage (which has to come out loudly if you are on your own). All the other things you "merely" do on paper, so nothing harmful may happen to you provided that you keep your notes under lock and key. You are still in a creative process that is in transformation. If the one person involved in your conflict by chance found your texts, this would solely lead to further problems and misunderstandings.

Now on paper you are completely with you, you look for and find a way by which you reach conditions and circumstances which make you healthy and naturally happy – for the benefit of all you need a harmonisation with your torturer at the end of your rewriting. Often it is not directly possible because this does not give you any satisfaction. I repeat: since it is nobody's business, on paper you may let off your rage until it is completely faded and your torturer has finally got the message that he / she did something horrible to you and apologizes to you convincingly. This rage is already part of your new reality at the end of which your torturer has become a better person. You write this *healing image* also in script-style, i.e. in present tense and in direct speech, the same as the pain image.

Please take care: in order to really experience this new reality emotionally you need to wholly stick to the rules and not write meta-texts. I will repeat the most important points for your orientation:

THIS IS HOW TO WRITE IN SCRIPT-STYLE

- Always define your problem/ conflict as "project".
- The writing is done best in an absolutely censure-free, undisturbed atmosphere (at night in the alpha- state).
- Provide some flawlessly working writing tools (block, pencil, pen or PC).
- Each protagonist begins with a new line.
- The event is written down in present tense and direct speech (as if it was to be staged and the actors have to play it).
- The names of the protagonists are shortened, e.g. M for mum, D for Dad.
- No comments will be put down, only (in brackets) indications for the action are given, e.g. (At what distance is he from you?) and for the mood of the protagonists (he shouts, she cries etc.).
- In a hand-written script you leave a broad margin on the right for later corrections or complementary notes etc. until the text is completely authentic.
- In a script written on PC you make a copy for later corrections so that you feel completely free to modify your emotions until they fit.
- Take care that these personal texts are not accessible to anybody but you.

Just try now, you cannot do anything harmful. Practice creates masters. If you need help – you can find it at the end of this chapter "Soul writing".

Your logic will of course protest against rewriting the conflict, since it knows that it was not like that, that in your childhood there was no loving person and no harmony like the one you wrote down or that you never showed such braveness and courage as in your text. However you already know from reading this book that logic has to submit to intuition and must not give any orders.

While rewriting your conflict, you create a new vibration in the relationship that is to be healed in your *project*. This new vibration created by you is real. Some even say that they can see it in your face because there is more light in it. You may notice that the symptom belonging to the conflict is often decreasing after the first rewriting.

Never let yourself be unsettled by your logic in this very early phase because then you will fall back into your former patterns with which you created the problem or which made you fall ill.

The new mental reality creates an overpowering effect. This is an incredible experience! You will stop being a victim and become a creator, you will be happy by your own design. Scientifically speaking you have created a new morphogenetic field which is having an effect on all people involved at the moment. By doing this you make them become better and more loving persons who create less and less negative things. This makes you breathe freely and all your cells will receive this new information. Peace has been restored.

As the cells do not react on nothing else than the neurotransmitters coming from the brain, they take this new information as their reality and act accordingly. The brain has sent these neurotransmitters believing that the new story is correct because it cannot distinguish between fact and fiction. It is not made for it. Synapses are generated on the base of a real as well as an imagined emotional experience. We have written this experience in the Now, so the new conditions will just arise. This is the art of *Soul writing*®.

Writing with the *KUBYmethod*® is not meant to be harassing or an addition supposed to be neglected, but an essential part of *Soul writing*®, otherwise this method does not work. When writing, two things happen:

First: All that is supposed to become manifest in the universe requires a spiritual impulse. When rewriting your cause the spiritual impulse first gets manifest on paper; comparable with a building plan: without it you cannot build a house.

Second: While writing you create a mirror for your condition. Without this mirror you cannot reflect this condition. So please read the text more than once and let it have an effect on you. You may also correct the text more than once, may expand on it or condense it until it has reached the intensity of the experience and synapses are formed. If you only turned the experience over in your mind, there would not be any reflection and therefore no evolution of consciousness. Consciousness is only attained by reflection and it is indispensable for healing or for solving your project.

With you former consciousness you have not been able to sustainably correct your pain or your limitations in life. This is the reason why you want to work with the *KUBY-method* now. The persons with which you were not in peace do not change by themselves. Since you want to develop and disentangle yourself from the karmic bonds, you have to do the first step. It does not make sense to wait until the other persons change. Now you take the change in your own hand.

To prepare your own reincarnation

The subjective reality in *Soul writing* in combination with the slow and sober thinking is also an important preparation for death or for the time after death in bardo (phase without a physical form). Because with *soul writing*® you aim at projecting your new next life. You may part from the idea that your future character with which you will enter another form / body at conception will be just the same as the one with which you leave your present body.

In bardo you will only continue developing when you have learned to control your thoughts while you are alive. Otherwise your uncontrolled thoughts will lead you to misunderstandings which distress you and make you commit mistakes, e.g. you will go straight to the persons and issues with which you are still connected by negative emotions like unrequited love, but also hatred and unreflected yearnings.

So it just depends on becoming aware of these driving forces and dissolving them so that you may be free to go where you want and where you will indeed be free in your next life. E.g. if you were a violent person in your former life, you have to take care where this aspect will take you. If you came back to Earth again with this trait of character, then your fate will not be an easy one. It would not be surprising if you were on the receiving end of violence as a means of education which you have to suffer in your new life. Especially as a man – even if you understand this karmic consequence – you may not escape from this consequence. There are many men who have spent various lives inflicting violence. Fighting was their life's purpose. In every generation you will find soldiers and violent males. If you belong to this armada of men, you may be irritated that you freak out regularly when things get tough on a psychological level – and maybe you also beat other people, even if in reality you do not want to. However you will only do this if you have been beaten too.

To reach the source of this conditioning, you can also use *Soul writing*. You will get a clear picture of the vibratory frequency of beating and there will be scenes emerging which are older than your present life. You will take these scenes seriously and plunge into them – although they may be a horrid thing to go through again – but you will not die of them (again) now. You now get the chance to rewrite this pattern, to transform it and to program it in a different way so that this (unconscious) vibration does not have to determine your future lives. A behaviour pattern only remains compulsory as long as you are not aware of its cause. This is what *Soul writing* does for you. Some people do not manage to completely dissolve the violence pattern in one life, because they are not aware of its source and they do not possess a tool for the search. If you wish to stop violent behaviour which you got accustomed to in many lives, this requires a thorough work of awareness. You may start on it right away.[42]

You know that you will die sometime anyway. Then at the latest you will become aware of what you have done. Or you might flee from it by becoming demented and thus repressing the recognition of your deeds or your life as a victim in a pathological way, but you cannot do so eternally. Your soul wants to get rid of such disharmony at some point, since it costs too much energy in the long run. You notice that you do not have control over yourself any longer. Something triggers you and you forget yourself, you lash about and / or become depressive. People often try to drown these feelings with alcohol. However this is only a short escape that may become a bad habit. In Germany alone more than a 100.000 people die every year from this addiction. They often exercise a terror regime inside their families which is promoted by this legal drug.

To overcome this suffering and any other form of pain, apply the *KUBY method®* – the earlier, the better. It would be best to start using it before wreaking havoc on future generations and before taking the problems into your next life.

I do not want to incarnate any more

Maybe you are someone who first reads this part of the book since you are virtually disappointed with the life that you have chosen and you would rather be left alone. It is true that by wanting to escape from all

---

[42] In my book *Healing – the wonder in us* you can find practical exercises to this process, which you may try out in writing. (see annex/media shop).

the stress and strain which entails living a life, there may arise the wish not to incarnate again as a human being if possible. But what else? As a nothing? Without taking any shape at all? I do hope that you know that with death only your shape drops off. The spirit that remains is immortal. Examine yourself: wherein lies the stress and strain which bothers you so much and makes your life miserable? Is it primarily your body or rather an emotional-spiritual strain in your mind? Probably you will answer: **both**. This means that you (still) have the opinion that your body possesses a life of its own independent from your consciousness and is virtually doing what it wants to do. Who do you think is the boss of your body? Who or what makes your cells behave in an unruly manner?

I can understand your wish not to incarnate any more, but basically it is an escape thought. The Nirvana you long for or the eternal paradise is an illusion, though a comprehensible one inconsistent with the universe. Because it would mean that there might be standstill. I am so sorry but no, there isn't. There is no such thing as a standstill in this Universe, and we do not have another one. Evolution is going on infinitely without a beginning or an end. It is difficult to imagine but mathematically logical in the cosmos (see e.g. the investigation and theses by Stephen Hawking and others).

Now if your evolution is also going on endlessly, it is primarily an evolution of consciousness before something is showing in reality, in real life. This power of spirit will stay with you, even if you die. Don't you believe that it may be advisable to harmonize your spirit in such a way that the stress and strain disappears from your life so that you can enjoy yourself? Self-love is the basis for everything because the universe is a harmonic fractal and on a very low energetic level at that. It is well-known that harmony needs the least energy. And harmony is tantamount to love. If you continue your evolution in this respect – by always asking: *What would love do?* – then you will die with a soul which cannot wait to realize itself again in a different body.

Just think of all the great ideas you once had. An idea which cannot be turned into action is frustrating. To be sure a painter does not only want to imagine his paintings. He yearns to see them on canvass. Only then is he satisfied and happy. Incorporeal love would not be the complete fulfilment either. Therefore your spirit too will want to manifest itself again. In so far you will be born again, never mind if you now have the wish to do it or not.

So just avoid your frustration with life as an energy which leaves its mark on you. It is no fun at all to come back into the world with this energy. And you will come back sooner or later anyway. If you stay away for too long, you will not be able to understand anything at all anymore because too many things have happened in the world in the meantime. This is frustrating and you strain yourself too (find more about it in chapter 4). You come into the world in order to make experiences, since only through these experiences you have the chance to go on developing into a harmonic, caring being. You still have enough time to get reconciled with your present life and love yourself.

Simply start now, then you will look into the future with happiness and excitement. Nobody else will do it for you. It is best if you learn the method of *Soul writing*®. I would love to help you with it.

If you need help

You may send your soul texts to my team of trained coaches or possibly to me. We will check them for their efficiency, write a comment and send them back to you.[43] It helps many people, especially when they realize that they get stuck and wonder why there is hardly any change in their situation despite the rewriting.

When looking at your text, my coaches and me /recognize – without having to know your whole situation – where and why your new reality does not show yet completely. You can also learn to feel this.

---

43 Please always send these texts as word.doc(x)-files for windows.

As I have made films since my school days, have studied and taught film-making, I constantly deal with the efficiency of images (scenes). As a movie-goer you will also know this feeling. You notice immediately which scenes work for you and which do not. If you have to (or should) cry, please register that you are a spiritual being who is doing fine with placebos = illusions.

If I have your *Soul texts* in front of me, I see the film which you remember (the so-called pain image): and if you mark the exact moment where your rewriting begins, i.e. your new film, then I will not have any difficulty to feel if this emotionality changes the behaviour of your cells which have got into disorder or if they are still lacking the harmony they long for. This is exactly what you will receive from us, a comment to your soul text.

Please read again the chapter *Soul writing – in script style* at the beginning of the annex. This procedure is the gist of the *KUBY- method*® by which you can harmonize your present problems. If you want to tackle certain topics in a more intensive way, you can find some possibilities on how to get assistance under "This is how you continue".

KUBY – the time after my death

When I am gone the *KUBY-method*® will simply be called KUBY. Only after one generation it will be the name for a tool and no longer for a person. These four letters are a special tool for the evolution of consciousness distinguished by the fact that it does not lay claim to any ideology. It works for every belief system or philosophy and for every gender too. It is true that KUBY has a primarily masculine character, but as a tool the term K.U.B.Y. is neutral, as an abbreviation for **Kreativ. Und. Bewusst. Yetzt.** *(Creative. And. Conscious. Now)*

Today it is normal that behind the tool KUBY there is still my person who has integrated his experience of making documentaries with it. The rules for the tool stem from this experience. If you do not observe these rules in *Soul writing*, K.U.B.Y. cannot work. The tool is only working as long as it is used expertly. This is logical with every tool, isn't it?

The expert thing with K.U.B.Y. is the before-mentioned neurological statement that our brain cannot distinguish between fact and fiction. This can already be seen in the development of our society as a whole. With the lightning speed in electronic evolution it gets ever more difficult to tell reality from make-believe. In the TV- media it sure is no longer possible. Everybody can fake everything. In the social media it is also getting more difficult and the rational landmarks for orientation are getting less trustworthy (cue: "fake news"). This means that the transition from reason to intuition is becoming more fluid.

Even if many people may be terrified: I believe that this development is good and necessary. Because thanks to it, reason is getting more and more powerless. At the moment it still plays up as a ruler. However, it cannot provide evolution of consciousness, since the latter stems from intuition, as shown before. Now if reason is becoming ever more diluted, people will find it more urgent to be able to trust their intuition. With K.U.B.Y. we learn to imagine our orientation with the help of intuition, therefore changing fundamentally our sensation of life.

When rewriting a *pain image* into a *healing image*, we declare imagination as our truth. This is unsettling for reason and lessens its power. By this process we achieve that reason subordinates to intuition and so establishes the hierarchy of *being* in which intuition comes first. It does not matter which term you give to this dominant position: God, Allah, Buddha, cosmos, inner wisdom, universal intelligence or Dalai Lama. Everyone who works with K.U.B.Y. uses these labels only to denominate his own term of truth with which he creates his own new reality that makes him healthy and happy and therefore produces an effect on him.

As a film-maker, I make use of this ability of our brain providing a real event for my audience. We do the very same thing with K.U.B.Y. to create a reality making us healthy and happy. As you know, efficient images even make your pulse rise and your heart beat faster, although there is no real reason for it. Everything you see in cinema has been imagined and invented. If you like, it is a complete illusion. James Bond is not James Bond, but an actor; however, you perceive him as the hero Bond. The fiction has to be staged so well that it is credible for you, then it has the effect of a real experience.

You do exactly the same thing with the scene in which you have suffered before, but now you have freed yourself from suffering and pain for the benefit of all thanks to your new film. If you achieve it on paper, it will also happen in reality.

We offer an intensive training course to properly use the K.U.B.Y. tool in order to spread it. The *KUBY-method*® has nothing to do with knowledge, as you may have recognized by now, since knowledge is connected to reason and therefore to space and time. What I know is already part of my consciousness. But if this consciousness is not enough to be healthy and happy in this and future lives, I have to expand it. This is where the K.U.B.Y. instrument is joining in. With it you have to restrain reason to its limits.

Every human being has got intuition in order to create new consciousness. This does not happen abstractly, just as music cannot be created abstractly. Intuitive insights are visible, music is audible. The resulting words are written down and can be read aloud. All this is real. K.U.B.Y. gets along without mysticism. There is normally a lot of ideology in mysticism. And ideological viewpoints always have an abstract base, like all religions. K.U.B.Y. only works in a very concrete way.

In your intuition you are not a thinking being, but a sentient being, a feeling person. We are talking of the *limbic system in your brain*. Of the not yet known. Of everything we retrieve from the repression without any joy. We make an effort to see pain, mourning, death and devil as the protagonists of our pain film. We do not have to know anything about it, we only look at the pictures and what they show us.

At the end of the process, when the whole scene has been fetched from the subconscious into the consciousness, we begin lo love these films. For example I love my paralysis, even though there appears sudden pain in my back or my legs. This pain is a warning from my soul. It wants to tell me to stop with what I am doing right now. With this pain, my soul is able to be louder than my ego. If remorse or a gut-feeling has not stopped me before, my soul sends me this pain signal. I have taken to stop then to reflect on my actions. Of course I have to reflect on them on paper in order to get the picture clear in front of viewers. Where and when did the pain first appear? Every pain contains a message that I want to know – that I become aware of. And I employ K.U.B.Y. to do that (even if my name would be different).

I can tolerate the pain, I do not muffle it with painkillers in order not to close the door to my subconscious by putting to sleep the bloodhound of my intuition.

Naturally I have taken painkillers or done something to get a break from pain on some occasions. But I have done it knowing that I put the hound to sleep or at least make it less fierce for some time. So I understand that others do the same thing sometimes. Only we must not take pain relief for the healing.

Intuition is our wisdom. The wisdom of the universe which is connected to our soul. Our soul is nothing but the personalized intuition, i.e. something for which our limbic system is the receiver. If I want to decipher the message of my pain, I cannot help but document the pain. All mankind, every single human being is full of pain, every one of us has once received and administered pain. This means that every human already has been victim and offender, man and woman.

Yet all that may be transformed. It is really entertaining to expand one's own consciousness when it is needed, even without pain or any suffering, simply for creative reasons. Healing as such is a side-effect of the expansion of your consciousness. A rewriting which is not entertaining is not what your soul wants you to feel and how it wants to be realized in real life. Health is still the most important thing, higher than love, money or God.

Do not forget: set an intention for the benefit of all. Intention means application, action. *The energy follows the intention.* That is a cosmic law just as the law of cause *and effect*.

Probing for the next life
(Example of a client)

The 85-year-old seminar participant Marta S. from Berlin draws intuitively card no. 64 in the self-healing navigator[44]: "I will leave my body healthily". Below it says among other things: *When I cannot serve my evolution in this body any longer, I will leave this body.*

This leads her to write the following:
I am convinced of the fact that I still have to fulfil a task in my life. I will stop looking for a sense in my life because I finally know why I am still here at 85. I will learn to create a new body with my mind. This is a completely new thought for me. I will deal with it intensely from now on.

Thanks to my *Soul writing* I have found out that I have lived in India in a former life and I want to go back there in my next life. I still wonder why I incarnated in this life in that little village I hated so much, with so many sisters and one brother and my parents who did not know anything but to quarrel and to pray the whole day. Their marriage was a catastrophe. Girls were not worth a thing, my parents only spoke of the little boy all day long. Why did I finish in the narrow cage with narrow-minded people and their Catholic make-believe piety? I wanted to take my A-grades and go to university. I was only able to do this at 78.

By now it has become clear to me that my husband and my child are leading my way: at 38 I married an Indian. At 47 we adopted an Indian baby. At 81 I get a lovely half-Indian grand-child and only recently I have bought myself a 60 cm high beautiful brass statue of the goddess Tara.

---

44 Clemens Kuby: *Self-healing navigator.* Set of 64 cards with an explanatory booklet. Kösel Edition. (see also "How to continue"/media shop)

I now have to fly again to India, although I had decided to stop travelling. I will fly to Bangalore. I want to reincarnate there and want to be someone in the IT-area, because right now I cannot even write a short message. I will also book a computer course in this life. In Bangalore I will get to know some young people and find out in what conditions I would like to be in my future life. I will do that before my 86th birthday.

I love India. Yet I will be born there as a boy and choose a family of musicians. Music is my hobby. Men do not have to fight for recognition in India like women do. In India men are freer than girls, they can walk in the streets at night, choose a wife of their own will and have sex before marriage. Moreover I want to spare my parents to have to get into debts for the rest of their life just to finance their daughter's wedding.

I am drawing another card from the *self-healing navigator* intuitively. It is no. 45: "All is fine because we love each other." It continues: *Whenever I need hope, health and joy, I first look at the healing picture I created in order to remember my good feelings.* – I am looking forward to my new project.

However I still feel panic when I think of dying. The god-fearing corset of my parents is not completely gone yet. My leaving the church has not caused it to fall off yet. However, since the seminar with Clemens, I take my life into my own hands as well as my future life. The thought of living in India in the future makes me happy and healthy. I can already walk better than before the seminar.

Love to all!
Marta, Berlin

Thanks

To whom do I owe the evolution of my consciousness which has been condensed in this book? I would have to have kept a precise diary to become aware of what made me aware. Often there were inconspicuous moments, but also the great dramatic conflicts of course. It was always a matter of love: from whom, when, how much, giving and taking love, confessing, reliable, enduring, neglected, misleading, authentic, open etc. My love always wants to realize itself, so my consciousness for it has to grow. Each disease, each accident, each misfortune – every single one of it is always "merely" a problem of relationship. Human beings do not have other problems. This is what I have explained in detail in this book. These problems supply the dramatic stuff by which consciousness has to grow.

I first want to thank my parents for the evolution of my consciousness. Moreover I have noticed that an encounter, a love, a conflict sometimes has an impact which can impossibly be the consequence of an experience in this life. There are incomprehensible forces of relationship which make my puzzle about where they might stem from. I cannot find a cause for them in this life. With this book I go beyond the limits of the physical life and suddenly there appears a person with whom I have been entangled, in a different role and different surroundings as the ones I know here and today. And I too feel differently than compared with my present life. I may admit these pictures in order to understand my soul. Understanding it is half the solution, since understanding means expansion of consciousness. These insights made me write this book. Therefore I thank all the persons from many lives and also from the present one who have contributed to the evolution of my consciousness and still contribute to it. It is impossible for me to name them all. I could begin with the Dalai Lama, who has helped me to evolve my consciousness persistently since 1987, after I met him for the first time when his car broke down in Ladakh.

I use filmmaking in order to venture into areas of consciousness which would not have been accessible to me as a normal citizen. The whole reincarnation history of Jamgon Kongtrul Rinpoche would have been impossible to know without my cameraman Valerio Albisetti. In order to understand it wholly, my cutter Stefan Weiß helped me among others.

I also want to thank all the participants of my seminars who have decisively expanded my consciousness due to their own awareness process. Naturally these seminars would not have taken place without the marvellous work of my team, Petra Schmid and Heidi Herschmann. They also organize my almost daily accompanying conversations with clients which very often slip into former lives, mostly because of an unresolved pain. Therefore we should not condemn our pain, but use it as a door-opener. Most of the pains have a history stemming from a former life and that is why they generate an expansion of consciousness by that fact alone.

For the very concrete, immense work performance of creating this book and her continued and valuable inspiration for the enhancement of the text, I would like to thank Ulrike Reverey, my lector who also did all my other books and the self-healing navigator cards of the Kösel publishing house. Without her I would not be able to write a book. I thank Kösel Publishing House for putting her at my side even after finishing her time in their company. I would not have known anybody who would have supported me with such soundness and deep comprehension for everything I write. Thank you very much, Ulrike!

I also thank the chief of program Usha Swamy as well as the president of the publishing house Tobias Winstel and all his team for bringing forth this book so that it could find its way to you, dear reader. Thank you!

Clemens Kuby

Who is who in this book?

In Christianity there are different schools like Catholics, Protestants and Orthodox, likewise in Tibetan Buddhism there are different traditions: Kagyü, Gelug, Nyingma and Sakya. Each of these faiths have their own leader.

Karmapa has been the leader of the *Kagyü* since 1110, the **Dalai Lama** since 1578 the leader of the *Gelug*. At the same time the Dalai Lama is the political leader of all Tibetans; this is what makes him so much more known than the Karmapa. When the now 14th Dalai Lama dies, the still young Karmapa will take up his role as the world-famous, spiritual teacher and the differences between the single Buddhist faiths will disappear more and more.

The Karmapa has incarnated 17 times in a conscious and planned way between 1110 and today. For the periods between his death and his next incarnation – a so-called seat-holder, a reliable proxy had been designed to exercise his offices until he could resume them again. In order to find those seat-holders the 16th Karmapa during the centuries has taught four students to also incarnate consciously at the same time as him. These four students are:

Shamar who incarnated 13 times from 1283 till 2014. In 1792 the then Dalai Lama issued a ban on the 11th and 12th incarnation of Shamar due to abuse of power. The incumbent Dalai Lama lifted this ban on the then 12-year-old Shamar in his 13th incarnation after fleeing into exile only after being bidden three times by the 16th Karmapa. At Karmapa's death this 13th Shamar replaced him (the 17th Karmapa Ogyen Trinley Dorje) as well as the 4th Jamgon Lodro Chokyi Nyima, both of whom we encounter in this book, by other students. This led to the fact that nowadays if you look in the Internet you can find two

17th Karmapa and also two 4th Jamgon. Whereas Shamar's Karmapa (Thaye Dorje) and "our" Jamgon have stopped being monks and are leading a normal life nowadays.

Situ has been another representative of Karmapa since 1377 until today with 12 incarnations.

Gyaltsap became another representative of Karmapa in 1427 until now with 12 incarnations.

Jamgon joined as a fourth representative in 1813 with 4 incarnations until today. In this book the transition from the 3rd to the 4th Jamgon is playing a major role.

Other persons

Tenzin, Jamgon's assistant, who survived the deathly accident of his master when he himself was 22, has administered Jamgon's legacy until today and has led the search for the incarnated 4th Jamgon.

Topga, the secular younger brother of the 3rd Jamgon, who lives in Nepal as a business man.

Pema, the mother of the 3rd Jamgon and of Topga, who lives in Kalimpong, West Bengal/East India. She died in 2012.

Yangki, the young mother, and Gampo, the young father of the 4th Jamgon (the reincarnation of the 3rd Jamgon) in Tibet.

Drupon Dechen, the abbot of Tsurphu monastery, 50 miles north of Lhasa. Tsurphu was and is the main seat of the Karmapas since 1110. Since 1985 Drupon Dechen looks after the rebuilding of the monasteries destroyed by the Chinese hoping that the 17th incarnation of

Karmapa will move in there, which is what happened with the only 7-year-old 17th Karmapa in 1992. (You might want to see the movie about *Resistance of the spirit* by Clemens Kuby.)

Books and works by Clemens Kuby

Books, audio-books, cards, films and audio-CDs

- The best-seller *En route to the next dimension* as paperback. Clemens Kuby's journey to healers and shamans. A stunning book.

- This book *En route to the next dimension* is also available as an audio-book (with excerpts on 2 CDs).

- DVD*: The cult movie *En route to the next dimension*. A special movie about spiritual healing which shows what you have always imagined but have never believed.

- The best-seller *Healing – the wonder in us* as hard cover. 320 pages with many practical exercises for your own self-healing process. A successful book in every respect.

- This book *Healing – the wonder in us* is also available as audio-book (with excerpts on 2 CDs), spoken by Clemens Kuby himself.

- DVD: The movie film *Healing – the wonder in us*. In this movie Clemens Kuby shows his own healing story and other cases of self-healing. A movie that goes under your skin.

- CD: The sound track of *Healing – the wonder in us*. This music has a healing effect.

- The book *Mental Healing. The secret of self-healing* resumes the mind expanding healing method by Clemens Kuby with lots of examples. A textbook for all who want to learn the KUBY method for themselves and for their healing work.

- DVD: *Live your movie.* Five soul conversations with Clemens Kuby, including the cases printed in the book *Mental Healing* exactly as taught by Clemens Kuby.

- DVD: *The human being – a spiritual being.* Explanations of fundamental knowledge with pictures about *Spiritual healing*; very entertaining and easily understandable.

- DVD: *Soul writing.* A documentation about the work in the seminars given by Clemens Kuby with the resulting consequences and success.

- The *Self-healing navigator.* With 64 cards; costly illustrated by Brigitte Smith. With a manual as well as an explanation for every card. Over the years the cards have proven a strikingly magical accuracy.

- DVD: *All is possible – The spectrum of self-healing. In 2.5 hours 26 different ways are shown to access self-healing.* A good DVD for entering in the matter. There is something for everybody.

- The small book *Healthy without medicine. The KUBY method* resumes shortly how this ingenious method works. A practical guide to change your way of thinking in everyday life, distinguishing themes for women and men and the different access to their intuition.

- The audio-book *Self-healing – get healthy on your own* reproduces 40 % of the text in the book *Healthy without medicine* in almost 3 hours of hearing.

- DVD: *Global Scaling – The melody of the universe. The scientific base for the intuitive processes of spiritual healing work according to the insights of Dr. Hartmut Müller.*

- DVD: *Self-healing in six steps – Joao de Deus.* When thousands of people experience healing, we can recognize how healing is brought about. Very exciting.

- DVD*: *Todas – on the edge of paradise.* A tribe of first people in South India visited by Clemens Kuby various times in four years. The Todas do not work and do not know fear.

- CD: The soundtrack *Toda – On the edge of paradise* will make you sympathize with a people without fear nor work to do and who sings and communicates all day long.

- DVD*: *The Old Ladakh.* Buddhism trilogy Part I. The Tibetan culture as it existed in the past. A cult movie honoured with the German Movie award.

- DVD*: *Tibet – Resistance of the spirit.* Buddhism trilogy Part II. How the Tibetans have been able to maintain their pacific character despite the brutality of Chinese occupation.

- DVD*: *Living Buddha.* Buddhism Trilogy Part III. A unique monumental epic about a person in two lives, the 16th and 17th Gyalwa Karmapa.

- CD: *Living Buddha.* A musical master piece. A mature spiritual experience of a very special kind: a symbiosis of Tibetan and Western culture.

- DVD*: *The making of Living Buddha* plus bonus material. It feels close to a whodunit the way how Kuby dealt with the greatest resistances and filmed *Living Buddha* in seven years.

- DVD: *Misery and peace in Tibet*. A movie with the Dalai Lama about the plight of the Tibetans, especially the women who have been neutered by the Chinese government.

Some of these movies are also offered for "streaming" on our website www.clemenskuby-shop.de. See further information in our shop or under the phone no.: +49 (0) 89 32 67 98 11

* These movies are available in English and German on these CDs.
For the streaming the movies in English and German are separate.

Promotion

Those who want to help distributing the KUBY method any further, please give a donation to the non-profit European foundation for self-healing promoting:

- to provide free knowledge about self-healing for interested people;
- to support people in need so that they be able to learn how to self-heal themselves
- to support informational events for self-healing in situ;
- to collaborate in financing scientific studies about self-healing

You will receive an official donation receipt for donations starting from € 100.– Phone: +49 (0) 83 41 9 08 22 01 or kontakt@shp-stiftung.eu; www.shp-stiftung.eu.) 86251 Schloss Blumenthal. Bank Account no. for donations: SHP- Stiftung (Foundation), IBAN DE02 7005 2060 0022 0897 34; BIC BYLADEM1LLD; Sparkasse Landsberg.

How to continue

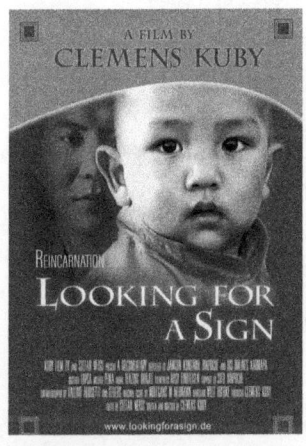

THE MOVIE
"Reincarnation – Looking for a Sign" is no motion picture. For 28 years Clemens Kuby has experienced up close the reincarnation story of Jamgon Kongtrul Rinpoche. In this book the tension of this extraordinary story is very noticeable. In the movie this is even more so since the spectator is experiencing LIVE something which he has never seen: a person in two lives. It is no problem showing something like that in a novel. But to be present LIVE when a man dies and see him again as a baby, is something the world has never seen before – at least not in a documentary film.

Since Westerners are so sceptical about the reincarnation theory, Kuby followed Jamgon's reincarnation with the camera until aged 20, before he published the movie. To do just that, many hundred hours of movie material had to be reduced to 108 minutes. These scenes however are the highlights of this amazing and incredible story. Those who combine reading the book with watching the movie will get the most profound insight in reincarnation. The movie transports you into a different dimension. The book wants to be read actively. The movie will stun you. Surely you will want to watch it several times in order to process the experience of continuity of life in your mind. After seeing this movie you will be a new person.

You can order the movie under www.clemenskuby.de/Film. It can be watched in two languages (English and German) in streaming mode or you can receive it as DVD.

Those who want to look behind the scenes can find lots of things on the Making-of the film on www.clemenskuby.de/Reinkarnation.

Do you want more?

THE WEBINAR

"**Reincarnation – nonsense or truth?**": This free webinar can be recommended to every sceptic who finds reincarnation a non-theme. Kuby picks them up at the place where most people in our culture stand. Naturally the concept of a singular life cannot be changed in one hour only. Therefore in this free webinar he explains everything that can be discovered in his detailed, 4-day seminar **Practised reincarnation**. Appoint yourself any time to the free one-hour webinar at: www.clemenskuby.de/Veranstaltungen/Online-Angebote.

THE SEMINAR

"**Practised reincarnation**": You get the biggest profit from the book and the movie when applying the concept of reincarnation on yourself. Every participant learns how to answer the following questions for themselves:
- How do I know who I was in my last life?
- How do I know if I only imagine the answer or if it is really true?
- How do I recognize who I was in my last life?
- How do I plan my next reincarnation?

- What consequences does this have on my present life?

Those who want to completely overcome the fear of death may visit this **4-day/4-parts seminar** either in situ or online.

In *Practised reincarnation* Clemens Kuby gives you the space and the time to become aware of your own eternal life and to set an intention for your evolution until the next and the second-next life. A profound and practical change of life will take place which will not only have effects on your present life. Get appointed to the 4-day/4-parts seminar any time at: www.clemenskuby.de/Reinkarnation.

THE MUSIC
Those who wish to get musical support for their feeling in order to go beyond their boundaries of physical existence, may listen to the music "I am going within" by Wolfgang M. Neumann. This music has got magic. It permits a direct flowing access to your intuition and in addition is a marvellous sound experience. (Some tracks are played in the film). Order as CD or download on www.clemenskuby-shop.de (with a free audition).

MEDIA SHOP
People interested in more books and movies by Clemens Kuby, find a great selection in the shop (www.clemenskuby-shop.de).

ABOUT THE AUTHOR
Born in 1947 Clemens Kuby, award-winning documentary filmmaker and best-selling author, has been paralyzed and has healed himself intuitively. After that he documented the phenomenon of self-healing powers in books and films. He became a speaker of world-wide fame and personally transmits his experiences of self-healing and the continuity of spirit in lectures and seminars.

www.clemenskuby.de

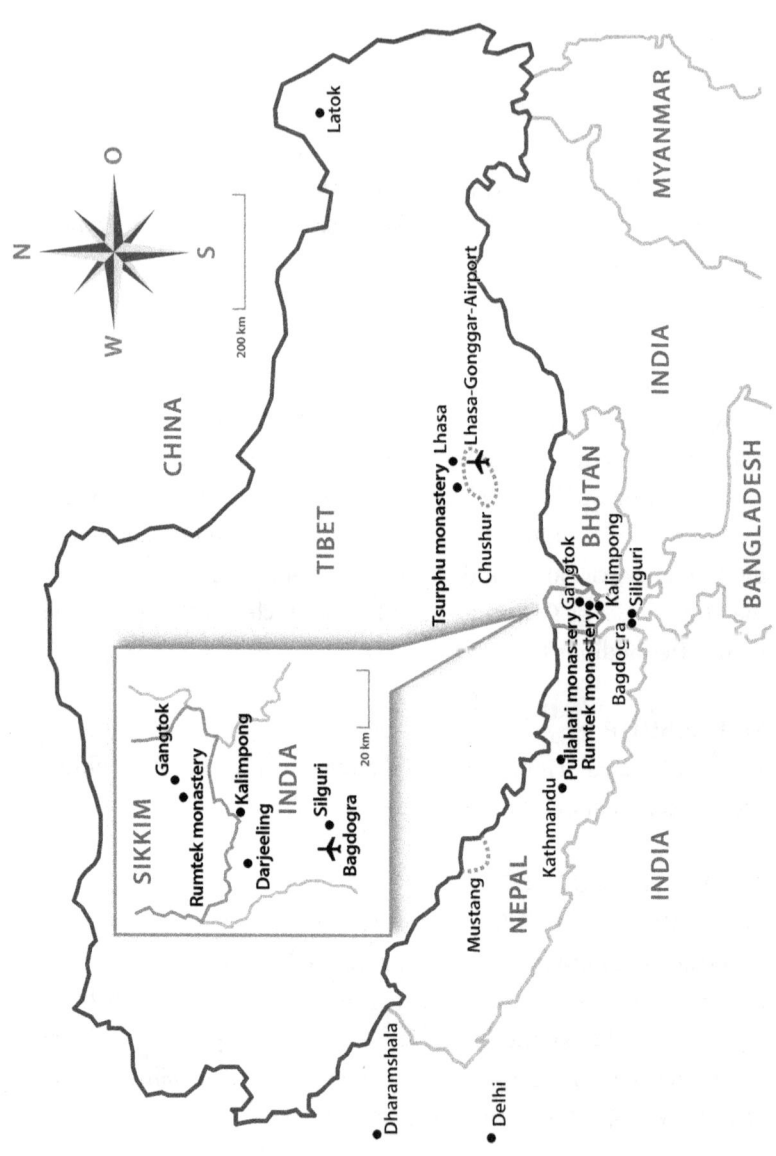

www.ingramcontent.com/pod-product-compliance
Lightning Source LLC
Chambersburg PA
CBHW031426160426
43195CB00010BB/623